HUMAN RESOURCES AND ECONOMIC WELFARE

ESSAYS IN HONOR OF ELI GINZBERG

ELI GINZBERG

HUMAN RESOURCES AND ECONOMIC WELFARE

ESSAYS IN HONOR OF ELI GINZBERG

EDITED BY IVAR BERG

COLUMBIA UNIVERSITY PRESS
NEW YORK AND LONDON 1972

LIBRARY OF CONGRESS CATALOGING IN PUBLICATION DATA
Main entry under title:
Human resources and economic welfare.

"Eli Ginzberg a selective bibliography" p.: 363
1. Manpower policy—United States—Addresses, essays, lectures. 2. Labor supply—Addresses, essays, lectures. 3. Human capital—Addresses, essays, lectures. 4. Ginzberg, Eli, 1911– I. Ginzberg, Eli, 1911– II. Berg, Ivar, ed.
HD5724.H845 331.1′1′0973 72-8331
ISBN 0-231-03710-4

PRINTED IN THE UNITED STATES OF AMERICA

CONTRIBUTORS

MOSES ABRAMOVITZ	Coe Professor of American Economic History and Chairman of the Economics Department, Stanford University
E. WIGHT BAKKE *	Sterling Professor of Economics, Yale University
DANIEL BELL	Professor of Sociology, Harvard University
IVAR BERG	Professor of Sociology, Graduate School of Business, Columbia University
KENNETH E. BOULDING	Professor of Economics and Director of the Program of Research on General, Social and Economic Dynamics, Institute of Behavioral Sciences, University of Colorado at Boulder
SUNE CARLSON	Professor of Economics, University of Uppsala and The Institute of Business Studies and Business Finance
FREDERICK H. HARBISON	Professor of Economics and International Affairs and Roger Williams Straus Professor of Human Relations, Princeton University
PHILIP M. HAUSER	Professor of Sociology and Director of the Population Research Center, University of Chicago

REV. THEODORE M. HESBURGH	President, University of Notre Dame
RICHARD A. LESTER	Dean of the Faculty and Professor of Economics and Public Affairs, Princeton University
THEODORE LIDZ, M.D.	Professor and Chairman, Department of Psychiatry, Yale University School of Medicine
ROBERT M. MAC IVER *	Lieber Professor Emeritus, New School for Social Research, New York
MARGARET MEAD	Curator Emeritus of Ethnology, American Museum of Natural History; Adjunct Professor of Anthropology, Columbia University
MELVIN REDER	Professor of Economics, City University of New York Graduate Center
ANNE ROE	Consultant in Psychology, Tucson, Arizona
GEORGE P. SHULTZ	United States Secretary of the Treasury, Washington, D.C.
BRINLEY THOMAS	Professor of Economics, University College, Cardiff, Wales
RALPH W. TYLER	Senior Consultant, Science Research Associates, Inc., Chicago; and formerly Director, Center for Advanced Studies in the Behavioral Sciences, Palo Alto, California
WILLIAM FOOTE WHYTE	Professor, New York State School of Industrial and Labor Relations and Professor of Sociology, Cornell University

* Deceased

PREFACE AND ACKNOWLEDGMENTS

It is generally the custom for a distinguished senior scholar and teacher to be honored by his students and by a small handful of immediate intellectual collaborators. A colleague setting about to prepare a *Festschrift* to be presented to Eli Ginzberg, however, finds it singularly difficult to be guided by this generally applicable norm.

His students, after all, include six American presidents who have benefited from his intellectual advice and from more personal guidance on an extraordinarily wide array of topics. A host of United States senators and representatives, charged with committee obligations to explore general economic policy questions—questions regarding youth, women, blacks, older persons, military personnel, and educators, to name just a few—have also served the American people better for having heard Eli Ginzberg's views and suggestions.

And his "immediate collaborators" include scholars, practicing professionals in law, medicine, social work, nursing, education, the diplomatic corps, personnel in the upper reaches of many of the nation's largest corporations and at all levels in trade unions, civil rights organizations, and religious bodies.

The decision to undertake the preparation of this volume, as a gift to be presented on the occasion of his sixtieth birthday, confronted me with a staggering array of choices. When the invitations were distributed, they went to those who are most like Eli himself: thoughtful students of the complex problems that inhere in the study of the uses and needs of people and of the prerequisites to the development of an efficient and democratic social order. I have sought to capture this much of the editorial judgment in the volume's title, one that, I hope, captures the span of Eli's interests and the nature of his essential values. The other qualification was that the contributors count themselves among Eli's admiring friends.

Some of the contributions that were to appear were sacrificed for reasons that Eli would well understand. Thus the list of contributors would have been slightly larger but for the good taste and judgments of governments, universities, and other organizations who placed new and staggering burdens upon would-be participants after they had enthusiastically agreed to join in this venture. Their best wishes have been recorded in warm letters.

The overriding majority of those to whom I wrote met all the deadlines, despite hectic schedules and conflicting demands, submitted stimulating papers, and were incredibly patient with the delays that inevitably accompany a venture involving many persons, publication headaches, editing efforts, and great distances. The fact that I was pressed into administrative service for a time at Columbia University, in the wake of my university's troubles, did not help speed the process.

One measure of Eli Ginzberg's places in America's social sciences can be inferred from the fact that the contributors represent thirteen American and two foreign universities, all of ranking importance in these sciences, and all of the disciplines one may collect under the present title. The fact that he has made significant contributions in all of these fields is the more remarkable when note is also taken of the number of agencies, public and private, that have spoken for substantial segments of his time, in Ethiopia, Israel, Japan, India, and innumerable other near and distant places in which his name means good advice, stimulating discussion and incisive judgment.

In keeping with the judgment that his birthday and the thirtieth anniversary of the Conservation of Human Resources Project, over which he presides, be exploited for scholarly purposes, highly personal tributes to our friend, colleague, and teacher have been placed at the end of the volume. For the same reason, the editor has not indulged himself in a public expression of personal affection in this preface.

But all of us here represented may record our deep satisfaction with the fact that we have come to know the finest of men. We give him, in these pages, the only gift that seems appropriate: a collection of thoughtful essays that reflect, in their individual ways, the many facets and attributes of Eli Ginzberg, but most especially his humanity.

It is a pleasure indeed to express my thanks to those who have contributed to this enterprise. The authors were responsive to their invitations, patient with delays, and tolerant of the editor's blue pencil. Dr. Anne Roe, for example, was obliged to sacrifice a number of helpful tables and charts for which references must suffice, while the others accepted an emendation here and a suggestion there in good humor. All wrote original pieces and all therefore gave generously of their time, despite busy schedules characteristic of accomplished people.

Less apparent contributions were made by Carol Levine, who assisted with editorial chores, and by Martha Chamberlin and Winifred Berg, who did all the detective work—tracking down footnotes and double-checking references—and who conducted the never-ending search for the errors that hound editors and publishers determined to present a readable volume. I am also indebted to these two colleagues, and to Heather Demree, Lillian Krasner, Joyce Woods, and Arlene Jacobs for their help with the many detailed management tasks involved in this enterprise.

Finally I should like to express my gratitude to Dean Samuel Richmond and to Professor William Newman, Samuel Bronfman Professor of Democratic Business Enterprise, and to the Samuel Bronfman Foundation. This foundation has facilitated a number of studies at the Columbia University Graduate School of Business bearing upon the role of business and the management of corporations in a free society. The support here acknowledged has facilitated the publication of this book to a most important degree.

Columbia University IVAR BERG
July 1972

CONTENTS

Human Resources and Economic Welfare 1
IVAR BERG

PART ONE

Reflections on Manpower Planning 15
RICHARD A. LESTER

Man as a Commodity 35
KENNETH E. BOULDING

Manpower, Capital, and Technology 50
MOSES ABRAMOVITZ

Human Capital and Economic Discrimination 71
MELVIN REDER

PART TWO

Manpower Policy during a Recession 89
E. WIGHT BAKKE

Human Resources as the Wealth of Nations 128
FREDERICK H. HARBISON

The Work Force in Developing Areas 142
PHILIP M. HAUSER

Foreign Subsidiaries and the Dynamics of International Economic Integration 162
SUNE CARLSON

PART THREE

The Family: The Source of Human Resources 177
THEODORE LIDZ, M.D.

Womanpower: How Is It Different? 198
ANNE ROE

More Effective Education for the Professions 229
RALPH W. TYLER

From Plight to Power 241
MARGARET MEAD

PART FOUR

"Grass on the Slag Heaps" Revisited 259
BRINLEY THOMAS

The Behavioral Sciences and Manpower Research 272
WILLIAM FOOTE WHYTE

The Corporation and Society in the 1970s 299
DANIEL BELL

PART FIVE

Tribute to Eli Ginzberg 341
THE REV. THEODORE M. HESBURGH, C.S.C.

Personal Postscript 355
ROBERT M. MAC IVER

A Personal Tribute to Eli Ginzberg 360
GEORGE P. SHULTZ

Eli Ginzberg: A Selective Bibliography, 1932–1972 363

HUMAN RESOURCES AND ECONOMIC WELFARE

ESSAYS IN HONOR OF ELI GINZBERG

IVAR BERG

HUMAN RESOURCES AND ECONOMIC WELFARE: A THEMATIC REVIEW

THREE major themes recur in the abundant literature that represents what in recent decades has come to be known as the manpower approach. The first emphasizes how much can be done through judicious policies in society to improve the economic and thereby the social circumstances of people. The second emphasizes that these policies must be rooted in a view of society that treats its components or subsystems as interdependent rather than as differentiated segments. The third emphasizes that no single social science discipline, or even pairs of disciplines, will be adequate to join the issues that need to be clarified on the way to policy formulation.

There are, of course, other significant themes. Thus one finds repeated urgings in this literature that data and analyses bearing upon work, the distribution of jobs, the impact of institutional forms, investments in people, unemployment and other related topics, be considered with an eye to comparative developments. And one is impressed by the interests expressed in the maintenance of democratic procedures and in citizens being served by their social institutions and public policies. These interests are given expression in the several reminders in this book that social, economic and political institutions are the means to a better life and not ends themselves to be served.

The invitations sent to the contributors did not specify that any of these themes should guide the treatment of a particular topic. The themes informed the editor's conception of the overall configuration of the volume, however. The results almost speak for themselves, and the volume may take its secure place on the relevant shelf of writings that began with Adam Smith's *The Wealth of Nations.*

This is not to speak to the merits of the essays but to the point that the manpower approach is not really an approach, in the disciplined sense, at all. The literature is rather, an aggregation of scholarly investigations whose common denominator is moral-philosophical, politically egalitarian and pluralistic, and intellectually eclectic rather than dogmatic. The professional backgrounds of the contributors and the intellectually diversified perspectives advanced in these essays thus reflect a number of the identifying characteristics of the larger body of literature to which these essays belong.

All of this is fitting, given the circumstances of the volume. Eli Ginzberg's extraordinary contribution to this bookshelf, listed at the end of this volume, fits the characterization of what is only in the nominal sense "an approach." It is interesting to note that his first book, *The House of Adam Smith,* sought to retrieve the work of the Professor of Moral Philosophy from misunderstanding claimants who could not recognize that the subject of Smith's title, as Professor Boulding points out, was labor. Eli Ginzberg's work furthermore, has covered the entire spectum of the social sciences and there is scarcely a professional social science society before which he has not made major presentations. Much the same can be said of the contributors to this volume: They have drawn from many wellsprings, have flavored their work with humanistic sensitivities and are comfortable in the many mansions that are the house of Adam Smith.

The essays themselves have been grouped under four main headings that relate to the "thematic" discussion conducted in these introductory paragraphs. Under the first are those in which the authors address themselves to a number of general questions. Thus, Dean Richard Lester clarifies the concept of manpower planning, identifies its role in the American social and economic system and compares this role with that of the market and that of large economic organizations vis-à-vis the development, allocation and use of human resources for gainful employment. While he concedes that the competing systems offer advantages, he favors manpower planning and argues that there must be assertive leadership from the top in the development of manpower strategies that are arrived at democratically, decentralized in their administration and in which there is latitude in the application of specific tactics "down the line." In all of this Dean Lester assigns a major role to manpower specialists who, through research and persuasion, may help top level leaders to resist dependence upon outdated dogmas.

The next three essays, while taking no essential issue with Dean Lester, inject some important cautionary notes about the development of systematic manpower programs and policies.

In Professor Boulding's view, one must be attentive to the peculiar qualities of labor. Thus, labor may not be treated as a commodity, for to do so is to invest the system of exchange with orders of legitimacy that have regularly been denied by "the sellers of labor." The additional facts, writes Professor Boulding, that sellers tend to remain sellers and buyers tend to remain buyers complicate further the easy imputation of legitimacy to labor markets.

While the process of exchange operates as an equalizer, the status relationships between employers and employees are nevertheless clearly those of super—and subordination, a fact that is not automatically reconcilable with democratic tenets. He concludes that institutional reforms, even well-intentioned "manpower approaches," aimed at the location of substitutes for the market, must recognize the social and individual need for the measurement and assessment of a worker's "value." Moral imperatives, meantime, require that we develop institutions that raise rather than lower this value. Professor Boulding, taking a chapter from Adam Smith, urges that good intentions will not prevent what is implied by the "manpower concept," too narrowly conceived, from obscuring man as an end in favor of social ends.

Professor Abramovitz argues persuasively, from a slightly different vantage, that another oversimplification may easily obscure the vision of specialists in a fashion that will inadequately serve lofty and salutary objectives. Thus he objects to the tendency of some to accept rather uncritically a distinction between manpower development, on the one hand, and capital formation on the other. It is his view that the two are interdependent, and he links the two through an examination of the developments of both capital and manpower in which he employs a common set of categories. "Capital formation" thus ". . . comprehends any deliberate employment of income to increase the productivity of resources . . ." including those, like education and training, that increase the productivity of labor. In his discussion, Professor Abramovitz eschews a view, implied by some in the late 1960's, that there are relatively constant ratios in the relationships among the various combinations of investments required for economic progress. It is his conclusion that the balance between "labor saving" and "capital using" and the "capital-and-education intensive" modes of production is an ever changing one, the dynamics of which bears constant observation.

Professor Melvin Reder urges a parallel synthesis upon us in an essay in which he draws together the efforts to develop a model of "human capital" and to understand the economic dimensions of discrimination. The result is that two bodies of material that have been treated as though they are analytically and empirically distinct become mutually reinforcing and thus individually strengthened in their appeal to the student of manpower development and manpower practices. His treatment of "discriminatory" employment practices will undoubtedly provoke considerable discussion in and out of the manpower fraternity.

Professor Reder, towards the end of his careful analysis, points out that ". . . the marginal costs of estimating the probable performance on-the-job of different individuals (in advance of trial and without using educational artifacts) may be too high, and the ability to make the predictions of differential performance among individuals too low to justify the cost of evaluating specific individuals." The Supreme Court, meantime, has recently held, in Griggs vs Duke Power Company (401 US 424, 1971), that educational requirements and tests must be demonstrably related to the jobs for which applicants are screened. It will be of great interest to measure the precise effects on employer costs and to determine whether the Court has simply made ". . . otherwise profitable selection methods . . . legally . . . unacceptable." This landmark case clearly will reduce the theoretical options confronting employers; an assessment of the economic effects of the decision will have to take account of Professor Reder's seminal discussion of information costs, of the role of stereotypes in managing "costs-per-hire," and of whether "employment 'discrimination' against persons culturally different from those hiring them often may be privately profitable."

This first part of the volume, then, offers us four cautionary views on each of four fronts that deserve the attention of researchers and policy makers. Pluralism without well informed guidelines, Dean Lester implies, will provide few solutions to the complex manpower equations that cry for attention. Beware that socio-political means do not displace human ends, cautions Professor Boulding. Professors Abramovitz and Reder add that we will be better able to deal with the sanguinary threat that we will be impaled on the horns of dilemmas in drafting public policy if we first avoid being split by false dichotomies. Collectively, these authors caution us against "directionless fragmentation" in policy making and research in the manpower realm, and against too easy ideological investments.

In the second group are a number of elaborations on and specifications of the positions adumbrated in the first segment. Thus Professor Harbison, picking up a theme in Professor Boulding's paper argues ". . . that human resources, not capital, income or material resources, constitute the basis for the wealth of nations," and goes on to specify the utility of a comparative view within which this wealth may be expressed. In keeping with the need to move from argument to propositional formulations, the author constructs two indicators, the level of human resources development and the effectiveness of human resource utilization, by which the true wealth of nations may be measured. Professor Harbison's suggestions will be well received by analysts seeking to find other measures to supplement those involving calculations of Gross National Products in evaluating the progress of nations.

Professor Bakke reports on an international conference at which the delegates sought to examine the role manpower policies might have played in preventing or ameliorating the most typical consequences for economic growth and development of anti-inflationary demand management. Once again, we learn that the issues involved are highly interrelated, and that policy is best informed when it is based on an understanding of the need for the *timely* and *selective* application of manpower measures. Professor Bakke thus shares the balance of optimism and caution that so strongly flavors other essays. In common with the other authors he directs our attention to the complexity of the whole, the need to recognize not only that differentiated policies are more reasonably likely to help solve socio-economic problems, but that they must be drawn in such a way that they do not lead to discontinuities and to aggravations of imbalances in an interdependent system in which one or another difficulty is attacked. These lessons are clearer for the author's sensitivity to comparative variations in economic processes.

Professor Hauser, meanwhile, shares with us a tentative design for labor force statistics that will, in due course, facilitate the very types of comparative analyses emphasized in other essays. His essay firmly, if politely and implicitly, reminds us that our analyses of manpower problems are only as good as our longitudinal and comparative data, and that far more attention needs to be given to the role of demographic dimensions and to careful construction of comparative models on which so much analysis hangs.

Finally, the second group of essays includes a brief theoretical statement by Professor Sune Carlson that directs our attention back to the units, in this case the firms, that play upon manpower developments. He does this in the context of a discussion that brings home, through an exploration of "knowledge factors" in the decisions of international business firms, the extraordinary role of intelligent, perceptive and skilled upper level manpower personnel. The assumption that managerial manpower can behave in rational ways has rarely been supported by an economist with so many inventive ideas about decision-making in so few pages. The fact that economic weights may be assigned to hitherto theoretically unappreciated management and professional functions is most encouraging. Many have long argued that "marginal analysis" might benefit from a more elaborate model to deal with the question of the productivity of distinguishable human "factors of production" than has been developed for nearly all but blue collar production workers!

There is no need to discuss in any detail the essays in the next part. Reflecting Eli Ginzberg's lifetime interest in "special cases of more general problems," Professors Lidz and Mead and Drs. Roe and Tyler comment on the family, on youth, on women and on professional manpower, respectively, and the essays are clear and self-contained.

Collectively the authors of Part Three highlight one of the points of this introduction, that an intelligent view of manpower policies must be rooted in findings and propositions emanating from all of the social sciences. While economics may be the best represented of these disciplines in the literature on manpower, it is clear that other fields may be overlooked only by those who refuse to put man at the center in efforts to discover the combinations of policy and institutional arrangements calculated to serve him. The result of such an oversight is likely to be a misbegotten reification of institutions at best; at the extreme, such oversights contribute to tyranny. In between, the authors tell us, are developmental hazards that must be attended as cultural, social and psychological problems, unamenable to solution largely by what is commonly regarded, even in broad terms, as economic policy interventions.

In the penultimate section, Professors Whyte, Thomas and Bell offer constructive suggestions on three related fronts. In the first essay Professor Whyte elaborates upon the importance of the multiple perspectives and methods available in the social sciences, highlighting thereby the shortfalls in several areas of professional social science training. To the extent that we who study manpower problems are responsive to Professor Whyte's commentary we will assure that our perspectives are more latitudinary, and that those who follow will be more sensitive to the many subtle questions that are gainsaid in analyses based on a single sovereign discipline.

Professor Thomas' essay, ostensibly about economic progress in Wales, makes a most important point more effectively by his use of ellipsis. Indeed his essay is a parable containing an important moral. Returning to a research site visited by Eli Ginzberg in the late 1930s, the author describes economic changes in a geographic region in a paper that serves to caution the student of manpower against the employment of static models. The substance of the essay argues compellingly for the view that social and economic systems are neither bounded nor long equilibrated, that change is constant and that we might well improve our characterizations and our forecasts if we were more attentive to lessons best called historical. We rarely see in the present all the elements of the future, Professor Thomas tells us, and our social analyses ought to be "open ended" in their construction.

Professor Bell rounds out this volume by directing our attention to the need for a companion volume! In the context of a discussion of the modern corporation he develops a suggestive two-fold classification of approaches to questions in the realm of welfare economics. The implications for manpower policy will be clear enough from a view that attempts to deal frontally with such important matters as social costs. Readers will recognize more clearly the degree to which Professor Bell's "economizing" and "sociologizing" models inhere in most of the preceding essays than they would in the absence of this explication. By delineating and elaborating upon these models he provides an overview that reflects, once again, a number of the themes characteristic of the essays in the volume, and of the nominal "field" to which they belong. In particular Professor Bell suggests that the analytical model in which individual interests are taken to be the ends emphasize a limited view of rationality, a view that leaves out assessments of society's needs. He thus brings us full circle by viewing in a complementary fashion the issues joined by Professor Boulding in the opening essay. He does so in an essay that redefines the parameters typically found in discussions of the public and private interests.

Much more could be said in this introductory section about the "manpower approach" and about manpower policy generally. It would be useful, for example, to develop the point that manpower policy ought not be viewed separately from other policies, an assumption that clearly informed the conference on which Professor Bakke has reported. And it would be useful, in this context, to develop the position that "workfare," as an antidote to welfare, does not include job-creating policies or policies geared to facilitating inflation-free economic expansion. None of the essays in this volume take issue with the need for work and none press hard against the view that favorable attitudes toward work would be much enhanced by a more positive policy regarding the significance of jobs in the society.

There is, furthermore, preoccupation with the nagging question of priorities in these essays, particularly Professor Bell's, but included in most of the others. One strongly senses the need, in arguments for strong, top-level leadership, in pleas that we avoid analytical fragmentation, in assertions about the centrality of individual men and women as ends, for clearer directions and, thereafter, for the types of research and policy formulations that will move us into the future with assurance.

But the editor invites the reader to draw some of his own "thematic inferences" at this point, and draws a line beyond which he has not elaborated upon the lessons for management and the nation—a subtitle of a Ginzberg volume—suggested herein. The authors do not require even as much of an intermediary role as I have sought to play in this opening commentary.

Though the occasion of collecting these essays has been a happy one for the editor, as the foregoing discussion may suggest, I express the sadness of all the contributors and many readers, indeed, over the news that Professor E. Wight Bakke and Robert M. MacIver died while the volume was in its final preparation. Both made important contributions to the "field" here explored and both were close to Eli Ginzberg. The loss of these two academic leaders is both a professional and personal one.

PART ONE

RICHARD A. LESTER

REFLECTIONS ON MANPOWER PLANNING

IN this country, manpower planning leads an ambiguous existence. It is favored or criticized without any consensus as to what the term really means or encompasses. Some commentators maintain that there is no need for manpower planning by the government; others insist that manpower planning, both public and private, is a vital element in economic efficiency and restraint on price inflation. Some say that manpower planning promotes political and economic centralization; others aver that it is a way of avoiding such centralization. Some contend that manpower planning is an essential part of a free enterprise system; others argue that it is contrary to the spirit and principles of private enterprise. Evidently there is a need to clear up some of the misunderstanding and confusion surrounding the concept of manpower planning and to examine its proper role in our economy and society.

MANPOWER PLANNING AND RIVAL SYSTEMS OF THOUGHT

1. One way of viewing manpower planning is as a systematic approach to the development, allocation, and use of human resources for gainful employment. It utilizes the method of rational calculation based on quantitative comparisons and projections of labor demand and supply in different sectors of the economy. As a conceptual apparatus it can be applied to achieve various purposes. One purpose, for instance, would be simply a production goal: the most efficient use of total manpower resources to achieve the maximum possible Gross National Product, subject to a minimum worker-satisfaction constraint. Another possible purpose might be a worker goal: the maximum on-the-job satisfaction of the members of the labor force, subject to a minimum total output constraint. A third over-all aim might be the assurance that all adults would have equal training and employment opportunity and a guarantee of a minimum standard of employment and earnings. These examples are for illustration; the matter of manpower goals under a planning program is discussed more fully in a later section.

As a process of thinking ahead to accomplish the most effective development and use of human resources, manpower planning must be concerned not only with goals but also with program operations and the integration of the plans of individuals, enterprises, and governments with the over-all public plan. The federal government has certain specified public responsibilities in the manpower field—for education, job training, the collection and dissemination of employment information, levels of employment and unemployment, provision for a public job-exchange system, and the promotion of equal educational and employment opportunities.

Part of the over-all responsibility of the federal government with respect to manpower is, therefore, to provide a set of plans that will enable the managements of firms, educational institutions, hospitals, cities, etc., to have a definite framework within which to proceed with their own manpower planning. Governments, of course, have definite social responsibilities (for . example, preparation and guidance for disadvantaged workers), which private enterprise cannot be expected to accept on an uneconomical basis. A significant element in manpower planning by the federal government may, therefore, be to provide at least financial support for parts of state, municipal, and company manpower programs. Need for coordination and integration of other manpower planning with that of the federal government (and vice versa) means, of course, that basic goals and priority decisions should continue largely unaltered for at least two years.[1]

Manpower planning is, so to speak, in competition with other systems of thought that often serve to limit its application. As a rationally oriented framework for programing, manpower planning may prescribe courses of action that seem to conflict with the orientation and prescriptions of other systems of thought and practice. The institutional reforms and programs for solving problems that are called for by manpower planning precepts may seem questionable according to, say, approaches that stress solutions based on the market mechanism or on collective bargaining.

2. The market system, like other systems of thought and practice, has its advantages and limitations as applied in the manpower field. Operating through individual purchase and sale, with prices determined by competitive forces, it enjoys the advantages of reliance on individual responsibility and self-interest, impersonal determinations, and freedom from bureaucratic control. The market mechanism can be assumed to work automatically, with no need for government to intervene or to plan. The market is supposed, as Adam Smith ex-

plained, to operate as an invisible hand, guiding purchases and sales, employment and output, according to relative prices moving freely to clear the market.

In the manpower field, however, the market mechanism has significant shortcomings for solving certain problems. Employment, including pay and benefits, training, transfer, and promotion, are often highly administered and personal matters. The market may fail to supply the information and guidance necessary for rational career and job choices. It may effectively exclude some suppliers, who experience so much unemployment that they become alienated from the whole employment system. The market mechanism may stress immediate gains or returns at the expense of serious long-term losses or damage—whether in the conservation of natural resources or protection of children from permanently injurious labor. And the market has proved quite deficient as a means of preventing or eliminating racial and sex discriminations in employment. It reflects social attitudes and social restrictions; it may not operate to correct social prejudice or bias.

The labor area has generally been a rather unruly part of economics. It fails to behave regularly as predicted by "market" models, whether the subject is occupational wage differentials, the employment effects of minimum wages,[2] or employment discrimination based on race or sex. With respect to the failure of the market to eliminate genuine discrimination against female workers and the need for some government action in that area, Eli Ginzberg has written:

> There are economists of Chicago, Columbia, and elsewhere who, predicating a single highly competitive labor market, have no doubt that these several attempts through legislation, administrative action, and trade union pressure to narrow and eliminate wage differentials between the sexes must result in a lowered demand for women workers. This straightforward conclusion of theirs is deduced from a model that has at best limited relevance and at worst next to no relevance to the complex forces that operate to determine the demand for labor and wage rates in multiple markets that

while competitive in some degree are non-competitive in many respects.[3]

Professor Ginzberg goes on to explain that sex discrimination and institutional factors may mean women do not have equal access to higher-level jobs and that the substitution of men or machines for female employees as an adjustment to the legal requirement of equal treatment, including pay, may prove to be impractical.

Negroes and ghetto residents likewise have good grounds for lack of faith that the market mechanism alone is sufficient for solving their employment problems. Their leadership has recognized the need for political and social action to break down employment barriers that the market failed for a century to eliminate. By themselves, market answers to ghetto manpower problems have proved too doctrinaire and ineffectual under prevailing circumstances.

3. In the labor area another approach or system of thought and practice is collective bargaining. Collective bargaining uses a form of representative democracy as a method of dealing with manpower issues—access to jobs; training and entrance to occupations; arrangements for lay-off, transfer, and promotion; and changes in the structure of compensation, mainly occupational wage differentials that can influence career choices.

Collective bargaining operates through negotiations between representatives of the employees in a "bargaining unit" and the management. The "bargaining unit" may be a plant, a firm, a group of firms, or an occupation or group of occupations in a workplace, a locality, or some other geographic area. Negotiations, when completed, generally result in written labor agreements that contain employee and management rights, work rules, wage scales, and other terms of employment, and provisions for interpretation of the agreement and adjudication of disputes under the agreement, usually according to a so-called "grievance procedure." Such agreements usually run for one, two, or three years, two or three years being the most common lifetime for labor agreements.

Provisions of labor agreements and union practice may serve to protect existing employees from market competition. Barriers to outside competition may take such forms as control of access to training or entrance to a skilled trade through apprenticeships; or control of access to employment in the workplace by union domination of hiring halls or by seniority provisions in agreements making length of service controlling in layoff, recall to work, and order of qualification for promotion; or control of the structure of compensation for different jobs, which influences their attractiveness to present employees and their appeal to outsiders.

The advantages of collective bargaining as a method of dealing with manpower issues are self-determination by the parties directly concerned and acceptance by the workers of the terms negotiated by their representatives. They are, in brief, the advantages of well-functioning industrial democracy.

The drawbacks from an over-all manpower viewpoint are especially prevalent with skilled-craft control, which tends to work against the interests of the disadvantaged elements in the labor force. The disadvantages of collective bargaining stem from such anticompetitive practices as arbitrary restrictions on supply, which limit access to training for, and employment in, a trade; exclusion by enforcement of excessive training requirements or periods, as under apprenticeship rules; and job control by forcing, through strikes, such large wage increases for particular occupations as to restrict employment in those occupations and in the industry. For example, building construction has faced this situation in recent years, with average wage increases of 15 percent in 1969 and over 20 percent in 1970. Under three-year agreements, the pattern of negotiated increases runs around $1.00 an hour rise each year in the skilled trades.[4]

Control over apprenticeship, union membership, and employment on jobs under union conditions has, in many instances, served effectively to prevent blacks and other minority groups from having equal opportunity to obtain work at rapidly rising wages in the skilled construction trades. The archaic requirement of four and five years of apprenticeship training to learn one of the construction trades such as carpenter or painter is, of course, absurd. A review by the bipartisan Construction Industry Training Board under the British Industrial Training Act of 1964 reduced the apprenticeship training period in construction from four or five years to one and a half or two years by a combination of classroom and on-job training.[5] Better still would be the practice of open national tests and certification of competence for skilled trades,[6] which would lead to competition by schools and industry for the most effective and economical ways to train skilled craftsmen. Such competition would undoubtedly reduce the period of training for a skilled journeyman in most building trades to less than a year.

As a method of helping to solve the nation's manpower problems, it is clear that collective bargaining, especially in local-market lines, can be counterproductive. It may be influenced by the demands and self-interest of the union's membership. Industrial unions in the mass production industries are less likely than many craft unions to try to exert control over labor supply and to restrict training opportunities. Thus, their policies may not conflict significantly with the manpower development plans of the federal, state, and local governments.

The distortion of the wage structure in a way that is contrary to the relative demand-supply situation in particular occupations and industries is perhaps the most significant way that collective bargaining operates against rational manpower policy. Under such circumstances, the "market indicators" (relative wages) give the wrong signals to workers in selecting and training for particular occupations and industries. This sort of misdirection has been especially evident in recent years as individual unions through economic muscle have forced their wage scales out of line and out of rational relationship with comparable jobs in other industries.

The Nixon Administration in 1969 and 1970, pursuing the illusion that fiscal-monetary restraint and the resulting induced unemployment would force negotiated wage increases to decline in conformity with market conditions, deliberately maintained a laissez-faire policy with respect to union demands and negotiated wage increases. Unions like the Teamsters, the building trades, and the printers took full advantage of this open invitation. The result was a serious distortion of the wage structure from the point of view of manpower allocation, not to mention the inflation-generating effects of a badly unbalanced structure of wages—the restoration of some balance generally means raising the low ones, not lowering the high ones.

4. As separate, highly administered manpower spheres, large business and government units offer still another system of thought and practice concerning manpower. They control a large part of on-the-job training, the career development and advancement, and the administered wage structure in the economy.

Large enterprises have their own industrial relations and manpower programs. They do their own manpower planning and have their own policies with respect to recruitment, selection, transfer, on-the-job and other training, advancement, and career development.

The large enterprise, of course, must focus on its ability to compete, progress, and (for business concerns) make profits for stockholders and to accumulate sufficient capital resources to assure its future development. A crucial element in the survival and growth of the large enterprise is an efficient work force and an able management. Therefore, the management plans and seeks to recruit, train, and retain highly effective working units. Generally, multiplant firms have company-wide manpower planning and manpower policies. Therefore, each company acquires and maintains a reputation in industrial relations and manpower affairs. The individual worker often selects a company to work for rather than training for an occupation. By tying to a large enterprise, he separates himself from the market and relies on administrative decisions in the enterprise for his career pattern.

Most large firms tend to follow similar or common types of industrial relations policies, and the manning decisions of governments under civil service provisions have much in common and also tend to be separate from market control. The fact that manpower developments in large enterprises are so subject to administrative determination and that large firms tend to modify manpower policy in a common pattern, helps to explain the marked changes with respect to the hiring of blacks and other disadvantaged persons in the late 1960s and early 1970s. When orders came from the top down to alter hiring standards and policies, the fact that so much operated by administrative decision made it relatively easy to shift to the new policy. Similarly the wage structure of a large enterprise is administered either under job evaluation, collective bargaining, or both. With on-the-job training and promotion from within, contact with the market is mainly at hiring in jobs, mostly at the bottom of the job structure except for management positions.

From this discussion of four different systems or approaches (manpower planning, the market collective bargaining, and manpower and personnel programs of large enterprises), it is evident that each plays a role in the manpower field. Often solutions to manpower problems need to draw on two or more approaches.

Part of the skill in developing and managing public manpower programs is to put together and carry out an appropriate combination of parts of systems which can complement and support one another. Of course, for some purposes and situations a mixture may prove ineffective because the parts work at cross-purposes. And, it may be intellectually satisfying, if rather impractical, to insist that reliance be placed solely on one system (say, the market) and that that system be carried out to its ultimate logical conclusion. Practical leadership selects pieces that can be made to operate efficiently together and makes them do so.

Thus, one important role for manpower planning is to develop program components of systems that will move along together and that can be administered successfully. This is a true leadership role. Because, as we shall see, manpower planning should operate at various levels, including at the top nationally, it can appropriately play a comprehensive leadership role. That is the sense in which one can speak of "comprehensive manpower planning" without implying central planning for detailed local application.

PURPOSES OF MANPOWER PLANNING

Whatever the approach and methods, manpower planning presumably is designed to accomplish a certain purpose or set of purposes. Supposedly, it should seek to make the best (or most rational) use of the nation's available manpower resources.

That broad generalization is, however, rather complicated in practice. In applying the principle of most efficient utilization of resources, each system of thought is likely to place its own special interpretation or stress on particular aspects of manpower utilization. Such differences can perhaps be brought out most clearly by first setting forth some of the purposes or aims of a public manpower program.

On the supply side, the possible aims or purposes of a public manpower program may include: (a) to attract and train a supply sufficient to meet current and prospective shortages in particular occupations; (b) to train and develop disadvantaged and discouraged workers so that they are able to get and hold gainful employment; (c) to improve the motivation and mobility of parts of the labor force by increasing access to and knowledge about jobs and transportation to them; and (d) to improve employment counseling and guidance so that occupations and career patterns are more intelligently selected and the transition from school to work is successfully completed.

On the demand side, the purposes of manpower policy might include: (a) to adjust pay and benefit schedules to attract workers to shortage occupations; (b) to induce employers to adapt recruitment, training, and jobs so that more disadvantaged workers can be employed; (c) to enforce equal employment opportunity in order to eliminate race, sex, or age discrimination in employment; and (d) to develop and carry out programs of job creation, especially for unemployed and underemployed workers.

With regard to the functioning of the market for labor services, the manpower aims might include: (a) good information available in a central location covering the whole market area and widely distributed and used; (b) removal of market impediments, whether unnecessary job or occupational requirements or other restrictions on labor mobility; and (c) quick and skillful matching of up-to-date job orders and current job applicants over the relevant area for the occupation (whether community, region, or nationwide).

In addition, there are purposes that are at the heart of a major national manpower effort. They include: (a) coordination of manpower policies with general economic and political policies; (b) establishment of priorities to serve as a basis for allocating resources to different parts of the total manpower effort; (c) systematic research and evaluation of the different parts of the over-all program as a means for determining future priorities and allocations; (d) advance planning for education and training (including the necessary capital facilities) in order to assure sufficient supply in occupations that require a long period of preparation; and (e) administrative leadership to develop coordination and a sense of goal achievement within the manpower effort and to attract and hold a high quality staff at important points in the manpower structure.

This great variety of purposes obviously cannot be achieved by a simple, single-system type of program. It is well to bear in mind that manpower programs have to be carried out through people on the local level. And the employment problems of some people (e.g., disadvantaged persons) often present a mixture of physical and psychological difficulties. Consequently, manpower programs need to be multidimensional and adaptable to local circumstances. And the more diversified and comprehensive a manpower program is, the greater are the problems of coordination and flexibility in application.

The matter of the priorities and weights to be placed on different elements in a broad manpower program brings one back to the question of the role of different systems of thought in working out emphases and resource allocations. Obviously, if one's manpower approach stresses the efficacy of the market mechanism, main reliance in a national manpower program would be placed on the Employment Service as a center of market information and as an efficient job exchange. Any elements under the program that may seem to hinder the operation of market forces (such as an unbalanced wage structure under collective bargaining or enforcement of antidiscrimination legislation) or that may seem unnecessary according to market doctrine (like government long-range planning for occupations requiring lengthy preparation periods, or special outreach activities that are more therapeutic than economic) would be considered interventionist and inefficient and wasteful. They are thought to constrict growth of the Gross National Product.

For the purpose of a manpower program, the collective bargaining approach is too narrowly based on a single firm or industry and too focused on the economic well-being of a relatively small in-group of suppliers. The main interest in collective bargaining is the terms and conditions of employment and labor relations in a relatively small section of the economy. Even within a bargaining unit, manpower development and the efficient utilization of manpower resources are generally left to management except as rules are established to promote the self-interest and job satisfaction of the employees in that unit.

The central labor federation (the AFL-CIO), which is designed primarily for publicity and political purposes, is broadly representative of most of organized labor. However, collective bargaining is conducted by the affiliated unions; the AFL-CIO does not participate in their bargaining or in rule-making in industry. Its influence on manpower policy is chiefly exercised in political terms.

The large enterprise also is focused primarily on its own problems and aims, which generally are not national manpower purposes. Although social responsibilities (particularly in the area of benefits for its own employees and support for local community projects) have received increased attention by large concerns, the priorities of each enterprise must be established in terms of its own purposes, particularly its own competitive power and its survival and well-being. The enterprise's manpower recruitment, selection, training, and promotion policies must be formulated according to its self-interest, which may be out of line with public manpower purposes. The enterprise's self-interest may only be coordinated with national manpower purposes in areas such as hiring of disadvantaged persons or training for shortage occupations, if those activities are made to the advantage of the enterprise through public measures like the employment and training requirements under public contracts, or public subsidies for certain types of training for particular groups, or by laws against racial or other discrimination in employment.

As in the case of collective bargaining, national associations of enterprises cannot provide the organizational breadth of interest and power to make enterprise manpower policies conform to national purposes. The U.S. Chamber of Commerce, the National Association of Manufacturers, the National Alliance of Businessmen, and the associations of colleges and universities, hospitals, and other nonprofit enterprises [7] are designed to promote the interests and special policies of their constituent enterprises. General, national purposes or goals are not and cannot be their primary concern.[8]

For the proper attention and emphasis on broad, national purposes, some central responsibility for planning and policy-making, and some administrative monitoring of programs, are essential. Systematic analysis and planning on the basis of informed projections are necessary to minimize shortages of well-prepared specialists in the professions. For occupations requiring a lengthy period of training and having a nationwide market, some national planning is clearly desirable.

Some sort of central manpower planning and supervising agency is required in order to provide the necessary top leadership function. That involves such activities as extracting and spreading the lessons of program experience, stressing the public and national interests in manpower programs, and fixing national manpower priorities and carrying through on their practical application. Above all, leadership at the top is necessary to spread a sense of purpose and mission throughout the whole operating organization. Only in that way can local units, including employers and labor unions, appreciate how their contributions fit into an over-all scheme.

Since 1963, the annual Manpower Report of the President

has served to explain the purposes and the over-all program of the national administration in the manpower field. The President has used the occasion to discuss the past year's accomplishments, the manpower areas needing special attention, and plans and directions for the future.

It is unfortunate that the first Manpower Report of President Nixon to the Congress in March 1970 contains no Presidential message on manpower policy and no explanation for the absence of that part of the Report. One can, therefore, only speculate as to whether the absence of a Presidential statement means that (a) the President's economic philosophy is not consistent with a comprehensive public manpower program; (b) the White House staff was unable to work out a consistent rationale for federal programs in the manpower field; (c) the bureaucratic hurdles and time constraints encountered in clearing drafts of a statement proved impossible to overcome; or (d) actual developments, such as growing unemployment and distorting and spiraling wage increases, made a Presidential manpower statement impolitic at that time. Hopefully, the grounds were practical and not doctrinaire or partisan political, because Presidential leadership and support are absolutely essential for an effective national manpower program.

Leadership at the top to achieve national purposes does not, or course, preclude decentralization of operations. As explained in the next section, variety in local conditions and reliance on state and local agencies for operating programs need not prove to be practical obstacles to national manpower planning, programming, and general monitoring.

LEVELS AND EFFECTIVENESS OF ADMINISTRATION

Much of the success of manpower planning rests on effective administration at the different levels of government. Since governments have social responsibilities and are subject to political pressures, program coordination and efficiency in manpower activities need the enforcement power of lessons of experience, persuasion of political leadership, and financial and other inducements.

Centralization of planning, project evaluation, and allocation of federal resources for manpower purposes can be compatible with decentralization of operations to state and local agencies, provided different levels of government are properly integrated and play a role in the planning process. It is important that the governors, mayors, and other elected officials have responsible roles in both the planning and operation of manpower programs. In that way, manpower programs can be adapted to the social and economic conditions at the local level, and localities can participate effectively in the overall program.

The degree of national guidance for manpower programs designed for a particular occupation or community may properly be made to depend on such factors as the following: (a) the geographical coverage of the market for the occupation (national concern and responsibility should presumably be strong for occupations with a nationwide market and weak for those having largely a local market); (b) the quality of manpower planning at the state and local levels; (c) the administrative capability in particular states and localities, especially in the agency that has the principal role in manpower operations. The type and amount of federal financial support provided for individual state and municipal programs are, of course, important. Block federal grants to states or cities have the obvious disadvantage that they permit local disregard of national purposes and priorities as well as considerations such as the efficiency of local programs and the quality of their product.

In a large country like the United States with a pluralistic tradition, the danger is that federal funds for manpower activities will be spread too thinly and misdirected and misused. Manpower planning is designed in large measure to avoid such inefficiency and waste.

Despite eight years of Congressional support for the concept of federal manpower planning and some painful lessons with poor coordination of programs, national manpower planning still encounters all sorts of practical obstacles and constraints. For example, the need to improve the forecasting of requirements for professional personnel, such as physicists and engineers, has been shown by the rapid change from shortage to surplus in 1969 and 1970. The year-by-year appropriation process, with little lead time, has contributed shortsighted planning, sudden shifts, and great uncertainty. The shifts have left ambiguous the extent to which resources for manpower purposes should be devoted to serving the disadvantaged or to training for professions and occupations threatened with shortages. In many communities it has not been possible to prevent the exploitation of manpower programs for personal or partisan political gain. And under existing methods of wage determination, little coordination between the structure of wages and labor-supply needs can be expected with or without manpower planning. In short, manpower planning is no sure cure for political, social, and managerial ills. It does, nevertheless, bring out rather clearly the real costs of particular barriers, mistakes, and misuses of funds.

Needless to say, manpower planning generally seeks to work with market forces to achieve its purposes. However, experience has indicated some of the practical shortcomings of purely market solutions to certain manpower problems. Thus, planning and administrative actions are, under some conditions, necessary in order to supplement market forces where they are not effective.

CONCLUDING OBSERVATIONS

This essay has attempted to put manpower planning in proper perspective. In discussing the role of manpower planning, a number of points were made, including the following:

1. Manpower planning is a complex process; manpower problems ramify throughout the economy and the society.

2. Systematic planning to meet special manpower problems (e.g., shortages in some professions or unemployment in the ghettoes) should be part of a general program, with priorities established nationally and with various sectors (federal agencies, states, municipalities, large firms, etc.) well coordinated with the national purpose.

3. Manpower planning is both a system of thought and a program for effective action. As a system of thought it is, so to speak, partly in competition with other systems of thought (e.g. the market, collective bargaining, and personnel management of large enterprises) and partly supplements and supports those other systems.

4. The market, collective bargaining, and large-enterprise manpower policies, singly or together, have serious shortcomings for manpower purposes that public programs generally, and national manpower planning especially, are designed to remedy.

5. Systematic planning seems essential, for government, which assumes certain community responsibilities, is not constrained by the profit criterion, and has a definite leadership function to perform in the manpower field. Planning at the top also provides a basis for manpower programs by enterprises, community organizations, and individuals.

6. The variety of possible purposes of planning and programs in the manpower field points to the need for objective evaluation of experience, careful determination of priorities,

and effective coordination of administration at various levels, in order to avoid the frustration of conflicting purposes and programs.

Much can be learned from the manpower experiments and experience since enactment of the Manpower Development and Training Act of 1962. Hopefully, we have the wit to extract a goodly measure of benefit from past experience.

If there is a message in this essay it is that we should face up to the fact that each of the four systems of thought and practice has the limitations of its virtues for tackling manpower problems. Under some circumstances and for some purposes, a particular approach may be not only ineffective but positively counterproductive. In deciding among manpower programs it must be recognized that their effectiveness may be greatly influenced by workers' motivations, opinions, and past experience.

Also account must be taken of the fact that manpower legislation, appropriations, and administrators are likely to be greatly influenced by the economic philosophy of political leaders and the general public, regardless of the lessons of actual experience or the results of systematic analysis. Old economic dogmas never die; they live on in the recesses of politicians' minds.

It is the task of manpower specialists, through research and other methods of persuasion, to educate those leaders whose mental bents were set before the 1960's, to explain that highly productive manpower programs can be developed, using the various approaches in combination in appropriate ways.

Above all, a constructive national program must include strong, democratically developed guidance from the top, with decentralization of administration and latitude of application down the line.

NOTES

1. For a further discussion of manpower planning, see R. A. Lester, *Manpower Planning in a Free Society* (Princeton, N.J.: Princeton University Press, 1966). Of course, for some parts of manpower planning such as training for the professions, planning must be on a much longer basis than two years.

2. On the failure of market models to predict the employment consequences of minimum-wage increases under legislation see, for instance, Thomas W. Gavett, "Youth Unemployment and Minimum Wages," *Monthly Labor Review,* 93 (March 1970), 5–6; Peter S. Barth, "The Minimum Wage and Teen-Age Unemployment," *Proceedings of the Twenty-second Annual Winter Meeting of the Industrial Relations Research Association, December 29–30, 1969* (Madison, Wisconsin, 1970), pp. 309–10; and R.A. Lester, *Economics of Labor* (2d ed.; New York: MacMillan, 1964), pp. 520–24.

3. Eli Ginzberg, "Public Policy and Womanpower," in Arnold R. Weber, Frank H. Cassell, and Woodrow L. Ginsberg, eds., *Public-Private Manpower Policies* (Madison, Wisconsin: Industrial Relations Research Association, 1969), p. 176.

4. See, for example, "Building Costs Push Steadily Upward," *New York Times,* Section 8, June 14, 1970, pp. 1 and 9.

5. Herbert A. Perry, "New Training Plan in Britain's Construction Industry," *Monthly Labor Review,* 93 (February 1970), 27–28.

6. In West Germany, the final written and practical tests for apprentices in a particular trade are common throughout the nation and the scales by which proficiency is assessed and grades into which candidates are placed are nationally standardized.

7. Eli Ginzberg has pointed out that government and other nonprofit sectors of the economy account for at least one-third and possibly two-fifths of all employment. See *The Pluralistic Economy* (New York; McGraw-Hill, 1965), p. 193.

8. With respect to disadvantaged labor, private industry generally seems to want the federal government to establish broad manpower policies and to provide financial support for training, which may not, however, be very effective. See John L. Iacobelli, "A Survey of Employer Attitudes toward Training the Disadvantaged," *Monthly Labor Review,* 93 (June 1970), 51–55.

KENNETH E. BOULDING

MAN AS A COMMODITY

THE live human body has always occupied a somewhat anomalous position in economics. We can define economics as the study of how society is organized through exchange and through exchangeables, which is at least a workable definition that seems to cover most of the field. The live human body, which we shall refer to simply as a person, occupies a central and yet at the same time a peculiar role both in the capital structure and in the network of transfers of exchangeables. Thus, the person is clearly a capital good in the sense that he is the source of benefits to his owner.

In a slave society, this relationship is extremely clear. Persons who are slaves are domestic animals, as much a part of the assets of their owner as cows or horses. They are bought and sold, they depreciate, they have a cost of upkeep, and presumably they produce a valuable stream of services. Their capital value depends on the discounted sum of the differences between the revenues derived from them and the costs incurred by their ownership. In a slave society, a slave gives off labor just as a cow gives off milk, and this labor presumably results in additions to the assets of his owner, the value of these additions being the gross value of the labor, and the value of these additions minus the cost of maintenance being the net value of the labor.

The total disrepute, both moral and economic, into which slavery has fallen suggests that the person or the capital good at any rate exhibits peculiarities which even a domestic animal does not. The moral attack on slavery rests on the sense of identity of one person with another and on a feeling of community, however fragile, with other members of the human race. "No man is an Island—any man's death diminishes me, because I am involved in Mankinde; And therefore never send to know for whom the bell tolls; it tolls for thee," said John Donne. Empathy, identification, pity, and benevolence are common phenomena in the human race. The man whose sense of identity stops at his own skin indeed is quite likely to end up in the madhouse. We credit these strange two-legged creatures we see around us, in outward appearance so much like what we see in the mirror, as having the same rich and complex inner world that we do ourselves. Therefore, we identify with them.

Slavery has long been morally unstable, although it was not until the scientific revolution made it relatively unprofitable that it became morally intolerable. As processes of production became more complex, requiring intelligence and skill on the part of the human operator and trust between the organizer and the operator, slavery became relatively unprofitable. To put the matter in another way, slavery was a system with a low horizon of development. Free labor, because of the greater richness of relationships which this made possible, had a very much higher horizon of development and productivity, so that the employer could hire free labor at higher and higher wages and still be better off than he would be under a slave system.

Once slavery is abolished, every man becomes, as it were, his own slave. The person is removed as a capital good from the accounting system. There are some apparent exceptions to this principle, in the case, for instance, of compensations for injury or death, and in certain special cases of long-term contracts and services, such as a professional baseball player. The person, however, still receives income by the sale of his services or activities and he exchanges this income for other goods and services. It would seem, therefore, that labor is clearly a commodity, for it is something which is bought, sold, and has a price in either monetary or real terms.

Nevertheless, the constitutions of both the International Labor Office and of the American Federation of Labor solemnly declare that labor is not a commodity. The feeling that some things about a person should not be subject to exchange, which is overwhelmingly strong in the case of regarding the person as a capital good, still clings somewhat to the purchase and sale of activities of the person for short periods, which is what we really mean by labor. It is clear, therefore, that even though labor *is* a commodity, it is a peculiar one; and its peculiarities are related in some degree to the peculiarities of the person considered as a capital good or as a commodity.

The problem here is essentially that of the legitimation of exchange and the exchange relationship where one of the exchangeables is either a person or some activity of a person. The problem of the legitimacy of exchange has been curiously neglected by economists.[1] At least since about 1870, with the rise of the marginalist school, economists outside the Marxist tradition have been unanimous in believing that exchange, if it is uncoerced, is beneficial to both parties. Otherwise, it will not take place, as either party has a veto on it. Consequently, it has been assumed rather generally, though implicitly, that exchange, which is even more clearly twice blessed than mercy, could hardly fail to be legitimate. Nevertheless, the attack on the legitimacy of exchange, especially in the labor market, has been severe and prolonged.

In the socialist countries the legitimation of the labor market has been achieved by the replacement of the private employer by the public employer. The labor market has not in general been abolished. Labor is still bought and sold and has a price, in fact, has different prices depending on the quality of the labor. But the fact that the principal employer is the national state or its creatures and agents sheds, as it were, a warm glow of legitimacy over the whole procedure. Socialism indeed must be regarded as a phenomenon arising out of a prior delegitimation of the market as an instrument of social organization, and the socialist state must be seen, in part, as an attempt to relegitimate it. The market is such an enormously useful beast that we cannot throw it away altogether. Indeed, the only alternative is the slave state in which all persons are slaves of the government. Nevertheless, the market is evidently a beast which is regarded with such hostility and ambivalence that it has to be bridled and tamed before it can be tolerated.

Even in capitalist societies, the same forces of delegitimation and relegitimation of the labor market are at work. Here this takes the form of the rise of the labor movement, resulting in collective bargaining, frequently with governmental encouragement. It also involves direct governmental intervention in the labor market in the shape, for instance, of a minimum wage or through social security taxes, which determine in part the form in which wages shall be paid. Thus, the feeling that a completely unregulated and competitive labor market is illegitimate is almost universal. Even though it is clear that human activities are organized in considerable part by exchange, we have a very strong resistance to any suggestion that they should be organized wholly by exchange.

Relations between persons indeed are organized by at least two other classes of relationships: on the one hand, by threat, and on the other hand, by what I have called integrative relationships, which is a large category that can be broken down again into such things as status, persuasion, identity, and so on. One of the problems in the legitimation of exchange at the level of the person is that exchange is a relatively uncomplicated relationship involving rather sparse uses of information and affect, whereas we have a rather strong feeling that relationships between persons ought to be at least moderately complicated.

It would be an interesting exercise, for instance, to try and find out what people really mean when they complain that something is "impersonal." Exchange indeed can be conducted quite satisfactorily between a person and a vending machine, or with anything else in the environment with which one could have terms of trade, that is, toward which one could direct output and from which one can get input. This is all that is strictly needed for a person to have exchange of money or commodities, especially where the commodity is standardized.

The activity of a human being, labor, however, is hard to standardize; and if it is standardized, the human being is treated as a machine much less complex than in fact he is. The very term "hands" for manual workers—indeed, the very term "manual," which means the same thing—suggests that workers are not really required to have any heads, that there is something undignified in being required to perform an activity which represents only a small part of the potentiality of the human organism. Adam Smith indeed noted this problem in his famous attack on the division of labor as productive of degraded human beings, degraded by the very specialization which made them productive.[2] It is a remarkable tribute to Adam Smith's profound insight that even though he recognized the virtues of specialization and the attendant increased productivity of goods, he also saw clearly that exchange, if left to itself to organize society, might produce a depreciation in the quality of human capital at the same time that it increased the quantity of nonhuman capital.

Another peculiarity of the labor market which may account for difficulties in its legitimation is the fact that the sellers of labor tend to remain sellers and the buyers tend to remain buyers. This in itself would tend to create semi-permanent castes of sellers of labor on the one hand and buyers of labor on the other. Considering also that the buyers of labor tend to be the active organizers of the productive process and the sellers of labor tend to be passive instruments, it is easy to see how a status differential appears, with the buyers of labor having a higher status than the sellers. The buyers and the sellers then become not merely castes but classes. This distinction is in rather sharp contrast, shall we say, to speculative markets, such as the wheat market or the stock market, where the buyer today will become the seller tomorrow, where there is no class or caste of buyers and sellers, and where the relationship between the buyers and the sellers is exactly symmetrical.

These status relationships in exchange are the key to much that is superficially puzzling. There is something still a little paradoxical about exchange. By comparison with either threat or integrative relationships, exchange promotes equality of status. A threat-submission system promotes sharp inequality of status between the one who threatens and the one who submits, of which slave labor is a good example. In order to get equality of status in a threat system we have to develop a threat-counterthreat system (eyeball to eyeball) which tends to be extremely costly and unstable. Equality here is bought at a very high price, for the escalation of such a system tends to ensure that a large amount of resources must be devoted to maintain the threat capability of both parties, which then cannot be used for the production of goods.

Integrative systems, likewise, are frequently built up on the basis of inequality of status. Thus, the relationship between parent and child, or between old and young, or between teacher and student, or between ruler and ruled, all have strong integrative components, but all imply inequality of status. The only integrative relationship, indeed, which implies equality is that of friendship, and this curiously enough is very much like an exchange relationship. If *A* and *B* are friends, *A* does something for *B*, and *B* does something for *A*. If the relationship becomes too one-sided the friendship then tends to break up.

Marriage, likewise, is supposed to be an exchange relationship involving even more division of labor than friendship. We could argue indeed that even the threat-counterthreat relationships also involve exchange, although in this case it is a threat to exchange bads rather than goods. If *A* does something nasty to *B*, *B* will do something nasty to *A*. In the exchange of goods, the equality of status is still more clear. By contrast, for instance, between the gift relationship, which always implies inequality of status with the giver having a higher status than the recipient, exchange is by its very nature reciprocal and symmetrical. If *A* gives something to *B* and *B* gives something to *A*, then there seems to be no reason why we should not reverse the statuses of *A* and *B*, since it would make no difference to the transaction.

We see this phenomenon in a curiously inverse way in the customs of retail trade, especially in those retail establishments which cater to classes which are higher in status than the retailer himself. Here we observe a traditional pattern of condescension on the part of the customer and servility on the part of the retailer. In the exchange, the retailer's goods and skill have in themselves an equal, or perhaps even a slightly superior status, to the customer's money. This equality implied in the act of exchange then has to be offset by status communications in the conversation, manners, and communications which surround the exchange. In the supermarket we may notice there is no such relationship. The checker at the exit gate is not obsequious, the customer is not condescending, and the very impersonality of the transaction oddly enough makes for equality.

It is at least a plausible hypothesis, therefore, that one source of the difficulties in the labor market is precisely the tension between the exchange itself, which operates as an equalizer, and the status relationships between the employer and the employed, which rise out of the fact that employers are a class who organize the activities of the employed into a process of production. In the utilization of labor, therefore, there has to be a dominance-submission relationship. Here again it is interesting to note that Adam Smith thought that the progress of the American colonies was a result of the fact that the colonists brought with them from Europe what he calls the "habit of subordination," and hence could be organized into political societies and into productive organizations! [3] This dominance-submission relationship which induces the worker to do what he is told rests on a complex set of human interactions. The worker may do what he is told because he respects the superior skill of the employer, or he may do what he is told out of fear of losing his job, in which case it becomes much more like the threat-submission system, with indeed overtones of slavery.

Again, there may develop a rhetoric for legitimating the position of the worker, as we find it, for instance, in the trade union movement, with the rhetoric of "an honest day's work for an honest day's pay." This emphasizes the legitimacy of the relationship, and in a sense the equality of fundamental status as between the employer and the employed. The boss-bossed relationship is seen simply as a convenient division of labor with the boss and the worker each "doing his thing," with each retaining a satisfactory identity in the process. It may indeed well be that the most significant result of the rise of the labor movement in the capitalist countries was the legitimation of the labor market which it fostered. The worker as a member of the union had a dignity as well as a security which the worker as an isolated individual in an atomistic labor market could not possibly enjoy, unless, of course, he had some kind of professional status arising out of some sort of professional mystique.

It is interesting to note incidentally that in the professions there is very little problem of legitimating the labor market—the lawyer, the doctor, the architect, even the professor—feels no threat to his status at all in selling his services to the highest bidder. The problem here indeed has been how to legitimate other arrangements which might be more socially productive than the labor market principle of fee for service. We see this especially in the medical profession, where there has been, and continues to be, very strong resistance to the abolition of the market for particular services and the organization of doctors in organized enterprises on a salaried basis. Among business executives and government bureaucrats, on the other hand, status has gone along with salary rather than with professionalization. This emphasizes once again the principle that where the seller of labor has a status independent of the fact that he sells it, as in the case of the professions, it is very easy to legitimate the labor market. Where, however, the seller is doubtful about his status, then we tend to get salaried workers, whose income is only loosely related to their output and is determined primarily by their position in a role structure. In the case of nonsalaried workers the labor market gets hedged around with organization of both labor and management, resulting in collective bargaining and what might be called industrial jurisprudence.

All this perhaps can be summed up in a question to the

employer: "Are you buying labor or are you hiring a person?" At one end of this extreme is the person who is hired to do a single specific task, as on the assembly line, and who is fired immediately if he does not perform the task precisely as instructed. At the other end of the scale, is the professor, or even the salaried executive, who is hired to "be" rather than to "do." That is, he is hired to fill a very loosely defined role and his activity, therefore, depends not on fulfilling instructions from somebody further up the hierarchy but in "doing his thing," according to his perceived identity. There are always limits, of course, often fairly sharply delimited, on what the "thing" is that a salaried person is supposed to do, but the limits are much broader than they are for "hands." The very distinction between salaried and hourly labor is one of status in the sense that the salaried person has an identity within which he has a certain freedom of action and capacity for originality, whereas originality is the last thing one expects from a hired hand—in fact, it would be severely frowned upon.

A considerable portion of the activities of the legal system arise because there is no market in the capital value of free persons, yet there has to be in society somewhere a substitute for this market in the shape of an apparatus which can evaluate the worth of persons, either to themselves or to society, under circumstances where this valuation is necessary for behavior. These occasions occur mainly at two quite different levels. On the one hand, the law is frequently called upon to assess the value of a person when his body has been damaged by another. Damage suits which seek to assess, and to force the responsible party to pay, the value of an injury to a person or the cost of his loss in a death to his dependents are a considerable part of the business of the law. It is a clumsy apparatus and certainly does not operate with any great justice. Many who are damaged receive no compensation at all in society and many receive what seems like an overpayment of their loss. Nevertheless, the very existence of this apparatus testifies to the need for making evaluations, particularly under conditions of loss, of the capital value of the human person. It is a very interesting and difficult question as to whether any reform of this system is feasible, for instance, in the direction of compulsory universal insurance against all losses of capital value of the person, without regard to blame or responsibility. Such a system might, of course, make for irresponsibility and for the production of avoidable damages, though we do not really know how elastic is the demand for doing damage to persons. One hopes that it is highly inelastic, in which case the system of universal human insurance might work pretty well. One would not really expect the problem to be much more serious than the problem of arson in the case of fire insurance.

At the other end of the legal spectrum, we can interpret the criminal law as in very large measure an attempt to assess negative values on persons whom society feels are on balance injurious to it. The criminal indeed is a form of human pollution, that is, as a person he is regarded as a negative good or a "bad" whose removal from society presumably increases the capital value of everybody else. Prisons are then seen as the septic tanks of society into which those persons who are regarded as discommodities are flushed. One can indeed have at least three theories of the operations of the criminal law—deterrent, custodial, or reformist.

Under the theory of deterrence, the justification of the criminal law is that without it more people would have negative capital values from the point of society, and that hence the cost of the criminal law can be offset by the increase in negative capital value of persons which would occur if the criminal law did not exercise its deterrent function. We still know very little about how much in fact the criminal law acts as a deterrent, although there is some considerable evidence that the effect is frequently, though not always, positive.

Whether the effect is large enough, however, to justify the cost of the criminal law itself is another matter and, of course, may vary considerably from one part of the law to the next. We abandoned Prohibition, for instance, because it became clear that the cost of deterrence was in excess of the depreciation of human values which the abandonment of the law would create. We may come to the same conclusion about marijuana. In this sense, the criminal law is supposed to act rather like effluent taxes in the case of pollution, by making the production of "bads," in this case of course bad character or negative capital valued persons, less attractive to the producer.

The reformative aspects of the criminal law, as reflected for instance in the euphemism "reformatory" for prison, is the human equivalent of the reclamation of garbage and sewage. There is no great optimism abroad about the capacity of reformatories to reform, and it is fairly clear that this aspect of the criminal law is very ineffective. It is too much like trying to reclaim the chemicals in smoke after it has left the chimney. The difficulty here perhaps is that the apparatus of the criminal law tends to be symbiotic with the criminal subculture. In many respects indeed the police are a ligitimated branch of the criminal subculture itself. Hence, reform involves a change in the whole subculture, which is very difficult, simply because the processes of transmission and the perpetuation of the culture are so universal and widespread within it that it is extremely difficult to impose other types of communication on it. Certainly the proposition that prisons produce more criminals than they reform is supported by a good deal of evidence. Part of the difficulty here is that deterrence and reformation are often incompatible, so that we have an extremely complicated social production function, the parameters of which are very hard to assess. The whole movement toward juvenile courts, for instance, is an attempt to separate the reformatory and the deterrent aspects of the law to some extent, but it is hard to tell how successful this attempt has been.

The other aspect of the criminal law, the custodial aspect, is unfortunately the easiest, and we continually tend to slip into it. The custodial concept, of course, goes far beyond the confines of the criminal law. We find it in the case of mental disease, old folks' homes, and even the ghettos. The custodial segregation of those whom society regards as having negative value is indeed an ancient institution and pervades all societies. The difficulty lies in the fact that this may be too easy a solution of the problem and hence too stable. If society can segregate those whose capital value is negative so that they will not depreciate the capital value of those who regard themselves as positive, then those who make the decisions for the society, who will of course always regard their own capital value as positive, may find this a very cheap solution, at least in the short run. Septic tanks, however, tend to fill up and overflow and to pollute the whole underground water system, and the same may be true of the social septic tanks implied in the segregation and neglect of the poor, the old, or the mentally and morally ill. A better apparatus for assessing the total capital value of the persons in society therefore is almost essential to any genuine social reform.

It is curious here how we seem to have come full circle. We have rightly rejected the concept of a market in human beings as such, because this perverts the concept of the value of a person, even though it may establish a dollar number on the slave block. Nevertheless, the measurement and assessment of the value of a person and the development of institutions which raise this value rather than lower it is perhaps one of the crucial problems of any society. Institutional reform in society, therefore, frequently takes the form of attempting to find substitutes for the market which perform its function in a more legitimate way. The person indeed is not a commodity, but he has something which commodities have—that is, value—and the study of a simple form of value—that is, commodity value—may throw a great deal of light on the generation, understanding, and even the measurement, of those higher forms by which true value of a person is to be measured either by himself or by society.

In an earlier paper,[4] written at the instigation of Eli Ginzberg for a conference he organized, I attacked the whole concept of "manpower" as implying that there is some single well-defined end of society to which human beings are subordinate. The manpower concept, it seemed to me, implied a political philosophy which made the ends of society or even of the national state transcendent over the multifarious ends of the individuals who composed it. My real objection to the manpower concept which I would make just as strongly now as I did eighteen years ago is that in effect it treats man as an intermediate good, not as an end in himself. I did not mean to imply, of course, that the manpower concept could not be used as a rhetorical device to organize certain aspects of the study of society, as Eli Ginzberg has used it very successfully. My protest was rather against assuming that this abstraction presented some kind of ultimate reality. I am as unfriendly to great societies as I am to great men and my ideal society is one which interferes as little as possible with the ability of little people to have a little fun.

Nevertheless, just as the rejection of the concept of the valuation of the person through the market and the rejection of the notion that man is a commodity does not exempt us from finding other institutions which will value the person in other ways, so the manpower concept, which in its crude form is a sheer affront to the dignity of the person, has its equivalent in the concept of the organization of the human community. The weakness of pure individualism is that there are no pure individuals. The human person finds his significance and his dignity as he finds an identity, and his identity is closely related to the community with which he identifies. To quote John

Donne again, "Every man is a piece of the continent, a part of the maine." It is the existence of this continent of community with which we identify which makes a purely atomistic economics unsatisfactory and hence makes the concept of a single well-defined end, toward which manpower may be directed, expressed in the welfare of community, much more attractive than it otherwise might be. We reject the concept of man as a commodity pure and simple, but not the concept of a person as a part of the valuable stock of society. We reject the concept of the person as simply a means to some nonpersonal end, but we recognize also that the person *has* nonpersonal ends for which he may willingly regard himself as the means. These distinctions may seem fine, but they are not hairsplitting. They represent indeed a watershed on one side of which society becomes an intolerable tyranny, on the other side of which it becomes a community which enlarges and makes more meaningful the lives of all persons within it. Finding where this watershed lies in practice is perhaps the greatest single task of the social and moral sciences.

NOTES

1. Kenneth E. Boulding, "The Legitimacy of Economics," *Western Economic Journal,* V, 4 (September 1967), 299–307.
2. Adam Smith, *The Wealth of Nations* (New York: Modern Library Edition, 1937), p. 734.
3. *Ibid.*, p. 532.
4. Kenneth E. Boulding, "An Economist's View of the Manpower Concept," in *Proceedings of a Conference on the Utilization of Scientific and Professional Manpower* (New York: Columbia University Press, 1954), pp. 11–26.

MOSES ABRAMOVITZ

MANPOWER, CAPITAL, AND TECHNOLOGY

THERE are two standard ways of viewing the process of economic growth. One sees it as the outcome of capital formation and technological and organizational progress, including progress made possible by enlargement of scale; the other as a process of transformation in the use of a country's resources, principally in the size, intensity of use, and training of its labor force and its occupational and industrial structure. The two views are sometimes regarded as competitive, sometimes as supplementary. The truth is, however, that manpower development, capital formation, and technological progress are so closely allied and so interdependent as almost to confound analytical separation.

The purpose of this essay is to elaborate and illustrate the theme of interdependence and to sketch some of the main lines of connection between manpower development on the one side and capital formation and technological progress on the other. This is an expository paper, making no claim to originality. The factual assertions on which the argument depends mainly refer to the United States, although some have a wider application. For the most part, they are in the public domain, reducing the need to make a show of empirical support, but not guaranteeing accuracy. These notes are, therefore, provisional and, even in respect to their factual content, subject to verification.

CONVENTIONAL VERSUS TOTAL CAPITAL FORMATION

The very distinction drawn between manpower development and capital formation rests in part on a conventional, but basically arbitrary, definition of the latter concept. Conventionally, capital formation refers to the use of resources to add to the stock of tangible reproducible goods useful in production. The fundamental idea underlying the conventional definition, however, has to do with any deliberate use of resources in ways which increase our potential productive capacity. In this more basic sense, it comprehends any deliberate employment of income to increase the productivity of resources, including uses which are not tangible but rather embodied in the knowledge, skills, energy, strength, location, or other qualities of people.

If we consider capital formation in this controversial but more truly basic sense, the most important category is, of course, expenditure on education, including both formal schooling and on-the-job training. There are, however, other important categories as well, including some expenditures for health care and recreation and for domestic and international migration and resettlement. The expenditures for education and training are themselves of the first order of magnitude. Indeed, Professor Simon Kuznets has estimated that, while the typical share of conventional capital formation in developed countries in the postwar period was about 30 percent, private and public consumption taking the other 70 percent, if one allows for "investment in man" through formal schooling and on-the-job training, the capital-formation proportion rises to 47 percent of the revised GNP, leaving only 53 percent for consumption.[1]

Needless to say, such estimates of investment in man rest on a number of shaky assumptions, variations in which might change the numbers significantly. In a final calculation, one would need to reduce the capital-formation share because not all the expenditure for education is either intended to or has the effect of raising the productive capabilities of people. On the other hand, the expenditures on education do not by any means exhaust our current investments in man. Expenditures for health care, public, household, and corporate, are partly undertaken to increase productivity. So are some of our expenditures nominally for recreation, including some significant part of the cost of supporting newspapers, television, and other communications media. Educational investment expenditures themselves might be expanded to include a large part of corporate and professional expenditure for travel, meetings, and trade and other professional literature. Perhaps most important, one would need to allow for the costs of migration and resettlement as workers and their families move within and between countries in their efforts to enlarge their own earning power and, by implication, the productive capacity of the economy.

Figures, as they now stand, can do no more than show that in a comprehensive accounting, industrialized countries now use a significant part of their total output for investment in man and that such investment forms a very large part, if not a major fraction, of capital formation, tangible and intangible. The Kuznets estimates do that sufficiently well. One can add that, in preindustrial times and in the earlier stages of development in countries now industrialized, investments in man were much less important both as a share of total output and as a share of the much smaller part of output used for capital formation. Expenditures for formal education were tiny; the industrially relevant part of literature or of other means of communication was insignificant. Travel and migration were restricted by the expense, difficulty, and dangers of transportation. All these avenues for using income to increase personal effectiveness were gradually enlarged in the course of the last century, and it is tempting to attribute the recorded acceleration in the pace of productivity growth during the last hundred years in good part to the enlargement of investment in man. This is too difficult a question to be pursued here.[2] Taking for granted the importance of such enlarged investment, how can we explain why people, acting individually and through public agencies, were willing to devote increasingly large portions of their personal income and of the government's revenue to the development of their productive capabilities, be it their own, their children's or those of other families? I shall try to look at this question from several angles and at the same time develop other connections among manpower development, capital formation, and technical progress.

THE IMPLICATIONS OF DEMOGRAPHIC CHANGE

The very small share of investment in man during the early stages of industrialization, roughly from the last third of the eighteenth to the last third of the nineteenth century, corresponds to two broad characteristics of that period. First, the demand for schooled personnel was small, which itself restricted this most important avenue of investment. (How it came to be larger is a question taken up in a later section.)

With the supply of educated people also limited, the earnings premium enjoyed by the fortunate was large, yet this did not induce a large responsive educational effort. For one thing, incomes were low, education was costly, and access to finance for most people close to nonexistent. But second, even a large earnings premium for schooled people did not necessarily signify a large return to an investment in education. In the same way, earnings differentials between countries or between places in a given country or between occupations, all of which were considerable in preindustrial times, did not necessarily offer a large return to geographical or occupational movement. One reason for this lay in the demographic conjuncture during preindustrial and early industrial times.

It is a commonplace that, during that period, both mortality rates and birth rates were high and that the difference between them—the rate of population growth—was small. The decline in mortality rates, concomitant in most industrialized countries with the onset of industrialization, is usually considered chiefly for its influence in accelerating the pace of population and labor-force growth. It is less commonly appreciated that the same decline in mortality rates was probably one of the forces behind the expansion of educational effort and the growing mobility of people across space and between occupations.

The high level of mortality rates a century and more ago meant not only that infant mortality was high, but also that the chance of survival through adolescence was smaller and life expectancy thereafter much shorter than it is today. Crippling morbidity was also more common. All these conditions effectively reduced the prospective rewards to investment in man. To spend eight or ten years in school beyond the age when earnings might otherwise begin, to forego these earnings, and to bear the other expenses of schooling was obviously less attractive when the remaining span of working-life was, say, twenty-five years, on the average than it is today, when it is forty or forty-five years. In the same way, the lengthening span of working life must have made people more ready to accept the risks and costs of seeking their fortunes in distant places and in new occupations.

A special consideration applies to women. Their chance of enjoying a material reward from schooling or other personal improvement was obviously limited so long as families were as large as they were through much of the nineteenth century. They were limited still more because high levels of infant and childhood mortality required more pregnancies for each surviving child. Smaller families and the decline in infant and child mortality together were forces helping to release many women to work outside the home and consequently to change traditional views about education for women.

TECHNOLOGICAL AND ORGANIZATIONAL PROGRESS AND THE SEX-COMPOSITION OF THE LABOR FORCE

In most industrializing countries, declining death rates were followed by declining birth rates, and these, together with the extension of life, meant a shift in the age structure of the population. The population of working age rose relative to the total population. In the United States, this change supported a rise in labor force relative to population during at least the half-century from 1870 to 1920 and perhaps longer and, by the same token, the growth rate of output per head. It would not have done so, however, had not the proportion of people of working age who were gainfully employed remained essentially stable. It did, however, remain stable—short-term fluctuations apart—even until the present time, in short, for at least a century.

A full discussion of the reasons for this remarkable example of secular stability would take us far afield. Its two chief elements, however, have in a sense already been introduced. Increased investment in man meant, among other things, more schooling. It required an ever-rising average age for entry into the labor force and, therefore, an ever-falling proportion of young people at work. By and large, the withdrawal of young people from work was offset by the entry of older women. Though each development had its peculiar causes, they also had common sources in the nature of technological and organizational progress, in the vast enlargement in the scale and urban concentration of economic life and in the accompanying rise in incomes during the last hundred years and more. I can best pursue my main theme by focusing sharply on these common causes.

I begin with the rise in the participation of women. We have already seen how fewer pregnancies and smaller families helped to release women from the home. Their release was also furthered by the appearance of labor-saving equipment for the household, by rising incomes and financial facilities which helped families buy such aids and by commercial substitutes for homemade food and clothing and for home laundering and cleaning. Progress in food preservation and packaging, the reorganization of retailing and the use of automobiles were, at least until recently, additional savers of women's time. Women have been pushed to work by the need to provide extra family income to support longer periods of schooling for children and even for husbands—a direct and obvious reflection of the forces supporting investment in man. Their way to employment has been eased by the availability of part-time jobs and by the general shortening of the working day and working week. Although the rise in men's wages tended, indeed, to reduce the need for married women to work, the higher wages the latter could earn if they did work proved even more important in drawing women into employment.[3]

All this is, in many ways, a twice-told tale. What needs to be stressed is that virtually every aspect of this story stems in one degree or another from a transformation in the nature of jobs. On the one hand, this transformation was itself a reflection of shifts in the scale of industry and of the urban concentration of activity and population, of technological progress and greater use of capital and of higher incomes. On the other hand, it gave women a chance to compete with men over a far wider range of employment and, in many types of work, to outdo them.

From the viewpoint of opportunities for employment of women, the transformation can be characterized as a growth of soft-handed at the expense of hard-handed occupations. It reflected four interconnected developments central to economic growth given the nature of technological progress during the last century:

1. With the rise of incomes, there was a shift in the composition of final demand toward the output of the service industries—principally education, health care, travel, and other forms of entertainment and recreation—in which soft-handed, or white-collar, jobs are relatively abundant.

2. The rise in productivity on which the increase of incomes depended, itself rested on technological progress of a particular character. This involved a huge increase in the overall scale of the economy, a much higher degree of specialization and a more intense articulation of functions which expressed itself, *inter alia,* in a heavy concentration of population in metropolitan communities. To support this particular technological structure, there was required an impressive relative growth of commercial services, specifically those of trade, finance, communications, and, most of all, governmental regulation and the provision of a wide range of auxiliary public services required for the operation of large cities. These again are employment sectors in which soft-handed jobs predominate.

3. The new technology meant not only this growth of social overhead, but also a growth of private overhead functions. Large-scale, heavily capitalized and roundabout methods of production required heavier expenses within individual firms for administration, finance, sales, intrafirm communications, supervision of production, personnel management, and the provision of services to improve the selection and retention of increasingly skilled and expensive workers.

4. Finally, though the demand for the output of overhead functions grew relatively rapidly, the productivity of labor supplying these functions rose relatively slowly, at least until quite recent years. Indeed, the whole process may be regarded as one in which overall productivity was increased by substituting soft-handed for hard-handed workers as a necessary adjunct to the adoption of the modern American technological mode. At all events, it was a process in which jobs suitable for both women and men replaced jobs suitable only for men.[4]

ECONOMIC GROWTH AND THE RISE OF EDUCATION

Of all the manpower developments of the present century, the great increase in the length of schooling enjoyed by people before beginning work is surely the most prominent. On the one side, the extension of schooling has meant a great reduction in the proportion of persons under 20 or 22 years old who work during most of the year. On the other side, the prolongation of formal schooling and the changes in school curricula have presumably made a significant, if uncertain, contribution to the rise of productivity and incomes.

That longer schooling has made a useful contribution to the effectiveness of workers is rarely questioned, however much the size of that contribution is disputed. In the same way, few doubt that the prospect of financial rewards associated with extended training induced people to seek longer schooling for themselves and their children, however hard it may be to specify the exact weight to give this consideration. Other forces were doubtless at work. The democratization of politics and of society would have made for an extension of schooling apart from any change in prospective earnings. So would the extension of life, the rise of incomes, and the enlarged access to credit facilities which wider segments of people have enjoyed. It remains true, nonetheless, that the costs of schooling beyond the primary grades, still more beyond secondary school, were and are very heavy in terms of fees and foregone earnings, and it is implausible to suppose that the great mass of Americans would willingly have borne these costs and supported the enlarged public expenditures for expanded school facilities had they not expected a large private return in terms of careers, incomes, and status.

My aim is not to settle these questions of weight and measure. I focus rather on a central fact on which the apparent contributions of longer schooling to labor efficiency, whatever that may have been, and the apparent financial attractiveness of longer schooling, both rest. This fact is the large earnings premiums which people with longer schooling have enjoyed, on the average, over people with shorter school experience. Viewed as indexes of the additional effectiveness of people with longer education, the premiums are the bases for approximative measures, however uncertain these may be, of the contribution of additional schooling to output and labor productivity. Viewed as a measure of additional earning power associated with longer education, they were the visible symbol of the prospective financial rewards which induced individuals to seek more schooling for their children and to support larger public expenditures for education.[5] The question I ask, therefore, is: why have persons with relatively more schooling continued to command attractively large earnings premiums even though so many of them have joined the labor force since the beginning of the century? Unless there had been an offsetting rise in the demand for more highly educated people, one would have expected such a large increase in relative supply to have been accompanied by a significant decline in the premium for longer schooling. Young people leaving high schools, colleges, and universities would have been generally disappointed by the advantages in occupations, careers, and incomes opened to them by schooling: and their discontent would long since have brought the secular boom in education to a close. Perhaps some decline in earnings premiums did occur in the earlier decades of the century. The data are too scant to permit a firm judgment. Yet as late as 1940, the spread of earnings associated with length of schooling was still wide, and since that time it has not contracted notably, although the rise in the educational level of the labor force accelerated.

An explanation for the persistence of the premium for education comes in two parts, and both reveal the obtrusive influence of technological progress and of the shifts in occupation which flow from it. We look, first, to the large change in the occupational composition of employment since at least the beginning of this century. The proportion of people employed in occupations characteristically filled by people with relatively long schooling has grown in importance; and rough calculations suggest that this shift accounts for something between a third and a half and perhaps more of the rise in the average school-level of the employed labor force since 1900. Some part of this shift may, indeed, have been due to a decline in the relative price of educated workers resulting from an increase in their supply. If so, it is presumably a small part since 1940, for the relative price of educated workers has fallen little if at all since that time. Before 1940, there may well have been a relative price decline which encouraged the growth of "education-intensive" occupations. Yet both before and since 1940, forces were clearly at work on the demand side which contributed substantially to sustaining the reward for schooling.

We note first that, among the principal industrial divisions of the economy, those in which the level of labor-force schooling is above average have been increasing their share of employment at the expense of those in which the level of workers' schooling is below average. In the latter group are the industries primarily concerned with the extraction, fabrication, and movement of goods, that is, farming, mining, construction, transport, and manufactures. In the former are the auxiliary industries concerned with distribution, coordination, and regulation as well as with furnishing those things the demand for which tends to grow rapidly with income—trade, utilities and communications, services, finance, and civilian government. Since 1948, and perhaps even earlier, the shift has rested in part on an increase in relative output. Before and since 1948, however, the shift has reflected a more rapid rise in labor productivity in industries directly concerned with the handling of tangible commodities compared to the service-producing or auxiliary sectors. A number of forces have combined to produce these results, but two are outstanding. First, the technology of power and machinery has so far proven more effective in saving the less well-educated blue-collar labor dominant in the goods-producing sectors and less effective in saving the white-collar, "education-intensive" labor which is dominant in the service-producing industries.[6] Second, the increase in scale, specialization, and articulation, on which the application of this technology rests, itself required an increase in the activity of those sectors providing regulation, communication, coordination, and finance.

Next, we note that these shifts in the occupational-composition of employment have been associated not only with changes in the industrial distribution of output and workers, but also with changes within firms and industries. Even in mining, transportation, and manufacturing, the white-collar, education-intensive jobs concerned with administration, record-keeping, communication, sales, and finance have grown at the expense of jobs more directly concerned with the handling of goods. And again, this was partly because efficiency gain called for enlargement in the scale of establishments and firms which was costly in terms of the overhead functions served by education-intensive, white-collar workers. It was partly because the larger scale of firms made profitable, and so encouraged, the growth of other education-intensive activities, like research and development, advertising, and employee-training. And it was partly because technical progress has, so far, been less effective in saving white-collar than blue-collar labor.

The second part of the answer is connected with the rise which occurred in the educational qualifications attached to most occupations. Some of this rise almost certainly has its origin in the extension of education itself. Employers depend on school records and diplomas to help them select applicants who are likely to meet their standards of intelligence, industry, and responsibility. When only 75 percent of all youngsters finished elementary school and only 40 percent were graduated from high school, an elementary school diploma could qualify its holder to be a clerk while a high school graduate might become a private secretary. When virtually every boy and girl finishes elementary school and three out of four obtain high school diplomas, mere maintenance of old standards means that clerks must have finished high school, and the boss demands that his own secretary have a junior college certificate or even a B.A. How far the increase in supply goes to account for an inflation of schooling requirements, we do not know. It may be, probably is, a major element of an explanation.[7] At the same time, developments have been taking place in both the worlds of work and of education which are manifestly calculated to raise the real value of schooling in the production of goods and services.

Some categorical assertions must suffice to put the case. From the side of industry, the content of jobs changed in ways which made formal schooling more useful. The machines which displaced labor became themselves more sophisticated and required more of the common school skills of reading and reckoning for their operation and maintenance. The enlargement of plants and firms meant not only more administrators and clerks, it demanded more paper work in all operations. Gas station attendants handle credit cards, check stock, and requisition supplies, and even the simplest mechanical operations have acquired peripheral record-keeping and communications functions. Manifestly, the expansion of the need for the clerkly skills has been all the greater at the higher occupational levels of larger organizations in whicn administration has more and more taken the form of consultation and decision on the basis of records, reports, analyses, committees and interpersonal and, in a sense, impersonal communications.

At the same time, the curricula of schools, colleges, and universities have come to include more that is of vocational, commercial, and professional interest and use. The high schools—partly in order to engage the interest and keep the attention of a much larger population of students, of whom only a minority were preparing for higher education or had a disinterested concern with impractical academic subjects—enlarged their program of vocational courses. Universities, led by the state universities, gradually embodied their goal of service to the whole community, in an ever-broader program of instruction in industrial subjects—for example, in agriculture, nursing, engineering, forestry, and mining.

The curriculum reforms were also a consequence of the growth of knowledge generally and of the increasing degree to which industry, commerce, and other activities, including education itself, have been made the subjects of formal disciplines and of the larger extent to which industry has come to rest on applied science. Professional training has become more complex and more rigorous as the scientific bases of the professions have become better established. Courses in engineering and medicine, including internship, to take just two examples, have, therefore, been extended and much more frequently involve postgraduate work. New disciplines came into being and gradually won a place in the esteem of students and their prospective employers. Business administration became the subject most frequently studied by college students, and the list includes journalism, public health, and education itself. Nor did this development stop at the level of professional training in normal four-year colleges and universities. The advance of science and its increasing application in industry have not only opened up many new technical and subprofessional occupations, they have also deepened the training regarded as useful in older occupations. These, in some cases, have so changed in character as to assume new names: kitchen managers have become nutritionists; dental assistants, hygienists; and masseurs, physical therapists. Training for these occupations has gradually been made the subject of classroom or laboratory study, and they have become the basic concern of the growing number of two-year community and junior colleges.

I conclude, therefore, that the rise in the level of schooling characteristic of most occupations is only in part an inflation of requirements due to to an increase in supply. The rest, like the expansion of employment in education-intensive occupations, is associated with technical progress, with the enlargement of scale it has entailed and with the evolution of applied science, the professions and their auxiliary specialities. These have made for a true expansion in the training which jobs demand and in the capacities of schools to impart useful skills.

EDUCATION AND TECHNOLOGICAL AND ORGANIZATIONAL PROGRESS

We now have to close the circle of interdependence between manpower development and technological progress. The advance of technology, by its effects on the scale of activity, the character of jobs, the level of income and the span of life has made for an increase both in the demand for, and in the number of, people with higher levels of schooling. At the same time, the enlarged number of educated people has itself fostered the advance of technology. This is manifestly the case insofar as larger numbers of scientists, engineers and administrators are directly concerned with the creation of new products, including new mechanical, electrical, chemical, and biological devices, and with exploring and improving the technology and organization by which they are produced. It is equally manifest insofar as the efforts of these professionals are better supported by larger numbers of auxiliary technicians. It is also widely appreciated that a generally educated population is better prepared, both as workers and consumers, to adapt to, and so to adopt, the novel products and services, the novel work routines, and the new locations which technical and organizational advance entails. Their adaptability lowers the costs and the risks of innovation.

The fundamental connections between manpower development and technological progress, however, are at once wider and less immediately apparent. If we assume that the character of our technological advance is given, we may well view the rise of educational effort, the withdrawal of the young from the labor force, and the offsetting entry of women as simply responses to the demands of an emerging technology with its implied requirements for "overhead" labor in the broad meaning we have given this term. As we grope uncertainly toward an understanding of technological change, however, it becomes more apparent that its pace and character are not facts entirely fixed by the nature of the physical universe and the state of basic science. On the contrary, they are themselves, at least in part, adaptations to the tastes and life styles of the people they serve and to the relative resource costs that they entail.

A more adequate view of the matter seems to proceed from the proposition that nature presents us, in each successive era, not with a singular path of technical progress, but with a choice among a variety of paths. Some entail much capital, little production labor, but much administrative effort; some involve a different mix of these elements. Some can be operated with small producing units and small firms; others require large establishments organized in still larger firms. Some can be successfully applied by producing units working at a distance from other units in the same industry and with little help from an auxiliary complex of establishments providing repairs, storage, distribution and advertising, finance and accounting; others require the full panoply of metropolitan business services and facilities. Some therefore, entail a great development of government services; others would do so to a lesser degree. And in the same way, some paths depend on a very wide extension of literacy and on an intense development of technical and professional skills, while others would be less demanding of formal education.

The path which this country has followed during the last century clearly has been a labor-saving, capital-using path—where labor means unskilled labor and capital includes not only the tools used by workers in direct production, but also the "social" capital required for urban population concentration and for administration, transportation, communication and finance and, perhaps most of all, the very large capital investments in schooling and on-the-job training. Compared with other countries, we early chose a capital-intensive and education-intensive technology and social organization, in part because it was cheaper in a country where labor—unskilled labor—was relatively expensive and where at least elementary schooling was relatively widespread.[8] We developed this technology and organization in part because a practice, once established, becomes, for a time, the object of progressive improvement.[9] More and more, we apprehend that technical and organizational advance is, to some extent, a matter of continuing exploration based on experience, a matter of learning-by-doing. Since the established mode of production and organization, in the history of U.S. industrialization was a capital- and education-intensive mode, it was the one in which we chiefly gained experience and tended to advance.

In part, however, we have followed the capital-using and education-intensive path because it appeared to be cheaper than it actually was. The full costs of a technology based on large and very dense metropolitan concentrations and on great expenditures for transport, communications, and administration are gradually revealing themselves: and it would be surprising if the direction of development in the future did not bend away from this path and toward one based on less dense population concentrations, on labor-saving in administration, and on some economy in social and private overheads. If so, this itself will have an impact on the need for schooling in preparation for work.

The full costs of an education-intensive technology are also now gradually revealing themselves as the period of schooling is extended and as entrance into the work force is postponed from the fourteenth to the eighteenth and now to the twenty-second, twenty-fourth, and twenty-sixth years, not for 6 or 10 percent but for 30 and 40 percent of the population of young people. It is not only that the expansion of public subsidies for education is being increasingly resisted as the aggregate size of the expenditure increases. It is also that the private costs, psychological as well as financial, of ever more protracted periods of schooling and hence of dependency come to be seen as out of balance with the physical and emotional maturity of the bulk of young people. Thus, it may be that for several reasons—from the sides of both demand and supply—we shall be slowing down the pace of education-using technical advance, even evolving a new path which is education-saving. Doubtless any attempt to assess the future relations of education and technological progress is in the highest degree uncertain. The character of technological and organizational progress may prove to be highly resistant to alteration. The schools themselves may finally learn to do their jobs of educating young people and of screening talent more expeditiously and cheaply, which would encourage the further development of technique and organization dependent on the use of people with more formal schooling. Nonetheless, one may well ask whether we are not now witnessing something of a climacteric in the trend of investment in man, at least in the United States. Needless to say, one should not expect to see our schools contract like the steel rail or the freight car-producing industries of earlier decades, but their long secular boom may well be over.

NOTES

1. The distribution according to the conventional definition of capital formation is based on unweighted arithmetic means of shares in fifteen countries, usually for 1950–58. The magnitudes for "investment in man" are based on T. W. Schultz' estimates of the cost of schooling in the USA in 1956. Kuznets' revised shares are calculated after reestimation of standard GNP data to eliminate intermediate output properly excluded. The stages in his calculations are indicated in the following figures:

	Shares of GNP components (%)	
	Private and public consumption	*Gross capital formation*
National accounts definition	77	23
Omitting intermediate products	70	30
Allowing for investment in man but excluding income foregone from capital formation and GNP	58	42
Adding income foregone in formal education and on-the-job training	53	47

See S. S. Kuznets, *Modern Economic Growth, Rate, Structure, and Spread* (New Haven: Yale University Press, 1966), Table 5.2.

2. The question is pursued by Paul A. David and the present writer in their forthcoming study, *Economic Growth in the United States.*

3. Cf. Jacob Mincer, "Labor Force Participation of Married Women," in *Aspects of Labor Economics, A Conference of the Universities—National Bureau Committee for Economic Research* (Princeton, N.J.: Princeton University Press, 1962), pp. 63–97.

4. It is perhaps only an incidental matter, though one of some importance, that, in many of the enlarging sectors, particularly in trade, finance, office work of many types and in some health care, educational, and recreational activities, part-time and intermittent employment proved tolerable for firms and effective, therefore, in attracting a supply of useful female workers with competing household demands on their time.

5. I am not arguing that the premiums can be wholly attributed to what schooling does to raise a person's effectiveness as a worker. So far as the contribution of schooling to productivity is concerned, it is enough if a substantial part of the earnings differentials associated with education can be so explained. So far as the inducement to seek more schooling is concerned, it is enough if people merely believe that the premiums are a measure of rewards of education.

6. Cf. Victor Fuchs, *The Service Economy* (New York: Columbia University Press for National Bureau of Economic Research, 1968).

7. This is a view emphasized and documented by Ivar Berg, *Education and Jobs: The Great Training Robbery* (New York: Praeger, 1970).

8. Cf. H. J. Habakkuk, *American and British Technology in the Nineteenth Century: The Search for Labour-Saving Inventions,* (Cambridge: At the University Press, 1967).

9. That technological progress tends to be capital-saving or labor-saving over a period of time because we gain experience in the kind of technology chosen in the past is an idea I owe to my colleague, Paul David. I have ventured here to give it a wider application than he himself might be disposed to do.

MELVIN REDER

HUMAN CAPITAL AND ECONOMIC DISCRIMINATION

THE literature of both subjects mentioned in the title of this paper bear witness to the powerful impress of Gary Becker's intellect.[1] However, the interrelation of the two has received scant attention. Becker himself found that discrimination might be responsible for racial differences in rates of return to schooling.[2] However, he did not consider the possibility that what is reflected in measured returns to investment in education may be substantially the consequence of "discrimination" against the uneducated, per se. The influence of Becker's views is such that in each of the above fields his work has been a major, and probably the principal, source of hypotheses for empirical investigation. As a result, empirical studies of the economics of racial discrimination and of investment in human productive capacity have constituted two separate topics with relatively little cross-fertilization.

It is my belief that both subjects have suffered from an inadequate examination of their interrelation. A fully developed analysis requires that we analyze the connection both of racial discrimination and of investment to employer hiring criteria. Though there are important differences, especially in our interpretation of economic theory, my view of the interrelations among hiring criteria, human capital and discrimination have much in common with that of Eli Ginzberg and his associates.[3]

EMPLOYER INFORMATION AND WORKER TRAINING

Most if not all studies of phenomena associated with the concept of human capital have ignored the role of information cost in its formation.[4] It is assumed that human capital is somehow created in the process of schooling or working on-the-job and that its creation reflects an alteration in the productive capacity of the worker.

But this assumption is not necessarily in accord with fact. To make the point clearly, consider an extreme case: suppose that in an on-the-job training program workers learn nothing that increases their productive capacity, and that employers are aware of this fact. Nevertheless the program may be of great value to an employer because it enables him more effectively than otherwise to distinguish among the following pairs of workers: those who are able to follow instructions and those who are not; those workers willing to submit to "industrial discipline" and others; and educable and ineducable workers. In other words, the aforementioned training program creates information about the workers involved which is of value to an employer. Depending upon whether the information is general or specific, the cost of training will be born entirely by the workers or shared by worker and employer.

Defining or measuring the *amount* of information employers have about worker capacity (or indeed anything) is as unnecessary as it is difficult. It suffices to specify the direction in which a quantum of information varies with changes in various parameters. Suppose, for example, that customary beliefs led employers wrongly to ascribe inferior productive capacity to black workers relative to white. Correcting this erroneous belief would shift upward both the production functions on which employers operated and the relative demand curve for black workers for any given firm. This would increase the quantity of black workers hired, at given relative wage rates and possibly their actual relative wage rate, as well. In short, correcting an erroneous belief about relative worker productivity is tantamount to an increase in employer information and it affects the economy in much the same way as a (non-neutral) technical improvement.

Whatever serves to dispel erroneous beliefs about the productivity of inputs shifts outward the production-possibility restraint of all affected employers, and is therefore "productive." If the culture of a society is such that erroneous beliefs can be corrected by activities that involve the expenditure of resources, then such expenditure is productive. If the time pattern of spending resources and receiving the benefits of increased productivity can properly be described as an investment process, then using resources to eliminate or reduce the effect of counter-productive beliefs is capital formation.[5] That is, using resources to reduce the degree of employer misperception of the relative productive capacity of black workers would (or might) be investment. But using resources to reduce or eliminate "market discrimination coefficients" (in Becker's terminology), that rest on tastes for discrimination combined with a *correct* perception of relative productive capacities of white and black workers, would not constitute investment.

The relevance of these remarks to our subject arises from the fact that education and/or training programs are usually thought to produce human capital. The basis for this belief is that these programs clearly entail costs (investment) during a short interval subsequent to which their participants are alleged to benefit from a larger stream of earnings (yield) than would be obtainable by otherwise identical nonparticipants. Accepting the customary inference that the gain in earnings is causally related to the costs incurred, it is convenient for many purposes of theory and policy further to infer that the investment process has embodied capital in the worker by giving him greater and/or more valuable skills.[6]

However, it is also consistent with the same body of data that there should have been no change whatever in the productive capacity of any worker. It could be that the effect of education or training programs is to certify or label those who complete them as possessing some level of competence and perseverance, but without in any way contributing to the attainment of that level.

Assume for a moment that education or training affects worker productivity *only* through the labeling of workers. The direction of this labeling effect is indicated by the change in the discrepancy between employer *beliefs* and "true values" of the marginal productivities of the workers involved.[7] That is, we assume that a change in employer information about the relative productive capacities of workers affects the rate of output that an employer can obtain from a given set of resource inputs only in consequence of changes in the accuracy with which he estimates worker capacities.

Consider two simple and extreme cases:

Case 1. The effect of training is completely to eliminate errors of estimate of the marginal productivity of any worker who undergoes training and to raise the estimate of the marginal product of anyone who undergoes training, but not to affect the estimated marginal product of non-trainees.[8] In this case, the demand price for the services of a trained worker will be greater than for a non-trained one, generating a return to investment in training which is the yield on the human capital (information) created by the training process. The employer information generated by training will increase both private and social marginal product, as well as the income of those trained.

Case 2. The effect of the training is to create a spurious difference between employer estimates of the marginal products of trained and of untrained workers; the true difference between *any* pair of workers is zero, which is (also) what the difference between any pair of non-trained workers is *believed* to be.[9]

Nevertheless, in case 2 training raises the wage rate of trained workers relative to non-trained. The difference between the wage rates of trained and non-trained workers constitutes a private return to any worker who undergoes the expense of training, but this return must come via transfers from the non-trained, and possibly from third parties; it is in no sense an increase in social marginal product. Indeed, these transfers may well involve a dead weight loss to society, but it is not relevant to our present purpose to enter into this issue. Obviously the above are only two of many possible cases in which education or training may affect relative demand prices for different labor categories.

In short, education or training often serves to label or certify workers. Whether such labeling increases the value of output obtainable from a given collection of otherwise identical resources depends upon the effect of such labeling upon the accuracy of employer estimates of worker productive capacity. If output is increased as a result of labeling, then the process by which the labels are attached constitutes social as well as private investment. But to say this implies nothing as to whether the labeling process (training) is an efficient way of increasing knowledge of worker capacities.

EMPLOYMENT DISCRIMINATION AND WORKER SELECTION

It is usually assumed that employer discrimination against members of particular minority groups reflects either direct distaste for certain kinds of contact with them, or fear that economic loss may ensue because of the aversion to such contact by workers, customers or both. It is not part of my purpose to deny the reality or importance of such distaste. However, many phenomena usually thought to be the result of discrimination may also be explained as the result of rational non-discriminating employee selection procedures, under conditions of less than complete information.

Let me suggest that race, or ethnic identity, and education are two related bases for choosing among job applicants. Assume that employers are always seeking the best job candidates available at a given wage rate and, contrary to fact, that the bases for judging the quality of any *individual* job applicant are independent both of his education and his race or ethnic background. Assume also that all employers believe that the probability of an applicant proving satisfactory is greater if he is white and if his years of schooling are greater, color given. Finally, assume that each act of hiring entails a positive, direct cost to the employer so that it is cheaper to fill a given job slot in n trials than in $n+1$ and that employers will therefore prefer applicants with a higher probability of proving satisfactory. Under these conditions, at equal wage rates, employers without a taste for discrimination will prefer whites to nonwhites, and persons with more schooling to those with less.

Briefly, let us spell out the consequences of these employer preferences for labor market behavior. Suppose that all job seekers believed that the probability of their being hired, upon making application, was the same for all jobs. Then, non-pecuniary benefits the same, job applicants will gravitate toward relatively high wage employers; thus, a firm paying a higher than average wage rate will attract a greater number of applicants per announced vacancy. Assuming, as of any moment, that the expected percentage of applicants for any job coming from any (education, race) cell is proportional to the percentage of the population of job seekers in that cell, a higher wage employer will be able to obtain "preferred" applicants (i.e., white with many years of schooling) more quickly than a lower wage employer.[10]

Assume that each firm learns from hiring experience and chooses an optimal strategy relating its wage rate, the desired characteristics of its hires and the length of time it is willing to continue screening applicants in order to achieve its objectives. Assume, for simplicity, that the number of applicants screened per time period is a diminishing function of the care with which they are screened; that increasing care (reducing the number of applicants screened per day) diminishes the probability of accepting an applicant who turns out not to be a continuing and acceptable employee, and that optimization leads to the choice of an "acceptable delay period" (*DP*) which determines how long the firm is willing to wait, on the average, to fill a vacancy.[11] Further assuming the distribution of *DP's* across firms to be uncorrelated with the wage rates offered, it follows that the high wage firms will tend to fill their vacancies with preferred applicants, leaving less preferred applicants to choose between continuing job search (unemployment) and accepting lower wage jobs.

If workers persisted in believing that the probability of being accepted to fill any one job vacancy was the same as to fill any other, less preferred workers would (presumably) distribute their job applications among openings in the same manner as more preferred.[12] This would result in the less preferred workers being unemployed a larger fraction of time spent outside the household than the more preferred. There is no reason, however, to suppose that the less preferred would not adjust their search efforts to the differential probabilities of acceptance, leading the less favored workers to concentrate on getting lower wage jobs and the more favored to pick among higher wage jobs. This adjustment would generate a wage-job hierarchy parallel to the education-race, or education-ethnic hierarchy but without implying the existence of a further parallel hierarchy of differential unemployment rates.[13]

The above argument serves to indicate the possible similarity of effects of workers' educational achievements and their racial or ethnic origins upon employer hiring policy. Either years of schooling, social origins, or both, may be used as an indicator of presumed performance on the job. When so used, they will adversely affect relative employer demand for less preferred workers at given relative wage rates, regardless of the "true state of affairs." In short, a "differentiated hiring policy" is compatible with an employer taste for discrimination, per se, against workers with particular characteristics; with an absence of this taste combined with a belief that these characteristics are associated with differences in on-the-job performance; or with some combination of both.

RATIONALITY, DISCRIMINATION, AND INFORMATION COST

The purpose of this section is to show how the presence of information costs can, in the absence either of a taste for discrimination or a belief in the inferiority of any specifiable group of workers, lead a rational employer to behave in a manner generally conceived to stem from prejudice. At the outset it is essential to recognize how difficult it is to distinguish between discriminatory behavior, on the one hand, and preferences for a particular standard of work performance, on the other. For example, an individual may be genuinely indifferent as to whether he is served by a person whose native language is different from his own, but would prefer easier communications. He may therefore, other things being equal, patronize establishments that employ only those who speak "his" language. In short, there is a real difference between a taste for discrimination per se and a preference for personal characteristics believed associated with superior service, but it is often very difficult to separate the two in real life situations.[14]

Granted the absence of a desire to select among job applicants on any basis other than the present value of their marginal products, a rational employer may still favor a member of Group *A* to one from Group *B* simply because the expected value of the marginal product of an *A* is greater than that of a *B*. This statement might apply even though a particular pair of applicants, one from *A* and one from *B*, were identical or even if the *B* were superior. This is so because the marginal cost of a more complete investigation of the capabilities of the particular individuals would be greater than the increase in the value of expected output at given factor cost resulting from greater accuracy in estimating marginal productivity of individual applicants.[15] That is, an individual may be denied a job he could fill to the employer's satisfaction simply because the profit maximizing selection procedure places him in a category of applicants whose *expected* marginal productivity is less than his own.

The cost of selecting job applicants varies with the method and the prices of the inputs used in the process. Obviously, ascertaining the color or years of schooling of an applicant are relatively inexpensive ways of screening workers and, depending upon their effectiveness, they may be used extensively. It is also possible that schooling, or school-related tests, are more effective in predicting differences in on-the-job performance among appropriately acculturated individuals than among others. If so, cheaper methods may be available (effectiveness the same) for choosing employees from among applicants with at least a specified number of years of schooling than for selecting from among other applicants. This would lead to a preference for "sufficiently" educated job applicants, wage rates and expected marginal productivities the same, simply because it was cheaper to distinguish acceptable from unacceptable applicants among this group.

It should be recognized that otherwise profitable selection methods may be eschewed because they are legally or socially unacceptable. Within the past fifteen years, and certainly within the past decade, overt use of race or ethnic origin as a basis for employee selection has become less acceptable than formerly, and its use has diminished. However, the association of years of schooling with race or ethnic origin, and the association of both with ability to pass various types of tests that reward verbal skills, makes selection criteria based on any one of these characteristics very likely to yield the same group of workers as a test based on the others.

STEREOTYPES, DECISION FUNCTIONS, AND DISCRIMINATION

It is not my intention to argue that educational requirements —or the requirements of educationally associated skills—for jobs are simply fig leaves useful in obscuring racial or ethnic discrimination. My hypothesis is that employee selection procedures embody a widespread cultural assumption that there is a hierarchy of merit among workers and that education, race, ethnic group membership, or patterns of conformity to dominant cultural norms all are correlated with such productivity-associated traits as workers' willingness to work and reliability. Individual variations in merit within groups may be acknowledged, but (until recently) were only rarely allowed to influence employee selection procedures. This might be attributed to cultural rigidity, but it is also explicable in quite different terms. That is, the marginal cost of estimating the probable performance on-the-job of different individuals (in advance of trial and without using educational artifacts) might have been too high, and the ability to make the predictions of differential performance among individuals too low, to justify the cost of evaluating specific individuals.

Evaluation of individuals as job applicants, and for many other purposes as well, is simply foregone to avoid expense. Instead, a small number of alternative stereotypes is specified and selection is made by identifying individuals according to one of a number of alternative stereotypes. One obvious stereotype is that of the immigrant (or member of a racial minority) who is uneducated, has bad work habits, and is prone to legal difficulties. Any screening device that generalizes from such stereotypes to an individual has adverse effects upon his or her chances for acceptance.[16] Discrimination does not arise from the use of one or another screening device, per se, but from the maintenance of the stereotype. So long as the stereotypes are maintained, evidence from any screening procedure is used mainly to decide which stereotype to apply.

In the language of economists, employer decision functions concerning hiring involve the specification of one or more stereotypes. Every applicant must be assimilated to one of these. (In the case where there is only one *articulated* stereotype, the alternative is the stereotype of not conforming to the articulated stereotype.) With each stereotype there is associated a binary decision function for each triplet of job, wage rate and state of the labor market.[17] The purpose of interviewing, testing and otherwise screening job applicants is to decide upon the appropriate stereotype with which to identify the individual. Once an individual is assimilated to a stereotype, the decision to hire or reject him is completely determined.[18]

The essence of employment discrimination lies not in the

screening techniques used to implement it, but in the stereotypes and decision functions used to process the screening information. It is not to the present point to explain the genesis of the particular stereotypes that influence current employer policy. Rather let us consider why stereotypes exist at all.

Suppose, for example, that there are two groups of workers with identical distributions of some measure of on-the-job performance. Group *A* consists of applicants from among whom employers can select with greater efficiency (obtain a higher measure of expected on-the-job performance profiles at given cost) because of greater familiarity with their differentiating characteristics than with those of Group *B*. That is, a desired measure of expected job performance for a given number of workers, chosen from a given number of applicants, is attained at less expense if all applicants are selected from Group *A* than if some (or all) are from Group *B*. Granted this assumption and the assumption that the elimination of all *B*'s is not too costly, the most profitable screening procedure will initially eliminate Group *B* applicants, and then select only among those from Group *A*.

To illustrate: employers might be quite persuaded that they are turning away many highly acceptable black applicants, but might correctly argue that by so doing they reduce (private) cost-per-hire because it is much more difficult to select good workers from among blacks than from among whites. Letters of recommendation for black workers are more likely to come from persons unknown to the employer (e.g. from other blacks); communication of intellectual capacity and attitude is more likely to be obscured by vocabulary differences and so on. Analogous problems have, of course, arisen in the employment of immigrant workers in a number of countries, and have led to similar consequences. Indeed, the additional screening cost associated with hiring workers culturally dissimilar to employers may be held down by utilizing bicultural labor contractors (padrones, etc.) to act as intermediaries. The earnings of the intermediaries are part of the extra hiring cost of the workers in question.

The implication of this point is that employment "discrimination" against persons culturally different from those hiring them often may be privately profitable. This is because of the greater cost of achieving a given degree of efficiency in hiring when the applicants are culturally dissimilar to the selector. These "selection costs" are principally costs of acquiring information. This suggests that relative wages among groups of otherwise similar workers will vary, *ceteris paribus,* with the magnitude of the "cultural distance"—difficulty of transmitting information—between a typical member of a group and the group's respective employers.[19]

But, of course, culturally different groups of workers will rarely seem "otherwise similar." Historically, cultural difference has been a matter for pejoration. And those who share less fully in the culture in terms of which the norms of performance are defined are, per se, judged inferior in that they have less schooling, less frequently pass tests, violate laws and customs more often, etc. Cultural divergence is sufficient for inferiority; but its effect is greatly reinforced when it is associated with physical dissimilarity.

Cultural divergence obviously generates the stereotypes upon which selection procedures operate. And so long as the divergence is perceived as a pattern, just so long will attempts to eliminate particular stigmata of cultural divergence as bases of employee selection *partially* fail in their purpose. Equalizing educational achievement between blacks and whites will not immediately cause a revision of employer opinion of black job applicants. More likely, its effect will be to create "cognitive dissonance," leading to confusion and subconscious attempts to find new selection criteria that will identify the old stereotype.

Hopefully, separating a number of different aspects of the stereotype of inferiority associated with blackness will shatter the stereotype itself. For example, if the average years of schooling, average performance on standard tests, etc., of blacks should become as great or greater than of whites, belief in the association of blackness with educational inferiority would weaken. A similar effect would result from a perceptible improvement in relative quit rates, absenteeism, and other aspects of work performance among blacks.

The effect of thus increasing the marginal cost of using an explicit racial stereotype in screening job applicants should, other things being equal, reduce the frequency with which such stereotypes are employed. Legislation that increases the difficulty of applying racial stereotypes, therefore, should lead to a gradual reduction in discriminatory practices. However, until the stereotype itself is shattered, prohibiting the use of one cultural trait in employee selection will tend to stimulate resort to others. Worse, unless the adverse prior underlying a stereotype is changed, even favorable observations may be interpreted adversely. As a bitter black has remarked "when black is beautiful, it will be better to be ugly."

NOTES

1. Gary S. Becker, *The Economics of Discrimination* (Chicago: University of Chicago Press, 1957).
2. Gary S. Becker, *Human Capital* (New York: National Bureau of Economic Research, 1964).
3. For example, Ivar Berg, *Education and Jobs: The Great Training Robbery*, with an Introduction by Eli Ginzberg (New York: Praeger, 1970); and Marcia Freedman, *The Process of Work Establishment* (New York: Columbia University Press, 1969).
4. A noteworthy exception is G. J. Stigler, "Information in the Labor Market," *Journal of Political Economy*, October 1962, Part II, pp. 94–105. Unfortunately, the implications of Stigler's article have not been much developed; the article is more cited than thought about.
5. Generally speaking, any stream of expenditures and receipts over time may be considered an investment process if synchroniza-

tion is not perfect; i.e., if at one or more moments expenditure occurs in advance of receipts.

6. Estimates of the returns from training or educational programs, virtually without exception, involve a comparison of earnings of (more or less comparable) workers who underwent training with the earnings of more or less comparable workers who did not. The costs of the program include tuition, out-of-pocket expense, estimated foregone earnings, etc.

7. For simplicity we assume that all employers have the same belief concerning the marginal productivity of any given worker.

8. That is, in the pretraining situation, the productive capacity of those workers destined to become trained was underestimated, but the capacity of other workers was estimated accurately.

9. It does not matter for present purposes whether the difference is created by exaggerating the marginal productivity of trained workers, underestimating the marginal productivity of others, or a combination of both.

10. The speed with which a job vacancy is filled—the mathematical expectation of the length of the interval between the moment the vacancy is "announced" and the moment it is filled—is an essential parameter of any employer hiring policy. In principle, the result of a random application process might enable the least attractive employer in the community to obtain the most desirable workers, if only he would wait "long enough." Therefore an employer's hiring policy cannot be specified until he decides *inter alia* how long (on the average) he is willing to let a vacancy remain unfilled. On this point, see an earlier paper, M. W. Reder, "The Theory of Frictional Unemployment," *Economica*, February 1969, pp. 1–27.

11. For a given employer, *DP* depends upon the characteristics of the firm's production process; the character of its product demand and upon its "loss payoff function in the event it misses its policy target." These factors are discussed in Reder.

12. This statement follows directly if we assume that all workers desire to spend the same fractions of their time in employment and in job search.

13. In practice, for many reasons, there may also be differential unemployment rates. See an earlier paper, "Wage Structure and Structural Unemployment," *Review of Economic Studies*, October 1964, pp. 309–22.

14. There are practical as well as theoretical reasons for distinguishing between a taste for discrimination per se, and a derived

demand for labor service that is biased against certain types of personal characteristics because they are associated with relative incapacity to produce certain kinds of services. The former is what Fair Employment Practice laws are designed to curb; the latter is not. However, attempts to indulge a taste for discrimination may masquerade as a desire to obtain or provide certain types of service and, conversely, attempts to promote equal opportunity may trench on freedom of consumer choice.

15. A method of screening job applicants is, in essence, a method of partitioning a group of applicants, A, into a set of subgroups, A_1—A_n. The "effectiveness" of the method may be measured, assuming all prices constant, by the (negative) difference in the expected marginal productivity of a member selected randomly from A, and one chosen from among A_1—A_n in such a way as to maximize the present value of the firm.

16. Except where the job and its wage rate are poor enough to be considered appropriate for the stereotyped individuals.

17. State of the labor market affects an individual employer's decisions by determining the relation between his actual and desired *DP;* i.e. in a tight labor market, the actual *DP* for a given wage rate, job and set of hiring criteria will tend to be higher than in equilibrium, leading to some combination of redefinition of jobs, raising of wage rates and lowering of hiring standards for given jobs.

18. Put in still another way, a stereotype is a device to evaluate information. That is, it establishes (or helps to establish) a "prior," in the Bayesian sense, that a given job applicant will perform satisfactorily. Given a favorable prior, adverse evidence on an applicant is ignored or explained away; the same evidence would be used as confirmation of an adverse prior.

19. It should be noted explicitly that it is assumed that members of inferior groups are all employees, and that employers must come from superior groups. This is not logically necessary, nor is it always the case. Where an inferior group contains potential employers, their ability to employ other members of this group without incurring the additional screening cost that must be born by employers belonging to the superior group is a source of economy of communication. This economy will tend to make the relative demand curve for an inferior group labor higher than if all employers all came from the superior group.

PART TWO

E. WIGHT BAKKE

MANPOWER POLICY DURING A RECESSION

IN 1966 and 1967 most Western industrialized countries experienced a recession which accompanied the initiation of fiscal and monetary measures designed to counteract increasing inflationary tendencies. The reduction in economic activity and employment found the administrators of manpower policy in most countries that are members of the Organization for Economic Cooperation and Development unprepared to respond rapidly and decisively to the problems presented. Early in 1969 the Committee for Manpower and Social Affairs of the OECD held, in London, a conference of manpower economists and government officials to review and examine their experience in this period. The object of the conference was to consider the question, "What contribution can an active manpower policy make to reducing the undesirable consequences for employment and economic growth of anti-inflationary demand management?" Actually the question might better have been phrased, "What *could* an active manpower policy *have done* had the manpower authorities been prepared and equipped for a rapid response to the downturn in economic activity?" Most of the positive contributions and the lessons learned were in answer to this question.

The following paper is based on some of the findings of that conference, in which I participated as general reporter.

Since World War II, discussion of the relation of manpower policy to general economic policy has focused on the utility of selective manpower measures in a period of economic expansion for (a) reducing the inflationary stimuli implicit in monetary and fiscal measures directed toward expanding aggregate demand (with its derived effect on employment); and for (b) supplementing the general and global expansionary impact of such demand management measures with the correction of structural imbalances and rigidities retarding production and growth in particular geographical, industrial, and labor force sectors. In terms of applied economic theory this contribution was defined as the utilization of manpower measures to move the curve (derived from the Philipps curve), representing the relation between a decrease in the numbers unemployed and upward changes in the price level, downward and to the left.

The key concept in the utilization of manpower measures for such purpose is "timely selective application." The practical and logical relevance of that concept is rooted, first in the easily observed phenomenon of "sectoral imbalances" in the overall system of economic activity and particularized employment, and second in the fact that the instruments of demand management are relatively general in their impact. The sectoral imbalances may refer to differential activity, productivity, and growth in different economic regions of the country, or in different industries. They may refer to differential shortages or surpluses with respect to certain occupations in such regions or industries and in different seasons of the year. They may refer to differential degrees of employability, or to differential opportunities to work, among different actual or potential members of the labor force. The differentials may create difficulties for the carrying out of desired public policy with respect to priorities in emphasis on export and domestically consumed production, with respect to the maintenance of stable prices, with respect to the increase in the welfare of certain groups in the population, etc.

If, so the theory suggests, manpower measures can be *selectively* applied, in a period of expansion-oriented demand management, to relieving, through training, manpower shortages where bottlenecks appear; if unused or ineffectively used workers can be expeditiously trained and transferred from places where manpower is in over-supply to places where bottlenecks appear; if unused or ineffectively used workers can be expeditiously trained and transferred from places where manpower is in over-supply to places where it is in short supply; if job producing industry can be stimulated in regions whose contribution to national production is relatively low; and if adaptability can be added to other ingredients of the employability of workers throughout the labor force, two consequences might be anticipated. The general efforts to expand effective demand would be amplified, but they would be amplified specifically in those sectors lagging behind the general movement, and the pressure on fiscal and monetary mechanisms to expand general demand sufficiently to provide full employment in those sectors would be reduced. The excessive wage and other resource-cost impacts of such policy-implementing mechanisms on those sectors already operating at high capacity would thereby be reduced. Undesirable inflationary consequences of expansionary demand management would be less pronounced.

The *basic* function of an active manpower program is the same in all stages of the business cycle. Manpower policy is one aspect of overall economic and social policy designed to achieve full employment in a way which contributes both to the maintaining of economic stability, productivity, and growth of the economy and to the economic and social security and satisfaction of individual people. In its own right manpower policy seeks to maintain a balance between the supply of and demand for labor whenever, wherever, and for whatever reason, rigidities or imbalances appear, and to focus its effort selectively and in a timely manner upon those sectors of the economy and on those segments of the labor force concerning which corrective action is needed either in the interests of the economy and society or in the interest of individual employers or workers. A continuing task of manpower authorities is to contribute to a balanced (neither overly inflationary or overly deflationary) state of the economy by rapid action to counteract partial imbalances (local and sectoral shortages and surpluses of manpower) whatever the causes of the imbalances. The beneficiaries are both individuals and the economic system. Individuals are beneficiaries by virtue of services performed for them personally and because their personal welfare is in a major way a function of the economic system.

When the economic system and the employment it offers is the object of restraint from overall demand management policy, as was the case in 1966–67, the number of workers who need personal service from the manpower authorities increases. But what is done has a bearing on the operation of the economic system also.

The particular functions of manpower policy, making more specific and amplifying the basic functions indicated above, and which are brought into focus by a recession, reveal the possibilities of this dual service: They are:

1. To reduce the burden of making a living without a job for an increased number of unemployed and under-

employed by providing temporary compensatory work and income maintenance and by expediting their return to more permanent employment through training and employment service activities.

2. To provide a productive alternative use, either through compensatory work or training, for the enforced leisure of the unemployed, productive from the point of view of both the economy and of the workers involved.

3. To develop improved human resources in readiness for the renewal of an expansion in economic activity.

4. To contribute to a renewed high level of employment without overdependence on inflationary demand management, and hence to reduce the dangers in a go-stop global economic policy.

5. To review and analyze continuously the nature of the societal and human forces at work and the experience in coming to grips with those forces.

The chief concerns of the governments represented at the conference, and the only ones discussed with the aid of empirical evidence, were the first two of these possibilities. The most specific evidence was provided by Sweden. The obvious expansion of manpower services related to adaptive employment of the increased number without normal work in that country is indicated in Table 1.

Assume now that, lacking the measures of compensatory employment and training, those adaptively "employed" by virtue of such measures would be recorded as unemployed, and further assume that all those so engaged would have been seeking employment, *i.e.*, considered to be members of the labor force. The figure of recorded unemployment in March 1967 would have been 102,200 not 42,100, and in March 1968 it would have been 151,200 not 51,900. The difference of 60,100 in March 1967 would have been in part accounted for by 33,500 engaged in compensatory employ-

TABLE 1

COMPENSATORY EMPLOYMENT AND TRAINING IN SWEDEN, MARCH 1966 TO MARCH 1968

	March 1966	*March 1967*	*March 1968*	*Increase March 1966–March 1968*
Unemployed Registered	35,300	42,100	51,900	16,600
Relief works	12,300	20,000	27,300	15,000
Sheltered works	9,900	11,600	13,700	3,800
Investment reserves	0	0	14,300	14,300
Extra building	0	1,900	5,600	5,600
Extra government projects	0	0	3,500	3,500
Total compensatory employment	22,200	33,500	64,400	42,200
Labor market training*	20,900	26,600	34,900	14,000
Total Adaptive	43,100	60,100	99,300	56,200
Total Unemployed and Adaptively Employed	78,400	102,200	151,200	72,800

* The figures on training are included here to indicate their proportion of the total as compared with that for compensatory employment.

ment and an additional 26,600 engaged in training, and the difference of 99,300 in March 1968 by 64,400 and 34,900 similarly engaged.

The manpower administration in the several countries derived a number of lessons from the attempt to expand their services in response to the increase in the number of unemployed in a timely and selective manner. The observation of the features and results of the recession itself and the experience in adapting their programs to these factors, moreover, raised a number of questions and issues germane to the implementation of manpower policy at any stage of the business cycle.

QUESTIONS AND ISSUES

What Is the Meaning of Full Employment? "Full employment" has been a declared national goal in all major industrial nations since World War II. Do all who use the term mean the same thing? It is clear that the quantitative meaning has changed over time. In the 1930s the reaching of a 5 percent or 6 percent unemployment level would have been a happy achievement. Beveridge's target of 3 percent held the attention for some years. In the 1960s politicians in European countries considered their political lives in danger when the figure approached, and certainly when it went beyond, 2 percent. Some ambitious advocates of full employment ask, "Why be satisfied with *any* unemployment?"

The most obvious possibility for an underestimation of the volume unemployment which measures the gap between the full employment objective, however defined, and realization, lies in the nature of the statistical ratio utilized. The two components of that ratio, the number unemployed and the labor force, are particularly subject to operational definitions which may distort results. If the denominator is the number of workers insured under an unemployment insurance scheme and the numerator the number of insured workers registered as unemployed, who among those actually without and desiring work are left out of the calculation? Even when the human components are those ascertained by a more comprehensive periodic sample survey, who among those actually without income-producing work (especially *adequate* income-producing work) are not counted?

A comparison of trends in the figures on employment and unemployment from 1965 in European countries emphasizes something of the size of this unrecorded group of people without work. The decline in employment was greater than would be anticipated from the recorded increase in unemployment. In Germany the decrease in those actively employed during the recession is represented only to the extent of 15 percent by the registered unemployed. In England the proportion is 50 percent, in France 40 percent to 50 percent.

Sample labor force surveys, like that upon which unemployment statistics in the United States are based, reveal more clearly the inadequacy of "registered" unemployment as an indicator of the size of the problem. In 1968 when unemployment was relatively low by American standards only 32 percent recorded as without and seeking work were those who had *lost* their last job and 19 percent were those who had *left* their last job. These are the groups who are most likely to be counted among the "registered" unemployed in countries.

These data raise several questions for manpower authorities. Are current nonmembers of the labor force who nevertheless are available for work if job openings are sufficient, a part of the "unemployed" whose numbers should be included in calculating how close we are to "full" employment? Do our unemployment statistics truly reflect the fluctuation in the intensity of the problem of utilized manpower? Do they give us an adequate clue to the clientele who are the appropriate concern of manpower measures, particularly those related to training and mobility? Are those who drop out of, or fail to enter, the labor market during a recession, but may be stimulated to first or renewed job seeking when economic activity revives, the responsibility of manpower authorities during a recession? If these people were to be included, the "unemployment" rate would be higher. Assume for example, 20,000 registered unemployed in a labor force of 500,000. Then

$$\frac{20{,}000}{500{,}000} = 4\%.$$

Now assume the inclusion of 5,000 nonentrants to, or drop-outs from, the labor force. Then

$$\frac{25{,}000}{505{,}000} = 4.9\%.$$

Another characteristic of the 1966–67 recession was that employment levels failed to recover to the extent which might have been anticipated from other indicators of economic activity that revealed recovery had begun. Had the managerial and technological response of firms to the problems of survival during the recession, and the failure of marginal firms, reduced the number of workers required to maintain the prerecession volume of production? The fact that the year-to-year increase in productivity was maintained at about the same rate from 1966 to 1968 as during the previous expansion in industrial activity, and in some countries was actually amplified, would re-enforce this conclusion.

Does optimism about expanding job opportunities generated by the observation of improving general economic conditions bring back (or for the first time) into the labor market persons who had not been job seekers and without work during the recession? Both the opportunity for, and the problem of, achieving a closer approximation to full employment would appear to be amplified when recovery takes place.

What Is the Effect in a Recession of Manpower Measures on the Redeployment of Labor? The movement of workers from sectors where they are underutilized or not productively employed is a central concern of the manpower authorities at all times. Since the object of one of the chief instruments of manpower policy, the Employment Service, is to facilitate this movement, the question arises as to whether this area of manpower activity can, as is suggested for training, compensatory employment, and income maintenance, be expanded as one form of response to the increase in unemployment in a general recession. A related question is whether the expansion of the abovenamed services actually runs counter to any desirable redeployment of labor.

The assumption of a *general* recession comes close to making the first a moot question since the general decline in employment reduces the chances that jobs will be available in other areas and industries. Unemployed workers cannot be moved to jobs which are not there. While job vacancies do not completely disappear, there is pressure on local authorities to fill whatever jobs are unfilled with local unemployed rather than to accept workers from beyond their borders, even if more qualified workers were available from the outside. When jobs generally are in short supply, any movement of the unemployed seeking work will be stimulated primarily by the need of employers for workers unavailable locally in the receiving area rather than by any spontaneous desire of workers to leave a high unemployment area or industry, or by the efforts of the employment services to expedite such movement.

There are, of course, in the midst of a general recession still labor shortage areas or sectors. Indeed, one of the interesting aspects of the 1966–67 recession was that reported job vacancies did not decline proportionately with the rise in the number unemployed as might have been expected. If, upon examination, the job vacancies reported represented more than a need for temporary workers, it would be foolish in the interests of both the economy and of the individuals, to fail to take advantage of the opportunity to move workers available into these vacancies. But the plausible conclusion is that the manpower facilities for expediting the redeployment of labor are not likely candidates for expansion during a depression. This does not imply the possibility of reducing the staff of the Employment Service, for placement of workers is only one of the important tasks needing continued and even amplified attention.

But the charge has been made that other manpower measures which *are* candidates for expansion during a recession, particularly compensatory employment and income maintenance, actually retard that degree of redeployment of labor which would be initiated by the spontaneous choice of unemployed individuals or by stimulus from the employment service administrators generated by their awareness of an unsatisfied demand for labor in certain areas or industries.

It is reasonable to conclude that the successful stimulation of job search, movement, and placement is a process in which the predispositions and mobility qualifications of the worker himself and the facilities provided by, and efforts of, the manpower authorities are full partners. Likewise, it is plausible to suggest that the reluctance of individuals to undertake a job search afield, to move, and accept the risks of an uncertain new job and life situation are reinforced by the availability of alternative work or maintenance possibilities provided by government in their present location. The personal predispositions rooted in the fear that, as a result of a search for something better, one risks the chance of losing the securities one has, are amplified during a general depression, however minimal those securities may be.

Economic security in the minds of the workers consists of more than job security, which for the unemployed, of course, is in a very low state. Established supportive contacts with family, friends, politically "in" persons, and community institutions are important ingredients. The availability of earnings from other members of the family employed in the present place of employment, legislative or contractual benefits in case of sickness, accident, unemployment or death dependent on continued attachment to the last employer, the perceived possibility of recall by that last employer, the consciousness of one's status as a respected member of a particular occupation are all-important. Even the wisdom of experience concerning how to get along and live in the present location is a source of economic as well as social security. Coupled with the uncertainty about reestablishing such securities in a new and unfamiliar environment and about the permanency of a possible job, and faced with the economic costs of movement (even when transfer allowances and initial living subsidies are available from the manpower authorities) it is little wonder that reluctance to search and move out of a present situation is at all times and predisposition of all but the unusually ambitious and risk welcoming unemployed workers. The numbers in that latter minority are reduced in a period of general recession.

It is always possible, of course, if conditions in the present location are desperate enough, that "any port in a storm" may become the objective. Particularly under such conditions, if adequate alternative government or private institutional provided compensatory employment or income maintenance are unavailable in the present location, might the unemployed make a "rational" choice to move to an area where rumor suggests the latter assistance is available. It is possible therefore, that the lack of that assistance from manpower and relief authorities might overcome the reluctance to move, and that the availability of that assistance can reinforce that reluctance.

In this way the inference can be drawn that the satisfaction of the objective to provide adequate work or maintenance is in conflict with the possibility of achieving a desirable redeployment of labor. But before that inference is permitted to influence policy, the concept "desirable" should be operationally defined in the light of the existence of opportunities for useful and productive work in the changed area, industry, or occupation, and consideration be given to whether that work is the kind which those inclined to move can perform and thus become self-supporting contributors to their own and society's welfare. In any case, the availability of compensatory employment and income maintenance are only a part of the structure of economic and social securities in his present location which the worker is reluctant to trade for a risky venture afield, and any impact of these two factors on the propensity to move is marginal to that whole structure. Such was the conclusion of the manpower economists and administrators at the London Conference.

Do Increased Expenditures for Manpower Measures Counteract the Impact of General Restraint Measures? Another frequently expressed concern is that the expenditures incurred for training and compensatory employment should not result in such an inflationary impact as to return the economy to the previous point on the trade-off curve.

In the attempt to initiate action of a sufficient amount to furnish an expansion of compensatory employment and/or training, in those sectors particularly hard hit by the measures of restraint, proportional to the increasing numbers of unemployed, the expenditures would of themselves increase overall demand, thus running counter to the restraining objective of fiscal and monetary measures. This would be particularly true when the general operations of government require deficit financing.

One answer to this concern is that the expenditures must be offset by raising taxes or reducing other expenditures. An OECD staff paper of January 1969 contains this line of reasoning:

> The fundamental analytical proposition must be that an expenditure of $X on training [or compensatory unemployment] tends to have a greater impact on unemployment than would a tax reduction of roughly equivalent magnitude or $X of other expenditures.
>
> In terms of contra-cyclical policy and policy designed to shift the trade-off, this makes sense. Presumably, the fact that the expenditures are so selective—reaching the unemployed very directly through training or relief works—means they can have a much greater impact on unemployment per dollar expended than would

less selective expenditures. Thus, a given absolute reduction in unemployment requires a smaller increase in expenditures and a smaller offsetting tax increase (or tightening of monetary policy) in order to restrain inflation. It is accordingly more acceptable and more likely to occur. The result is an improvement in the position of the trade-off brought about by using training and other selective policies to mop up the unemployment created by a reasonable restrictive general fiscal and monetary policy.

Another answer to the concern that manpower expenditures may undo the influence of general demand management measured when the objective is restraint is that manpower measures can be selectively applied to the correction of labor market imbalances in those sectors, geographical, industrial, or occupational, where, because unemployment is already severe, a further reduction in employment would be meaningless from the point of view of fighting inflation. If this justification is to be substantiated, the measures must be concentrated and largely limited to such sectors.

There is at least one possibility which could have a contrary effect. There could be a spillover demand effect on other sectors where restraint was desired. Intersectoral flows can thus result in adding to the demand for goods and services in already high demand areas.

This is especially likely to occur in the case of any major public construction projects. Since it is estimated that less than one-third of the total costs of new public construction are attributable to on-site labor and about one-half attributable to material, the impact of activity will, of course, be felt in other parts of the economy. If these other areas are also in a depressed state, the "selective" compensatory employment process is simply extended to them. If, however, the secondary areas affected are not in need of compensatory effort, or in fact are among those areas in which restraint is deemed necessary, the new construction approach may actually increase the inflationary pressures which the restraining policies were intended to correct.

These and other answers to the concern over the possible inflationary effect of expenditures for manpower measures, that is an effect on general demand opposite from that intended by general measures of restraint being applied to "cool down" the economy, may be briefly summarized:

1. Manpower expenditures are not normally applied to those sectors where close to capacity performance has produced the situation leading to inflationary pressures. They are applied selectively to those sectors where underutilization of manpower and other resources is the normal situation which is aggravated during a recession.

2. The increased manpower expenditures in a recession are made largely on behalf of the unemployed whose pressure in wage negotiations, if present at all, is not likely to be on the side of large wage increases.

3. Expenditures for training and compensatory employment are made to many who, in any case, would be receiving some income maintenance from public funds. The net increase in public expenditures would not, therefore, be represented by the total outlay.

4. The payoff in the future contribution of the workers involved to production would, to some degree, compensate for present expenditures.

5. In case the restraining measures were to be introduced to relieve a particular situation, say a balance-of-payments problem intensified by inflation, selective manpower measures could conceivably do a more focused job than general deflationary measures, without the danger of inducing a general recession. If, in so far as labor shortages in general or for particular skills stood in the way, the capacity of export or import substitute industries could be increased by manpower measures selectively applied in precisely those sectors, a general recession might be avoided.

6. Even if it were decided that, in view of the

increased expenditures, taxes needed to be proportionately increased or tax allowances reduced, the positive benefits to individuals and to industry and to the community from manpower measures are offset advantages.

7. The very statement of the issue suggests that the problem of avoiding an inconsistency between a demand management policy which restrains demand and manpower policy which, to the degree of expenditures, increase the demand sectorially is one of synchronizing and coordinating the two.

8. Finally it should be noted that the need for restraint does not continue forever. A point is reached where once more the need is for reflationary measures. At that point, the manpower expenditures exert an impact in the same direction as the more global reflationary measures, and can be tapered off as these become effective if that is necessary, in the interests of stabilization.

Are Timely Short-Range and Sound Long-Range Manpower Measures Inconsistent with Each Other? Implicit in the problem of utilizing manpower measures in response to cyclically declining employment is the need for timely and rapid action. Those who understand the long-range significance of manpower measures for the strength, stability, growth, and viability of the economy, however, may well point out the dangers in gearing decisions to short-range cyclical situations. Training, compensatory employment, movement of workers, regional development, employment service operations, improvement of the employability of the disadvantaged groups, even income maintenance, must be organized and carried out with long-range goals and effects in mind. Certainly this latter assertion emphasizes a premise with which no rational person could disagree. Of course, the needs which justify government action in these areas are those which continue to evolve over time. Policy and plans and action must necessarily be responsive to that fact. And if action in response to sudden and unforeseen problems were to inhibit or retard steady progress toward the long-range solution of the problems presented by these needs, the warning would indeed be justified. But this need not be the case.

Indeed, the more normally observable situation is that the failure to take timely and rapid action with respect to immediate problems results in an interruption of such progress. There is, therefore, no necessary incompatibility between rapid and timely, in contrast to deliberate and steady, action to deal with problems of the labor market. Quite the opposite. Short-range and long-range, immediate and eventual, detailed and overall, are simply adjectives describing different continuously experienced aspects of the same problems. It is only common sense to prepare for and take the kind of action called for by the aspect of the problem which requires attention.

Moreover, rapid and timely action should not be equated merely with action in response to short-term cyclical changes. Timeliness is an essential characteristic of action whatever its objective, and whenever it takes place. The removal of structural imbalances in the labor market, the encouragement of long-term economic productivity and growth, the control of population growth, the raising of the level of living, etc. are all long-term objectives. That they can be so characterized does not eliminate the need for rapid and timely attention to immediate obstacles that arise to their attainment or to unexpected opportunities that are presented for increasing the chances of their attainment.

There is no reason why rapid manpower action in relation to cyclical changes in production and the derived changes in employment should not be planned and prepared for as a part of a long-range attack on structural and secular trends in the labor market. Indeed, unless they are planned and prepared for, they are likely to be ineffective, as we shall see in the next section. An effective apparatus for manpower action in relation to cyclical changes cannot be easily created at the moment when an acute need for action to relieve employment difficulties becomes manifest. In a very real sense, rapid action can be simply the setting in motion of action anticipated as necessary in a long-term plan. Any long-term plan which does not provide for contingencies and emergencies, which all experience indicates will arise, can scarcely lay claim to being an adequate plan.

There is no reason why manpower authorities should not be guided by the venerable experience that large and difficult-to-manage problems *build up* from unattended-to smaller and detailed problems. This is no less true of cyclical crises than of secular trends in structural imbalances. One of the major contributions of manpower policy to overall economic stability and growth is the recognition that timely and selectively applied measures can prevent the accumulated buildup of sectoral problems into a huge problem for the total economy.

This is well recognized with respect to the problem of inflation during the period when demand management policy is directed toward increasing aggregate demand. It is no less true during a period when that policy is directed toward restricting aggregate demand. The unemployment resulting from deflationary measures builds on itself. Sectoral imbalances are worsened. The capacity of unemployed workers to contribute to renewed productive activity declines with time. The popular demand increases for stimulation from fiscal and monetary measures to absorb the unemployed, to restore production to desirable levels, and to provide expectations encouraging to investment, before inflationary tendencies have been brought under control. The contribution of manpower measures to the prevention of this situation, a situation which increases the difficulties of achieving long-range manpower goals, depends upon the *timely* application of those measures.

To reduce by rapid and timely action the necessity for exaggerated dependence on stop-go measures, to set to work immediately on the development of skills the lack of which may create bottlenecks when employment opportunities expand, to use at once the opportunity to increase the adaptability of temporarily unemployed workers to future changes in occupational demands, to provide, before unemployment has taken its toll, work or training which reduces the chances that unused skills and working habits will deteriorate—such rapidly instituted efforts are definite contributions to the achievement of long-range results. That their effectiveness is dependent on the quality of the effort is obvious. That the effectiveness of the best effort is limited unless made in a timely selective fashion should be equally obvious.

What Are the Requirements for Timely Response of Manpower Measures to Declining Economic Activity and Employment? As indicated at the beginning of this paper, the manpower authorities in most OECD countries were not prepared to make a timely and adequate response to the unusual tasks thrust upon them by the recession of 1966–67. The positive answer to the foregoing question must therefore be based, not on the observation of what most of them did, but on an examination of the obstacles they faced and what might have been done to reduce the impact of those obstacles.

COMMITMENT TO PREVENTATIVE ACTION. The requirements are germane not only to the action taken at the moment of the onset of a recession, but to what has been done before. It is a truism that the difficulty of initiating and carrying out timely and adequate adaptive action when a recession sets in is inversely proportional to the degree to which the size of the problem encountered has been reduced by previous action. The size of the redundancy problem in a declining industry may present a problem of overwhelming proportions to the manpower authorities during a recession if the ultimate reallocation of resources including manpower, long foreseen as necessary, has been continuously postponed. The need for attention to the manpower problems in certain export and import-substitute industries will be difficult to solve by rapid action if the need for retraining has not previously been anticipated and responded to. The numbers of the disadvantaged (operationally defined as the least employable in terms of the changing occupational requirements of technological and organizational developments) can well be increased beyond the point at which their problems, aggravated by a recession, can be dealt with by rapid action, unless previous attention to their problems has been a focus of effort. The alleviation through rapid action of the problems of the unemployed workers during a recession will be made possible to a greater or lesser degree in accordance with the way in which basic structural and regional problems have been handled prior to the cyclically induced unemployment of these workers.

Possibly the most significant lesson to be derived from the experience of the immediate past is that the volume and direction of selective manpower measures during the 1960s was not sufficient in any OECD country to prevent the need for general disinflationary measures reminiscent of the traditional stop-go, or go-stop, policy. Perhaps the necessity for such measures was postponed by the anti-inflationary impact of selective manpower measures. Possibly the size of the problem faced by general economic policy makers was mitigated by those measures.

In any case the value of such a lesson is to emphasize the need for manpower authorities—and indeed all determiners of governmental economic policy—to increase their efforts through selective measures to make possible a growth in production and employment without inflation by reducing labor market imbalances as soon as they are anticipated or realized, and to maintain for the workers of the nation a sustained level of opportunity to work or prepare for work when, in any sector or region, that opportunity is reduced by the operation of private or public economic policies directed toward objectives other than the maintenance of a high level of employment.

The maintenance of a full employment society requires a commitment to preventative, not merely remedial, action. The remedial approach to government action with respect to the volume of employment characterized what might be termed, an "unemployment society."

During that earlier day when large fluctuations in employment were considered inevitable, and when unemployment was itself regarded as one of the necessary regulators of free market operations, remedial measures *after the event* rather than preventative measures before the event predominated. The role of government was primarily to correct rather than to initiate in respect to the particularized operations of the labor market. The focus of attention was on meeting the consequences of unemployment rather than on giving the kind of direction to the economic activity of the nation which would avoid imbalances in the supply of and the demand for labor. A certain "wait and see" attitude was not considered unreasonable. And the concern was with operating each institution as an entity in itself rather than on shaping an integrated set of institutional instruments ready for whatever immediate adaptive action and emphasis a changing employment situation demanded. We are still learning how to live with full employment. Our institutions and procedures are not fully geared to the requirements of anticipatory and rapid responsive action essential to avoiding the consequences of "letting nature take its course." The ways of thinking of many of us are still more consistent with "figuring out what to do" after a problem arises rather than with planning and being ready to take alternative immediate measures contributing to the attainment not merely of short-term, but of long-term objectives.

LONG-RANGE SHORT-RANGE PLANNING. It cannot be emphasized too strongly that the most effective short-term action in response to the onset of a recession is that which is taken within the framework of a long-term plan. Rapid action in the face of an unexpected change in the labor market or an emergency, to say nothing of that in response to recurrent and easily anticipated changes, becomes under such circumstances simply a setting in motion of that part of a long-range plan designed for dealing with such contingencies. Furthermore, the request for official authorization and support for such short-term action is more likely to be forthcoming if the need for such timely authorization and support has been forevisioned in a long-term plan.

The importance of long-range planning will be evident from the discussion of the next requirement, namely of flexibility.

FLEXIBILITY OF FINANCING, PROGRAMS, PERSONNEL, AND FACILITIES. The achievement of flexibility is best considered by reference to specific types of manpower actions, compensatory employment, training, employment service, unemployment insurance, and other forms of income maintenance. However, one requirement, related to financial arrangements, is relevant to all aspects of manpower effort, especially when the form of desired adaptation is an extension or amplification of the service under consideration. This extension and increase in the volume of activity related to compensatory employment, training, and income maintenance is, by all odds, the major adaptive device for achieving the objectives of manpower effort in response to a cyclical decline in employment.

If manpower administrators possess the authority to shift expenditures from one year to another and this possibility is supported by a system of multiannual budgeting, the administrative flexibility would be increased. The multiannual budget method, however, is likely in practice not to achieve the desired result, i.e., a reservoir of funds for emergency use, since under the pressure of interest groups and legislators for expenditures during a boom period, the decision to postpone expenditures until needed for a countercyclical purpose is politically unpopular.

It is unlikely that the needed enlarged budget for manpower measures can be precisely formulated prior to a recession (this process begins normally from twelve to eighteen months before the authorized financial resources are to be used). Even if it were possible to predict a general slowing down of economic activity as a consequence of contemplated fiscal and monetary restraints, the specific sectoral impact of that result, leading to determination of the what and where and the degree or size of the effort would still be difficult.

The only assurance then of the possession by the manpower authorities of the financial resources for timely and decisive action at the very onset of recession is the "contingency budget" which would not have to await the long process of Congressional or parliamentary action. Parliamentarians are loath to forego their declared authoritative control of government expenditures. But some modification of that absolute control, and the authorization of a high degree of discretion for manpower authorities to initiate that modification, is a *sine qua non* of timely, responsive, and hopefully, anticipatory action on their part. Several alternatives are available, each successive one offering an expanding degree of discretion in the making of expenditures within the framework of a contingency budget:

a. The release of additional funds could depend on legislative action requested by the manpower authorities.

b. The funds could become automatically available

under certain conditions evidenced by the behavior of specified economic indicators, *but* subject to legislative review and veto.

c. The funds could become automatically available under certain conditions evidenced by the behavior of specified economic indicators, *unconditionally*.

d. The manpower authority could be granted full discretionary authority to use the funds under certain legislatively defined conditions.

The last two methods are clearly the most likely to result in the possibility of timely selective action.

The economic indicator which is normally used to trigger the exercise of such discretion to expand the scope of manpower services is the unemployment rate. Several problems have been encountered in this matter. If the rate used is the national aggregative rate, it covers up the sectoral variations which are the pertinent figures for triggering *selectively* applied expansion of manpower efforts. Also there is some question as to whether the overall unemployment rate is as sharp an indicator of the need for manpower services as, say, the variation in the *numbers* unemployed for, say, fifteen or twenty weeks or longer. Whichever indicator is used, the provision (as in the recent Administration Manpower Bill in the United States) that the figure must be above a critical point for three successive months is completely unrealistic for the setting in motion of timely action that prevents the escalation of an undesirable situation. The action is actually postponed for four months since it is normally a month after the observation that the figures become available.

FLEXIBILITY IN COMPENSATORY EMPLOYMENT EXPANSION. Compensatory employment is normally considered to be the least flexible of possible manpower measures with respect to timely adaptation to the meeting of a cyclical decline in normal employment. A major factor contributing to this conclusion is that the allocation of projects providing various forms of compensatory employment is frequently considered to be a political device for increasing the popularity of the legislator in the locality to which the project is allocated. Considerations of the political advantage from such projects, rather than their utility for adapting employment possibilities to sectoral needs as envisioned by manpower authorities, is likely to govern. Another factor is that the initiation of such projects lies normally with departments or ministries acting independently of the manpower authorities. Unless the manpower authorities can be given authority to determine the time and place for such projects, it is difficult to see how they can be utilized as a part of a selective manpower program.

A consideration of the several types of compensatory employment, however, suggests that there are variations in rigidity among them. *Public works* of the new building and construction variety (whether of the public or private type), are most difficult to vary in relation to short-range cyclical movements. The time required for approval of plans and specifications, the authorization for launching, the completing of contractual arrangements for operations and delivery of supplies, the mobilization of a labor force, especially of highly skilled workers, is such that the eventual carrying out of such projects is likely to be accomplished after the peak of the immediate need for additional employment has passed. Several countries have, however, undertaken to have all stages prior to actual construction in readiness. If such a "pipeline" concept of public and/or private construction is implemented, such projects hold some possibility for timely action. In any case a number of countries have found it possible to speed up or retard such building and construction in response to opposite trends in the employment situation.

Public works of the maintenance and repair variety are somewhat more flexible. On the whole, work of this sort is of shorter duration, and therefore more useful in responding to short-run cyclical fluctuation, particularly if preplanning has taken place so that the schedule of postponement and release can be made consistent with the concentration of activity at the time needed.

Public works of the reforestation or other public lands improvement type, granted that the "pipeline" concept of preparation governs, are still more flexible. Since they are more labor-intensive than the other forms, they have an added advantage when compensatory employment for the unemployed is an immediate problem.

Additional production orders by government departments is a device which has the advantage of keeping workers, who might otherwise be laid off, working for their normal employers. Its utility as an adaptive and selective manpower measure is weakened by the fact that the manpower authorities do not issue the contracts and that the contract issuance is frequently a slow process. Also there is a limit to which the inventories beyond immediate needs can be built up by the several departments.

Expansion of government services, that is, the expanded engagement of unemployed persons in preplanned government service activities, for example, in the fields of education, health, recreation, libraries, museums, research, etc. can take up some of the slack in the demand for labor in the private sector. Such projects normally require a large component of white-collar workers and, while such occupations are a less volatile area of cyclical employment fluctuations, they are not wholly insulated from the effects of demand-restraining measures. The possibility of combining such compensatory employment with training for permanent careers in government service, or indeed in private industry, should be considered.

TAX ALLOWANCES AND OTHER SUBSIDIES IN FAVOR OF MAINTENANCE OF PRIVATE EMPLOYMENT. The political possibility of differential tax or subsidy treatment for selected areas, industries, or firms is not equally available in all countries. But where such a taxing policy is possible, it would appear appropriate to consider such measures for encouraging continued, if not expanded, production and even investment, in those sectors particularly hard hit by an overall policy of restraint. The critical necessity in the case of tax rebates, as in the case of other forms of direct or indirect subsidies made to employment creating enterprise, is that the timing and duration of such measures and rules governing allocation of awards be controlled to avoid continued dependence on such measures, to minimize the danger of continued stimulus arising from their use when the peak need has passed, and to balance the relief needs of particular sectors with the need for the relocation of resources, including manpower.

An innovative form of tax rebate is that used to encourage the accumulation by firms of tax-free "investment reserves," to be released by the government on advice of the Royal Labor Market Board in Sweden, with limits set for the period during which they can be used. In the recent 1966–67 recession these were released with favorable effects on employment, although previous releases had not been so well-timed.

Although there is an advantage in the possibility of speeding up the job-creating private investment by such measures, there are also difficulties. Unless a government agency is empowered with the discretion to act under a previously granted general mandate, in response to an immediate change in the employment situation, the protection of the taxing prerogative, normally jealously guarded by parliamentarians, and the time required by the parliamentary process is likely to preclude the rapid action required to make the rebates or other subsidies effective when needed. This problem, of course, is avoided in the Swedish system of investment reserves. The encouragement, through tax relief, of the accumulation of the reserves is an established policy. The release can be focused and in principle be selective and timely.

A particularly interesting form of employment maintaining,

if not expanding, subsidy is the system of "productive unemployment assistance" as developed, for example, in Austria. Under this system, as a substitute for paying out unemployment insurance to a laid off worker, the employer is subsidized up to an equivalent amount if he agrees to maintain the worker on the payroll. If such payments can be made under regulations limiting them to short periods, they have the advantage of subsidizing employment rather than merely relieving the burden of unemployment. Since adequate empirical evidence is lacking respecting experience with such a plan, it is difficult to judge whether it can be successfully utilized to ease the impact of adverse cyclical movements in employment. This method, however, involves basically the substitution of one form of government expenditure for another, and is most applicable in a country where both forms are largely government-financed.

FLEXIBILITY OF TRAINING EXPANSION. Like compensatory employment projects, expanded training projects cannot be set in motion in a timely fashion simply by providing that contingency funds shall be available. A major requirement is that provision be made for the expanding and contracting of the teaching staff on relatively short notice. The achievement of such flexibility is hampered by the demand of trainers employed by the manpower or coopted agencies for the same kind of employment regularity as that experienced by teachers in the public schools. Swedish and Canadian manpower administrators have approached this problem of expansion and contraction by drawing on a large cadre of temporary instructors from industry whose training work is likely to be reduced during a recession, and likely to be increased when the recession has run its course. The permanent nucleus of instructors is maintained, even when public training activities are once more brought to a normal volume, by assigning those not needed for current instruction to curriculum development and new teaching devices and methods.

If the training activity is to be selective by reference to different sectoral needs, a portion of the teaching staff will need to be mobile enough to implement this selective approach, and the expectancy that such location shifts may be necessary needs to be understood from the beginning by the members of that staff.

In order to assure the availability of facilities and equipment for variations in the amount of training offered, manpower authorities need to have on hand a roster of auxiliary facilities and equipment and to have made contingency arrangements with the managers of those facilities and that equipment. Such contingency plans and arrangements may well be entered into with firms, voluntary associations, vocational schools, proprietary and public schools offering approved training.

Many administrative arrangements such as period of attendance, number of classes per trainee, number of trainees per instructor, class size, shift arrangements, staggered entry, etc., can be so ordered as to provide the flexibility needed to adapt to an uncertain fluctuation in the volume of training needed and desirable.

The extent and variety of courses offered will determine the extent to which the needs of workers, the variety of whose qualifications and circumstances widens as the level of unemployment rises in a recession can be met. They will need to vary in length from a couple of weeks to a couple of years, and vary in content from those providing very broad and basic elementary studies to those preparing trainees in very specialized and narrow occupational skills. The courses will need to start at a level assuming different degrees of basic education, for some quite limited, for others quite advanced. If they can be organized in stages so that one who moves from one stage into employment might, at a later time, take up his training where he had left off, so much the better. Some workers may be characterized as "skilled" only by reference to techniques which are on their way out, and their skills must be updated to take advantage of new processes.

It has been customary in the development of training programs, both private and public, to gear the type of training to the kinds of jobs which have a high probability of being available in the area in which the training occurs. Such training is specific-job oriented. It has been considered not only a waste of money to train people for specific jobs that were not likely to be available, but a blow to the morale of trainees if no training-related job was available when they had completed their course.

Such concerns are natural and inevitable if the concept of matching specific supply with specific demand is the only one governing the establishment of curricula in training programs. It certainly is one highly important guideline principle that specific job training should be directed by the probability of specific job openings.

But is specific job training for specific vacancies the only appropriate principle for determining the nature of the curricula which may provide a useful vocational experience for the larger than normal number of persons who find themselves without gainful employment in a recession? Is there not opportunity for experimentation in the kind of training curriculum which increases general orientation to a changing occupational structure and develops adaptability for facing up to the problem of changing occupations over time? Of particular utility during a recession when employers are able to be more selective in their choice of workers, are courses, such as those widely developed in Canada and the United States, for those with basic vocation-related educational deficiencies, courses not aiming immediately to confer any practical specific-job oriented skills. At a higher level of this broader-than-specific job training are the following: the Swedish approach to offering individuals "open-ended" courses, and their general courses for members of the building trades; the

Danish method of permitting individuals to go through series of increasingly advanced courses providing basic scientific information related to a number of occupations; the English development of basic, then more specialized, "modules" of training which can be combined in a number of ways. Moreover, to the extent that the opportunity for "renewed" training throughout life is incorporated as an objective of the general training system, that system will be better geared to the unusual strains, or rather opportunities, experienced when and where imbalances in supply and demand for various skills occur, especially during a period of restrained economic activity.

Much of the anxiety that the trainees will be trained only to find no jobs in which their acquired skills can be utilized, would not be relevant if, over time, one operational definition of training implanted both in the minds of both manpower authorities and workers was basic and general preparation for adaptability.

The wider the variety of types of training constituting the going system of training, the more flexibility it has for selective attention to the variety of training needs, always present, but increasing in scope during a recession.

COORDINATION AMONG MANPOWER SERVICES. At all stages of the business cycle, coordination among the administrators of the several particular manpower services is essential. Functionally no one of the services is self-sufficient. The fact of necessary interdependence, however, does not guarantee synchronized interaction.

The several types of manpower services were not accepted as a government responsibility at the same time in accordance with a concept of the overall mission of manpower policy. Their introduction into the structure of government operations occurred frequently under the sponsorship of different ministries or departments with the aim of aiding or expanding their particular operations. The principles for allocation by legislatures of the administration of measures to particular ministries or departments has not been consistent over time. At all times, therefore, the smooth coordination of the various forms of compensatory employment (e.g., public works, expansion of public service, sheltered workshops, additional production orders, subsidization of private enterprise), of training, of the employment service, and of various forms of income maintenance, has been a difficult task.

In addition to the compelling necessity for continuous synchronization of the services, several advantages become particularly revelant during a recession and essential to timely action. The information gathering and distributing function of the employment service gains added significance for all agencies. This matter is discussed below. The introduction of a training component into those projects of compensatory employment conducted under government auspices is desirable in order to avoid the possibility that such employment could become a permanent way of life for the persons involved. The need for intensification of the job development, counseling, and placement activity of the employment service for the increased numbers involved in compensatory employment and training during a depression is evident, and partly for the reason just indicated. The provisions for income maintenance are essential to undergird the carrying on of other services in accordance with the requirement for effective achievement of their specific mission as services, unfettered in the pursuit of that objective by being operated *primarily* as maintenance-income-producing projects. The key word is syncronization of income maintenance payments with other measures designed to bring the unemployed worker into renewed contact with productive opportunities or to better prepare him for that employment relationship.

Another very important service of the system of income maintenance to the other aspects of manpower policy is that, incidental to the payments to individuals, a record is kept of the whereabouts of the unemployed individual. If a recession is prolonged, the tendency is to lose track of marginal workers because they no longer have contact with either jobs or public agencies which identify them as members of the labor force. This *de facto* exit from the labor force, as we have seen, makes an apparent, but not real, reduction in the observed problem of nonutilized manpower, and hence provides governments with an inaccurate conception of the size and the nature of the problem which faces them at the moment or will face them when the need for increased resources of manpower becomes apparent. Though this service is incidental to the task of adequate maintenance of unemployed workers, it is nevertheless important to the effective continuous balancing of labor market resources of supply of and demand for labor. The desirability of having an up-to-date and full roster of those who can potentially be benefited by the full range of manpower services provides a supporting argument for extended benefits in a prolonged depression.

A constant subject of debate among students of manpower systems is the relative advantages of the highly centralized responsibility for the initiation and conduct of manpower services in an independent agency (as best represented by the Swedish arrangement) and the dispersion of responsibility for these services in a number of agencies and at a number of levels of government from federal to local (characteristic, for example, of the arrangements in the United States).

The advantages of the centralized independent agency system become especially evident in its capacity to respond in a timely and synchronized fashion to the challenge to the manpower services in a recession. The need for rapid decision-making to trigger the direction and scale of timely action is difficult to satisfy when the dispersion of responsibility is widespread.

SYNCHRONIZATION OF MANPOWER WITH GLOBAL ECONOMIC MEASURES. Moreover, the significance and potential of manpower policy as a collaborative partner in all aspects of government policy in response to cyclical movements in economic activity is unlikely to be given due weight and priority by administrators of the other aspects of policy unless the needs and claims of manpower action are continuously represented by a single spokesman. The necessary cooperative predispositions and pattern of action cannot be set up ad hoc when the need for cooperation arises. The need for the cooperation is present both when demand management policy is directed toward expansion, and when it is directed toward restraint of economic activity. An important manpower function in both cases is to anticipate and prevent or correct undesirable consequences of demand management policy, in the first case an exaggerated rise in the price level, in the second case, the increased individual and societal burden of unemployment.

At least two requirements for effective and timely collaboration are evident, in addition to a conviction on the part of policy makers and administrators in the areas of government operations oriented toward both selective and global objectives that a synchronization of their efforts is essential and feasible. These requirements are: (a) organizational and administrative liaison arrangements making agreement on synchronized measures mandatory and feasible; and (b) the possession of information about the proven or probable impact of measures taken by one group on the problems faced by the other group and of their probable consequences for the operation of the economy.

The requirement for organizational arrangements which make collaborative interaction among responsible officials feasible and possible has been the object of a variety of experiments. The most direct approach, as indicated above, is to concentrate the great majority of agencies relevant to manpower operations into an independent or semi-independent agency whose director is in continual collaborative relation with the heads of other economic policy implementing agencies or ministries. The more frequent approach is to place responsibility for the administration of manpower measures in the hands of a subdivision or of several subdivisions of a particular ministry or department. This locates the manpower people in a status in which their influence on policy and practice synchronization must be mediated through a minister or cabinet member. Their influence is dependent on the degree to which the minister or cabinet member is able to obtain consensus among his peers as to the priorities for government action and expenditure. The controlling factor of financial resources for operations makes it inevitable that whoever has the largest influence in the ultimate structuring of the budget, whether a Director of the Budget or the Minister of Finance, shall have a large *de facto* voice in determining the extent to which manpower measures can be utilized effectively in complementing, through selective action, the actions taken by those responsible for global economic and industrial and trade policy.

Whatever the allocation of functions, regular and periodic meetings between ministers or cabinet members or their deputies are necessary in order to assure that decisions on action related to one type of policy will be made in the light of the mutual and reciprocal impacts of policy implementation in one area on the problems and actions in another area, and in order that the greatest possibilities of complementary activity among the several forms of action be realized. The kinds of information required are suggested below.

RELEVANT INFORMATION. Success in the effort at synchronization of global and selective manpower economic measures is also related to the adequacy of the information possessed by those responsible for planning and implementing the synchronization. They need to know specifically how the implementation of one policy affects the situation to which implementors of other policies will need to respond. It is plausible to assume, and empirically verifiable, for example, that an expansionary or a restraining action in general demand management will affect differentially different geographical, industrial, and labor force sectors. The implication for labor market policy is to govern the timing, location, and extent of selective measures in accordance with the sectoral need disclosed by those anticipated or realized differential effects. But obviously one does not plan for, marshal the resources for, assign facilities and staff to action in general. When, where, to what extent, at what cost, is the need for action to be anticipated? Knowledge of such facts and agreement on the part of the negotiators as to their significance for coordinated policy and action are essential to translate the predisposition and the opportunity and the possibility of synchronized action into readiness for such action itself.

The above conclusion is logically derivable from the premises as to the basic function of manpower policy as one instrument of economic policy. It suggests the desirability for summarization and analysis of practical experience as well as theoretically and empirically oriented calculation of the probable differential sectoral effects of the different options available for those concerned with demand management. Does a reduction in central government expenditures at particular times create a particular sectoral problem for the manpower authorities? Are differential results of demand-restraining measures to be anticipated with respect to particular industries (e.g., industrial and residential construction, the several manufacturing sectors, materials, various service sectors, etc.), and in significant groupings of industries (e.g., investment-consumption goods, export-import substitute goods, durable-nondurable goods, etc.)? What are the differences in the effect on employment in general and in different industries and regions from the choice to use monetary or fiscal measures? Are there differences to be anticipated if open market operations or interest rate manipulation is used? What differential sectoral effects on cyclical or structural movements can be expected to result from different policies as to:

1. The emphasis placed on taxes or reduction of government expenditures?
2. Incentives to increase or to decrease private investment?
3. The kinds of taxes used: general sales, value added, income, employment, social security?
4. Expansion or contraction of particular budget items?

Are some manpower measures better adapted than others to meeting the anticipated variations in the labor market and employment problems?

General policies are brought to the point of implementation after a choice of options in such detailed matters. The input of both manpower and fiscal and monetary authorities to the synchronization of their respective policies is made effective in part by their common understanding of the ways in which the choices of each with respect to the available options lead to consequences to which the choices of the others, both as to type and extent of action, must be adapted.

ANTICIPATORY INFORMATION. The most obvious requirement for timely action is that information be available to manpower authorities which enables them to anticipate the need for action and therefore to have their resources marshalled in readiness. In addition to the prognosis of probable sectoral effects of global economic policies referred to above, the continued perfection of the instruments for forecasting probable changes in the quantity and quality of both labor demand and labor supply, and as to when, where, and with what intensity the changes are likely to occur, is a clear need.

Two of the chief forecasting problems met by manpower authorities, whose approach to imbalances is selective, is that statistically based forecasting depends largely on reports of *past* economic activity, and that the statistics are chiefly aggregative in nature. Information which becomes available after the event makes possible *remedial* action at that time. But if reliance is placed only on such statistical information to trigger action, there is a real possibility that the action will be undertaken after the appropriate time and need for it has passed. Something more than after-the-event information is needed, even though that predictive information can disclose only probabilities.

Forecasting with respect to the sectoral changes to which selective manpower activity responds is difficult unless the highly aggregated data most easily available can be sufficiently disaggregated to make such forecasting of sectoral developments adequate to indicate the need for selective response.

The systems for advance notice of separations and vacancies developed in several countries with the cooperation of the employment service, employers, and trade unions are worthy of careful study by the manpower authorities in all countries. An essential source of knowledge about short-range employment changes is the employer whose decisions will effect those changes. The manpower personnel whose function puts them in a position to gather and collate that information are the employment service's employment officers. No estimates by expert forecasters can take the place of the ascertainment by employment officers of the intentions of employers in the area whose workers become their "clients" when they are laid off or separated. Continuous contacts with individual employers, trade associations, and trade union officers are essential. Systematic exploration of the probabilities, the analysis of the data gathered, the laying of plans, and the concentration of manpower administration forces where disemployment is anticipated is a *sine qua non* of timely and effective response.

This fact is so obvious that a number of countries have by

agreement between the employment service and employers, or by compulsory legislation, formalized the procedure for obtaining advance notice of where and when changes in the volume of employment are likely to take place. In other cases employers are given certain advantages with respect to other manpower services on condition that they give advance notice of such contemplated changes.

Such information is normally used locally. However, in view of the likelihood that a general recession will reduce work opportunities in all the firms in an area, and that declining industries are frequently the chief source of employment in particular areas, the hope for finding vacancies to which the local unemployed can be referred will depend to a larger degree than normally on information concerning job openings farther afield. A number of countries are experimenting with technical facilities, such as teletype and computers, to provide immediate transmission to wider than local areas of the details of requirements for jobs available (as well as details of the job seekers' qualifications). Developments of this sort are in the experimental stage and at the moment are concerned solely with data on registered requests for workers on jobs. When perfected with respect to these data, their utility may become apparent for the transmission of predictive data also.

FREDERICK H. HARBISON [*]

HUMAN RESOURCES AS THE WEALTH OF NATIONS

ACCORDING to economic doctrine, the wealth of nations is measured by income, or more precisely by GNP or GDP per capita. A wealthy country is a high-income country; advanced nations are by definition those with high GNP per capita; and underdeveloped countries are characterized by very low income per head. Rates of growth, or progress along the road of modernization, are most commonly measured by annual increments in national income or product expressed in monetary terms.

But should income maximization be the supreme or even the primary objective of national economic policy? Are not other goals—for example, minimization of unemployment, maximization of education and knowledge, limitation of population growth, or improvement in the environment—of

* The author is grateful to Mrs. Joan Maruhnic, Research Assistant, for the editing of this paper and the preparation of the Appendix.

equal or greater importance? Perhaps in their devout commitment to GNP as the primary measure of progress, economists have developed a "tunnel vision" perspective of modern societies. Although I still belong professionally to "the church of economics," I am among a small but growing group which argues that GNP or income as the major target of national development should lose its "sanctity." [1]

The central thesis of this paper is that human resources, not capital, income or material resources, constitute the basis for the wealth of nations. Capital and natural resources are passive factors of production; human beings are the active agents who accumulate capital, exploit natural resources, build social, economic, and political organizations, and carry forward national development. Clearly, a country which is unable to develop the skills and knowledge of its people and to utilize them effectively in the national economy will be unable to develop anything else.

At the outset, a definition of terms is required. "Human resources" are the energies, skills, and knowledge of people which are, or which potentially can or should be, applied to the production of goods or the rendering of services. Thus, the term connotes man in relationship to the world of work, and such work involves producing things and providing services of all kinds in the social, political, cultural, and economic development of nations.

The "human resource approach" to national development, therefore, is people-oriented, though it does not presume to encompass the full range of human ambitions or endeavor. Man may work to live; hopefully he lives for much more than work. Indeed, the energies and skills of people as members of the labor force are but one dimension of human development which embraces as well the thoughts, motives, beliefs, feelings, aspirations, and culture of human beings beyond and outside of work. But in economic terms, the wealth of a nation can be expressed in terms of the *level of development* and the *effectiveness of utilization* of human energies, skills, and knowledge for useful purposes.

To develop this thesis, let us make a crude statistical comparison of the development of ten countries from three different perspectives: national income or GNP per capita; generating capacity of the educational system; and health (see figure 1). Five of the countries are relatively advanced: the USA, the USSR, Sweden, Israel, and Japan. The other five —Colombia, India, the United Arab Republic (Egypt), Kenya, and Tanzania—are all less developed countries. (This choice was intended to simplify the presentation; it would be possible to obtain comparable data for over a hundred countries for the mid-1960s period.)

The first indicator expresses development on the basis of GNP per capita. The second measures development according to the Harbison-Myers index of secondary and higher education. (The index is the sum of the secondary school unadjusted enrollment rate plus an arbitrary weight of five times the third level unadjusted enrollment rate.) [2] The third estimates health development on the basis of the number of doctors and dentists per 10,000 population. In each case the top-ranking country is given a value of 100, and the measure of development of the others is a percentage of the highest value for that indicator. The comparisons, as shown on the chart, are rather interesting.

Measured by GNP per capita, the USA is far ahead of all other countries. Sweden's level of income is only 70 percent of that of the USA; Israel has about 35 percent, followed by the USSR with 25 percent; Tanzania, the lowest of the ten, has only 2 percent.

The rankings on the indicator of educational development are somewhat different. Here the USSR is in second place with about 60 percent of the level of the USA; Israel and Japan are next at about 45 percent; Sweden follows at 40 percent. In the less developed countries, Colombia is slightly

FIGURE 1

INDICATORS OF DEVELOPMENT

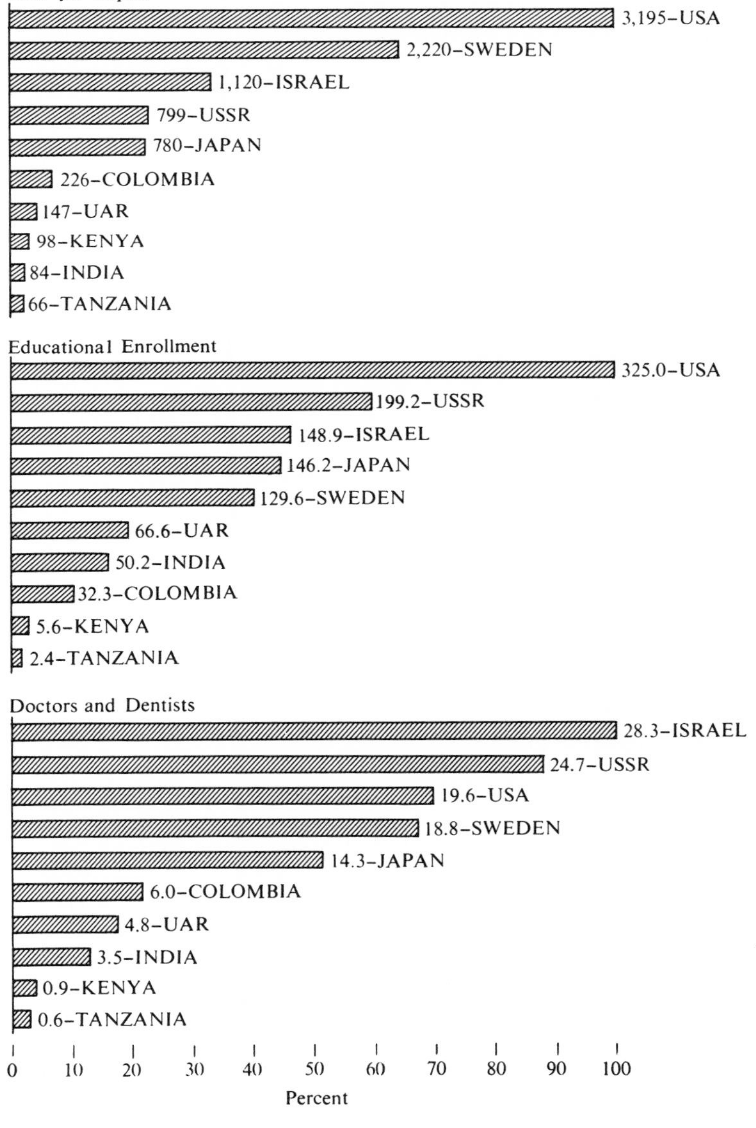

above the UAR with both close to 30 percent, followed by India with 15 percent, and then by Kenya and Tanzania far lower, with a little less than 2 and 1 percent respectively. Note, however, that India, Japan, and the UAR are many times more advanced relative to the United States on the educational index than on the income indicator. Thus, in these cases, GNP per capita grossly underestimates development as measured by secondary and higher education enrollment ratios.

More striking, however, is the ranking on the health development indicator, i.e., doctors and dentists per 10,000 population. Here the United States is not in first place at all; indeed it scores only about 70 percent of the highest country, Israel, and comes in a very poor third after the USSR, which holds second place. Sweden is only slightly below the USA and Japan is not far behind. The less developed countries, characteristically, have very low scores.

These indicators of educational and health development perhaps raise more questions than they answer. At best they are only proxies which suggest levels of development. For example, there may be much better indicators of a nation's health than the number of doctors and dentists in the population. It is possible on the basis of presently collected statistics to construct somewhat better measures. Figures on hospital beds per 10,000 population and life expectancy are available for many countries. Likewise, primary school enrollments and per capita expenditures on public education can be added to secondary and higher education enrollments in an index of educational development.

The analysis up to this point suggests that a truly meaningful index of development and utilization of human resources should include many more indicators of health, education, and employment. Admittedly, quantitative data presently available in most countries are far from adequate for construction of such an index. Yet, it is possible to suggest the kinds of data series which would be needed and which could be developed with reasonable effort.

In order to measure the *development* of human resources, data on educational achievement (e.g., completion of school-years at primary, secondary, and higher levels) are needed as well as enrollment ratios. An information series on numbers of persons in the labor force with specified strategic skills (from artisans, craftsmen, foremen, and master farmers to writers, musicians, artists, engineers, scientists, and managerial personnel) should be attempted.

An index of health development should include indicators of life expectancy at various ages, infant mortality, incidence of critical diseases such as parasites, malaria, and tuberculosis, and availability (i.e., geographic distribution) of health care. Indicators of nutrition would also be appropriate, for example, various measures of calories and/or proteins consumed.

A measurement of *utilization* of human resources would be more difficult to obtain. Statistics on unemployment are hard to come by and often are not comparable. Measures of underemployment and malutilization of skills still lie beyond the frontiers of present knowledge.

Two other types of measures would also be desirable. The first is an indicator of progress toward population limitation. The second would be indicators of reduction in disparities between the rich and the poor, the educated and the uneducated, the healthy and the unhealthy within a nation. Countries such as Sweden and Japan would rank very high on indicators of this kind; the newly developing countries would be the lowest scorers; the United States might fall somewhere in between.

In short, a composite measure of development and utilization of human resources using the types of data mentioned above could be designed. Though far from perfect, such an index might be as statistically valid as present indices of

GNP or national income. The major shortcoming of such an index, as in all other quantitative indices, would be the failure to measure the qualitative dimensions of education, skill, knowledge, and health. In other words, statistics may not adequately represent facts. But, quantitative measures can identify major areas for ascertaining the facts through more in-depth qualitative analysis.

Supposing an index of human resource development and utilization could be devised and accepted as a primary measure of progress in modern nations, what might be the likely consequences?

Increasing GNP would no longer be the supreme target of economic policy. The human resource approach would alter priorities and choices considerably. For example, education would become more of an end in itself and its contribution to national development would no longer be calculated simply as a component of national income. The health and well-being of the labor force would be measured by criteria other than those of increasing the income productivity of the labor force. The contributions of scientists, artists, and intellectuals would no doubt be given higher value on a human resource than on an income index. The United States would no longer be considered as so far ahead of all other nations, and the ranking of many nations on a scale of modernization would be changed quite significantly. Indeed, the strategies of development in this and other countries might be very different. The human resource approach to modernization certainly would call for substantial revision of economics textbooks.

A policy of "maximizing" human resource development and utilization, however, would *not* mean that the growth of national income would necessarily decline. Human resource indicators and GNP are, after all, quite highly correlated. Many eminent economists, such as T. W. Schultz and Gary Becker, have demonstrated the contributions of investments in education to national income generation. Rising national income, therefore, would be one of the expected consequences of maximization of development and utilization of human resources. Thus, the human resource approach in no way implies that income growth is irrelevant to national prosperity. It would simply substitute a process of setting targets and measuring progress in human rather than materialistic terms.

There is a growing recognition—in the less developed world as well as in the advanced countries—that higher income per se does not provide a better standard of living. Indeed, if income alone were to be the yardstick of development, then the less developed countries must abandon the hope that they will ever be able to narrow the existing gap. Despite substantial progress in development, the evidence is clear that income disparities between rich and poor nations are widening. But the less developed world can catch up in human resource development and utilization. And in the advanced countries themselves, the concern about the environment and human values is beginning to overshadow the mere quest for greater affluence. The human resources approach to development is not a new idea by any means.[3] But, it is perhaps an idea whose time has come. It certainly warrants more serious and systematic exploration.

INDICES OF DEVELOPMENT

There is, quite surprisingly, a vast amount of figures, statistical series, and other quantitative material related to the development of more than 100 countries though it is of varying quality and usefulness. And, with few exceptions, it fails to measure any aspect of development very accurately. But, the available data, if used with caution, can be used to chart at least the broad dimensions of various aspects of modernization and development.

It is also possible to construct indices of development comprised of a number of individual indicators or variables. The particular "taxonomic method," briefly described below, is explained in greater detail and applied to many country groups and indices in our recent monograph.[4] This technique is a relatively simple, though lengthy, process.

First, indicator values are converted into quantities which can be added together. This is done by standardizing these values based on the mean and standard deviation of each indicator using the following formula;

$$\frac{x_j - \bar{x}_j,}{s_j} \qquad \text{where} \qquad j = 1, 2, \ldots, m \qquad [1]$$

and

$$\bar{x}_j = \frac{1}{N} \sum_{i=1}^{N} x_{ij} \quad \text{and} \quad s_j = \left[\frac{1}{N} \sum_{i=1}^{N} (x_{ij} - \bar{x}_j)^2 \right]^{1/2}$$

These standardized values then replace raw values and result in a new matrix. From this new matrix countries may be ranked according to their performance in any particular area of development. This is a familiar process in international comparison. However, multiple dimensions make ranking of countries with respect to many indicators simultaneously more complicated. (Assumptions must be made as to whether an indicator is a "stimulant," or a "retardant" to development; a high per capita gross national product would be a stimulant, while a high dependency ratio would act as a deterrent to development.)

A ranked relationship is then established by determining the difference between the standardized value for each country and the highest country for each indicator. Typically no country will have the highest value for all indicators composing a particular index. For example, a country may have the highest value for first-level enrollment rate, while another has the highest value for per capita public recurrent expenditures on education. An "ideal" (hypothetical) country may be created, comprising the highest (or best) value for all indicators within a particular index. A ranking of differences from this "ideal" country is termed the "pattern of development" or simply the distance of each country in the matrix to the ideal country as derived by the following formula:

$$c_{io} = \left[\sum_{k=1}^{m} (D_{ik} - D_{ok})^2 \right]^{1/2} \qquad [2]$$

where $i=1,2, \ldots, N$ and o is the maximum standardized value. The larger is this number c_{io} the greater is the distance from this particular country to its potential high point within the set. This is similar to the familiar concept of ranking countries by means of a single indicator.

Another way of ranking countries for a particular index, or group of indicators, using the taxonomic technique, is called the "measure of development." The ideal country is designated as "0," and a simulated percentage distribution from the ideal is discerned by a simple calculation (See equation [3]). The measure of development is a more recognizable way of showing relative development, since the range is definitely limited (0.00 to 1.00). In other words it is a function of the pattern of development and the "critical distance" from the so-called "ideal" country. The following formula may be applied:

$$d_i = \frac{c_{io}}{c_o}, \qquad [3]$$

where $$c_o = \bar{c}_{io} + 2s_{io}$$

and $$\bar{c}_{io} = \frac{1}{N} \sum_{i=1}^{N} c_{io}$$ (the mean of the pattern of development),

and $$s_{io} = \left[\frac{1}{N} \sum_{i=1}^{N} (c_{io} - \bar{c}_{io})^2 \right]^{1/2}$$

In the above equations d_i shall be called the measure of development. The closer d is to 0 the more developed is the country, and the closer to 1, the less developed the country. The measure is constructed in such a way that it is always non-negative. It can exceed 1, but the probability of such an event is small so, in the majority of cases, the following inequality holds:

$$0<d<1$$

Three indices of development for the ten countries, calculated in the above manner, are illustrated in Figure 2. (Only the measure of development is plotted.) The indices are comprised of: (1) GNP index—GNP per capita in U.S. $; (2) educational effort index—first, second, and third level enrollment ratios (adjusted for length of schooling and relevant age group in population) and per capita recurrent expenditures on public education in U.S. $; (3) health index—doctors and dentists per 10,000 population, hospital beds per 10,000 population and life expectancy (at birth) in years.

The relationships are not too dissimilar to the initial exercise in the body of the paper which used only single variables for economic and health assessment and an earlier composite for education. However, except for the GNP index which uses only one variable, no country is "ideal." Sweden moves up in rank on the educational index because of its high per capita expenditure on education. The rankings in the health index do change when the other variables are considered and the differences among the "advanced" countries are not so marked. But again the United States is nowhere near the top. The actual values for pattern and measure of development for the health index are given below:

Country	*Pattern*	*Measure*
USSR	0.9365	0.1667
Sweden	0.9793	0.1743
Israel	1.4071	0.2505
USA	1.4832	0.2640
Japan	1.5875	0.2826
Colombia	3.5355	0.6294
UAR	3.7550	0.6685
India	3.9243	0.6986
Kenya	4.5935	0.8178
Tanzania	4.7117	0.8388

FIGURE 2

INDICES OF DEVELOPMENT

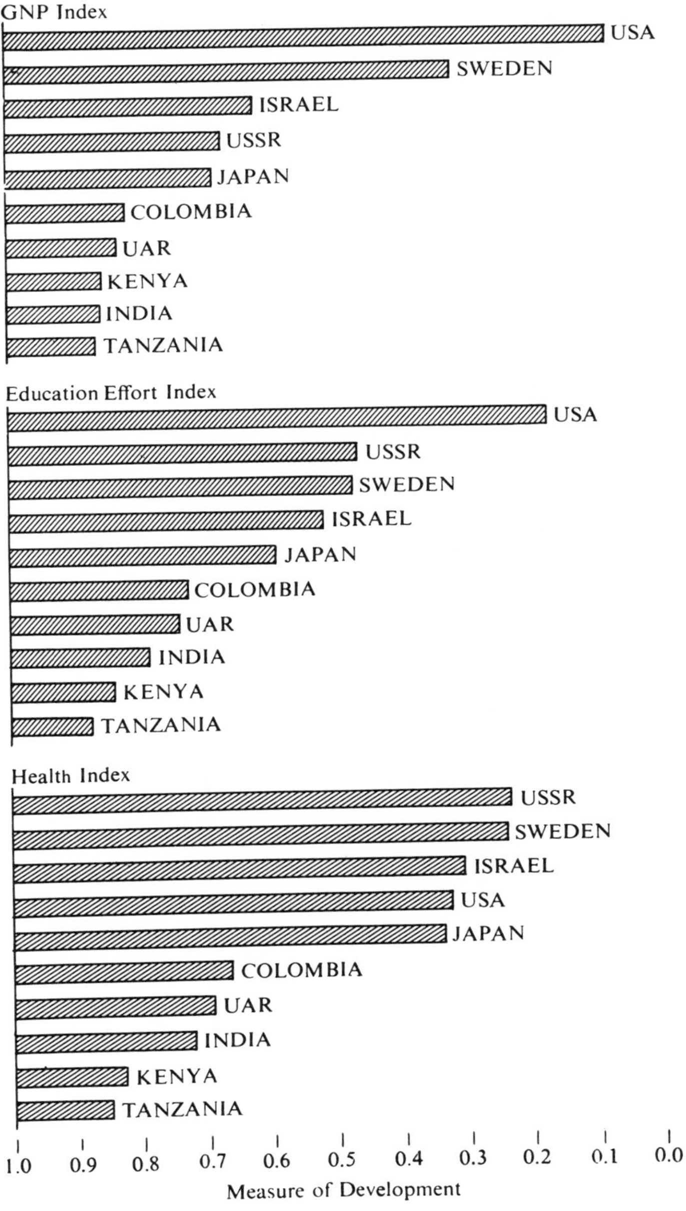

The group of countries in this exercise were chosen merely for purposes of demonstrating the taxonomic technique. Certainly no such disparate small group would or should be measured by the same criteria.

As elaborated in the previously mentioned monograph, the taxonomic method can also be used for other purposes. By means of additional calculations countries with similar characteristics for a particular index may be grouped so that targets for planning may be designed. "Optimal graphs," a visual presentation of differences among groups, may be drawn from these further calculations. One feature of the taxonomic method that could have far-reaching applications is that a country can be added to a group of countries even though some of the data for particular variables in a given index may be lacking. In other words, it is possible to "manufacture" data that can be used as "approximations" of missing variables. Of even greater interest to planners are the possibilities for intracountry comparison. A particularly fruitful area for analysis is continued study over time. It would be possible for an underdeveloped country (or region within a country) to set targets by comparing its progress with those of a more developed country which had been at the same level five or ten years before.

A great deal more work needs to be done before the measurement of human resource development and utilization will be more than educated "guesstimates" or proxies for accurate target setting. Data reliability and index construction are areas which demand more study. Nevertheless, the work that has been done and is now going on definitely point to the need and the worth of continued effort in the measurement of human resource development and modernization.

NOTES

1. For further elaboration of this viewpoint, see in particular: International Labour Office, *Toward Full Employment, A Program for Colombia* (Geneva: 1970). For a short summary, see Dudley Seers, "New Approaches Suggested by the Colombia Employment Program," *International Labour Review* (October 1970).

2. Frederick H. Harbison and Charles A. Myers, *Education, Manpower and Economic Growth* (New York: McGraw-Hill, 1964).

3. Among recent attempts to construct indicators of human resource development, see the following: Panel of Experts on Methodology of Human Resource Indicators (Paris: Unesco, 1969 and 1970); U.S. Department of Health, Education, and Welfare, *Toward a Social Report* (Washington: U.S. Government Printing Office, January 1969); Frederick H. Harbison, Joan Maruhnic, and Jane R. Resnick, *Quantitative Analyses of Modernization and Development* (Princeton: Industrial Relations Section, Princeton University, 1970).

4. Harbison, Maruhnic, and Resnick. See also Z. Hellwig, "Procedure of Evaluating High-Level Manpower Data and Typology of Countries by Means of the Taxonomic Method" (unpublished working paper for UNESCO), 1967.

PHILIP M. HAUSER

THE WORK FORCE IN DEVELOPING AREAS*

THE presence in a culture of the concepts of "work" and "work force" may, in historical perspective, be regarded as indications of modernization. That is, as soon as a series of activities is designated as work and people who engage in such activities are considered as a work force, a society has already traveled down the road toward modernization. For to designate a particular set of activities that fill the life space as "work" is a differentiation that probably did not exist in the minds of people themselves for most of the time that man has been on the face of this earth.

* The "new approach" described is the product of a Workshop of the Organization of Demographic Associates consisting of population centers and their affiliates in Southeast Asia. The Workshop was held in Hong Kong in February 1970. The working group which developed the approach included: You Poh Seng, Chairman (Singapore); N. Iskandar (Indonesia); Nibhon Debavalya (Thailand); Yoichi Okazaki (Japan); Bernardino A. Perez (Philippines); Evenly M. Kitagawa, Rapporteur (USA); Philip M. Hauser (USA), and Paul Demeny (USA).

The efforts of nations to differentiate in a population that part which consists of "workers" is also a relatively recent phenomenon. The United States, for example, did not develop a consistent approach that permitted the definition and a count of workers and their characteristics as a subgrouping of population until 1870. Only from 1870 is it possible to construct a reasonably comparable historical series on the size and composition of the work force. Before then the censuses of the United States either contained no inquiries in respect of workers or had very limited inquiries.[1]

Thomas Jefferson, creative genius that he was, as President of the American Philosophical Society petitioned the Congress of the United States, prior to the Census of 1800, to include among the census questions an inquiry into ". . . the vocations of our fellow citizens" so as, among other data, to "ascertain more completely the causes which influence life and death, and to furnish a curious and useful document of the distribution of society in these states . . ."[2] Jefferson listed a number of categories by which "vocations" might be classified. The designations he set forth were broad categories of occupations. It is amusing that professional persons included "scribes in general." That is, anyone who could write was considered a professional person.

Jefferson's petition to the Congress in 1810 was in "the greater wisdom" of Congress ignored. But in a desultory way, beginning with the Census of 1820 and then irregularly, inquiries were included in the census on the "vocations" of the people. The inclusion of such inquiries can be interpreted as an indication of a society undergoing change, change of a character that led the Congress to become interested in the "work force" as distinguished from the rest of the population. There was no interest, however, until 1870 in continuous comparable measurement of the work force. It may be inferred that in the agrarian, preindustrial, preurban United States such statistics did not have much relevance. That is, why should there have been an interest in knowing how many workers there were and what kind of work people were doing when, in 1790, 95 percent of the population lived in rural areas—on farms or places having fewer than 2,500 persons? At that time there were only 24 urban places in the United States and only two of them—Philadelphia and New York—had populations in excess of 25,000. To have an inquiry on vocations at that time did not occur to most people because it was obvious that almost everybody was doing something on a farm or working in nonfarm family enterprises! There was no particular point in differentiating those who were working from those who were not.

These considerations help to illuminate the problem of work force measurement with which the developing nations are confronted. Until recently there was little reason in these nations for differentiating workers from others in the population. As in the early experience of the United States there was no perceived need for aggregated statistics on the size and characteristics of the work force. In the developing nations, not until post-World War II developments and the adoption of programs of economic development was there a felt need for information about human resources. This need has become an increasingly pressing one as the developing nations have continued to strive for higher levels of living.

THE GAINFUL WORKER APPROACH

The identification of workers so as to make possible a count of the work force, and the determination of its characteristics, requires both a conceptual framework and specific technique of measurement. In the development of work force statistics in the United States a relatively simple conceptual framework and technique of measurement evolved—which became known as the "gainful worker" approach.[3] In the gainful worker approach an inquiry was made of every person above a specified age as to his "profession, occupation or trade." If the person reported a profession, occupation or trade, he was considered a "worker," and the aggregate of such persons constituted the work force. In the United States the lower age limit was 10 years until as recently as 1940. In the 1940 Census it was raised to 14 years of age and in 1970, to 16 years. The changes in the lower age limit is, of course, a specific indication of the arbitrary character of designating a subgroup of the total population as in the work force and reflects the prolonged schooling and changing laws for compulsory education.

In 1820 an inquiry in respect to vocation was restricted to persons, including slaves, engaged in three classes of occupations: agricultural, commercial, and manufacturing. There was no such question in the Census of 1830. In the Census of 1840, the vocational question was asked for a longer list of specified occupations. In 1850, for the first time the inquiry applied to every "profession, occupation or trade" but the question was restricted to free males over 15 years old, omitting females and slaves. In 1860, the question was required of all free persons 15 years old and over. The applicability of the census inquiries to broader categories of vocations and of the population may be interpreted as indications of the increasingly felt need for information about the work force as the United States underwent transformation from an agrarian society to an urban and industrial society.

The conceptual framework and techniques of measurement utilized in the U.S. Census from 1870 through 1930 had as their objective the identification and count of "gainful workers"—all persons who usually worked at "gainful labor." A "gainful occupation" in census usage is an occupation by which the person who pursues it earns money or money equivalent or in which he assists in the production of marketable goods.[4] Conceptually then, the gainful workers of the

United States consisted of those persons who reported a gainful occupation in response to the census inquiry.

To obtain a count of gainful workers and their characteristics required specific techniques of measurement. These consisted of the form of the question, instructions to enumerators for obtaining responses from the population, the actual procedures of enumerators in the field in performing their duties. The editing, coding, and tabulation of the responses also influenced the results. Examination of census statistics from 1870 through 1930 indicates that although the concept remained essentially the same, the techniques of measurement varied so as to produce discontinuities in the data. The nature of the variations in techniques of measurement have been described elsewhere.[5] In general, differences in the instructions to enumerators and in their implementation resulted in significant variations in the extent to which persons were reported in the work force, especially women and children, and other persons of marginal relationship to the work force. Especially volatile were responses to the gainful worker question of persons engaged in family enterprises, including farms and in part-time work. In consequence, although the concept utilized was essentially the same, data adjustment is necessary to trace trends in the size and composition of the work force between 1870 and 1930.[6]

THE LABOR FORCE APPROACH

The Great Depression of the 1930s, which for the first time in the history of the nation led to an insistent demand for measurement of unemployment, pointed up inadequacies in the gainful worker approach to meet the needs of the complex, interdependent, highly vulnerable economy of urbanized and industrialized United States. The obviously increasing volume of unemployment after the stock market break in 1929 led to the inclusion in the 1930 Census of questions relating to unemployment. The publication of the 1930 Census unemployment figures produced widespread dissension and debate about the meaning of the data and eventually to an evaluation of the conceptual framework and techniques of measurement employed.[7] It was clear that unemployment continued to increase during the decade but in the absence of direct measurements there was considerable confusion among the general public, political leaders, and also technicians about the actual volume of unemployment. Estimates, based on indirect methods, varied in magnitude with the position of the estimating agency on a continuum ranging from conservative to liberal. That is, organizations identified with management provided estimates of unemployment considerably lower than organizations identified with labor.[8] The fact is that during most of the decade of the 1930s the actual volume of unemployment remained unknown even while the demand for dealing with the human distress produced by unemployment was mounting.

The work relief programs developed during the decade to provide income flow for the unemployed included programs for white-collar workers. Among the work projects mounted, to determine those eligible for work relief, were various surveys to measure the unemployed on a local basis. In consequence, the 1930s witnessed the emergence of a series of new conceptual frameworks and methods of measurement in an effort to ascertain not only members of the work force but also, their employment status, that is, to determine whether they were employed or unemployed.[9]

The diverse conceptual frameworks and measurement techniques used, in due course and with the benefit of hindsight, made clear the inadequacies of the gainful worker approach for the measurement of the total work force as well as employment status. It became apparent that the gainful worker approach, since it had no specific time reference, produced an occupational return even if the person was not actually working at it. Furthermore, it omitted persons who were seeking their first employment if they had no occupation to report. Second, since the gainful worker approach was not based on any "activity" as such, occupations were often reported by persons who were long since retired from the work force or who were neither working nor seeking work at the time of the census enumeration.

As recognition of these deficiencies of the gainful work approach became apparent, experiments were conducted, climaxed by "the Enumerative Check Census," as part of the Census of Partial Employment, Unemployment and Occupation[10] conducted in 1937 by the Government, which resulted in the development of a new conceptual framework and new techniques of measurement. The new approach, first utilized in the Census of 1940 in the United States was known as the "labor force approach." [11]

The labor force approach, in an effort to correct the deficiencies of the gainful worker approach for the measurement of the work force as of a given period of time and with due attention to employment status was based on a "behavioristic" rather than a "status" response. That is, the person was asked to report on his actual "activity," specifically the activity of "working" or "seeking work." Second, the labor force involved a specific time reference. That is, the activity to be reported was that during a given specified week. Thus, in contrast with the gainful worker approach, "new workers" who had no occupations to report could report that they were seeking work during the specified week and thus be included in the labor force. Moreover, a person with an occupation as a "status" rather than as an activity, as for example, the retired railroad engineer, since he had not worked and he was not seeking work during the census week, would not be regarded as a member of the labor force.

The labor force approach conceptually then included as

workers those persons above a specified age who were either "working" or "seeking work" during a designated week. The labor force was made up of two major components by employment status—the employed and the unemployed. Although the census work force inquiries included questions relating to occupation (and also industry, class of worker, and other items) the occupational return was no longer the basis for determining whether or not the person was in the work force. On the contrary the occupation inquiry became an auxiliary question asked only of those persons who were in the labor force, that is, who were either employed or unemployed during the specified week.

Although the effort to obtain a measurement of the work force in a specific labor market was based essentially on a behavioristic approach with a specific time referent, the complexity of employment patterns in the economy did not permit a rigid adherence to these criteria. For example, the employed, it was decided, should appropriately include not only those who were actually at work during the specified week but also those "with a job." Persons "with a job" who for various reasons did not actually work during the week would include such persons as those on vacation, temporarily ill, temporarily unable to perform outdoor work, such as in construction because of bad weather conditions, etc. Such persons, it was decided, actually constituted part of the labor force, that is, were part of the supply of labor in relation to the demand for labor during the specified week even though they were not engaged in actual work activity. Similarly the "unemployed," it was decided, should appropriately include not only persons actively seeking work but, also, those who for specified reasons were not actively seeking employment during the period under observation but who were actually part of the labor supply. Such persons would include, for example, the worker in the one-industry town who was not actively seeking work because the plant was shut down but who would return to work as soon as it reopened. It would also include persons not actively seeking work during the week because of temporary illness, etc. Thus, the labor force concept, while based on an "activity" approach, nevertheless encompassed persons with "status" relations in including both inactive employed and inactive unemployed.[12]

Needless to say, the implementation of the labor force conceptual framework also involved complex problems of measurement. Discontinuities in the labor force statistical series over time can be attributed primarily to measurement problems which included variations in methods of estimation; and, in variations in data processing. These problems need not be detailed here.[13]

In general, then, the labor force approach as compared to the gainful worker approach comes much closer to providing measurement of the work force in a given labor market at a specified period of time. Furthermore, in having a definite and specific time reference, the labor force provides a relatively clear-cut benchmark for the anchoring of series of measurements over time, including measurement of changes over periods of time as short as one month. It became possible, therefore, with the labor force approach to develop a monthly series of measurements of the work force, a task not possible with the gainful workers approach.

APPLICABILITY OF THESE APPROACHES TO DEVELOPING NATIONS

As the developing nations became increasingly aware of the need for measurement of the work force, they naturally used the experience of the economically advanced nations as a basis for designing their work force statistics. The developing nations had the choice of employing the gainful worker approach or the labor force approach or some modification of either. The advantages and disadvantages of the respective approaches were pointed out by the United Nations and its specialized agencies, especially the International Labor Organization.[14] In the censuses of 1950, 1960, and 1970, as well as in various current sample surveys, the developing nations have employed one or the other approach as recommended. It has been apparent for some time, however, both among the personnel in the developing nations as well as among the experts throughout the world that both of the approaches which were based on the experience of the economically advanced nations have serious shortcomings for the measurement of the work force in developing areas. This should not be too surprising since both approaches were designed to meet the needs of economically advancing or advanced nations.

Gunnar Myrdal has perhaps been the most explicit and comprehensive critic of the "modern approach" to the measurement of the work force.[15] He regards the approaches utilized in economically advanced nations as incompatible with "reality" in the developing nations as "logically inconsistent," and as based on value premises which are inappropriate to the developing areas. Some of his criticism is equally applicable to the proposed new approach, in the sense that the new approach also involves consideration of labor input as a "quantity" without regard to "quality"; does not take into consideration low nutritional and health levels, nor the relative immobility of labor.[16] Nevertheless, the new approach does deal with some of the inadequacies to which Myrdal refers, and specifically represents an approach more consistent with the reality of work arrangements in developing areas than is either the gainful worker or labor force framework.

In recognition of the inadequacies of the gainful worker and labor force approaches for developing nations the members of the Organization of Demographic Associates in Southeast Asia undertook to devise a new approach to the measurement of the work force. This approach, still tentative and subject to change through actual experimental use, is described in the materials which follow.

THE PROPOSED NEW APPROACH

Both the gainful worker and labor force approaches are based on the assumption of a monetary economy in which the major portion of the work force are "employees," in a contractual relation to an "employer." In the developing nations, however, a large proportion of "work" is actually performed in the household as part of a family enterprise both in the agricultural and nonagricultural sectors. Developing nations characteristically have "dual" economies with the monetary sector, including smaller numbers of workers than the nonmonetary sector. The recognition of these facts constitutes the starting point of the proposed new approach and accounts for the major functional sectors into which the population is divided. Since even the very young contribute to sustenance activity in developing areas the age cutoff for the workers is set as low as 10 years of age.

It is proposed, then, that the population 10 years of age and over be divided into the following four major categories:

I. Work for wages or profit
II. Work outside the household without monetary payment
III. Work inside the household (or an institution) only, without monetary payment
IV. Other (residual category)

I. Work for Wages or Profit. Category 1, those who work for wages or profit, include essentially the workers in the monetary sector of the economy or the modern sector of the work force in the country. Compared to the work force in economically advanced countries, such persons constitute a relatively small proportion of the total. This is the sector that the labor force approach does identify well, because the labor force approach was developed to measure the work force in an economically advanced nation.

For analytical purposes and because of its policy implications, it is proposed these workers in the modern sector be further subdivided as follows:

A. Work for wages

B. Work for profit, own-account workers.

In effect these two groups parallel employees and own-account workers as reported in the class of work categories in the labor force approach. But within each of these groups further differentiation not normally obtained in the labor force approach is proposed. In Category IA, "Work for wages," the following differentiations are suggested: 1) only one employer; 2) more than one employer; 3) commission workers; 4) casual workers.

These subcategories would provide information not now available on the network of employee-employer relations in the monetary sector.

Similarly, within Category IB "Work for profit, own-account workers," the following differentiations are proposed; 1) with paid employees only; 2) with unpaid family workers; 3) with both paid and unpaid workers; 4) with not paid or unpaid workers; 5) contractor for workers; 6) rentiers (living on investments).

It was realized that these differentiations call for more detail than may be feasible in continuous surveys or even a decennial census. But it was felt that for experimental purposes an effort should be made to distinguish these various groups of workers with the possibility that consolidations could be effected depending on the actual distributions ascertained.

II. Work Outside the Household Without Monetary Payment. The second major functional classification of workers includes persons employed in the nonmonetary sector of the economy but outside their own households. This would include workers who do not receive monetary payment and who, it is proposed, at least at the onset, be further subdivided into categories as follows:

A. Payment in kind
B. Without any payment (exchange labor or not exchange labor)
C. Nomadics (hunters), fishermen, etc.

Persons in Category IIA "Payment in kind," it is proposed, be further subdivided into: 1) unpaid servants; 2) sharecroppers; 3) apprentices and trainees; 4) others—job squatters, etc. Thus, Category II along with Category I would in effect account for all persons engaged in work outside the household (or institution) in which they resided. These persons, in most developing areas, would account for a relatively small proportion of the total work force.

III. Work Inside the Household (or an Institution) Only, Without Monetary Payment. This category will probably include most of the work activity in the developing nations. For in the agricultural sector, which is the major sector of the economy, and in much of the nonagricultural sector, work activity is essentially a family enterprise and is performed inside the household (or in an institution such as those of religious orders) without monetary payment. It is proposed that this category be subdivided into four groupings as follows: 1) unpaid family members working on farm or family enterprise (whether or not performing household duties or attending school); 2) unpaid family members working in putting-out system (whether or not performing household duties or attending school); 3) both a and b type work; 4) household duties only.

Here again, it is proposed that an effort be made experimentally to obtain the detail indicated so that consolidations can later be effected on the basis of empirical distributions.

IV. Other (residual category). The remainder of the population 10 years of age and over is to be subdivided into the following residual groupings: 1) school only; 2) disabled; 3) retired and pensioners; 4) inmates of institutions (other than those included above); 5) other. In effect, this category of persons would be persons not in the work force. Moreover, the subgroupings would all be residual groupings of those persons of similar status who were not included in Categories I, II, or III. For example, persons in school in Category IV would include only those students who did not fit into any of the other groupings and would, therefore, not include all persons in school.

Special Notes. It is proposed that each of the categories and subgroupings proposed above be subdivided into the agricultural and nonagricultural sectors of the economy. In effect, then, the population 10 years of age and over would be sorted into major groupings on three axes, namely: 1) in monetary or nonmonetary sector; 2) at work inside or outside household; 3) in agricultural or nonagricultural sector. No decision was reached on the order in which these differentiations would be made, and it was hoped that experimental work would provide the best answer. Next, it was recognized, although the age limits should be set as low as 10 years of age in developing areas, that provision should be made for tabulating persons by single years of age up to age 14 at least. This would permit better international comparability over time as age limits were raised with increased schooling and possible provision for compulsory school attendance.

It was decided that a specific time reference was to be made an element in the new approach although no firm decision was reached on the matter, and this was also to be left to empirical determination based on experimentation. The major alternatives were, of course, the single week or the single month if recurrent surveys were to be taken. For a decennial census the year might be utilized but this would introduce ambiguities that would preclude continuous measurement.

It is also proposed, although it was recognized that initial experimentation would be very much complicated, that dual statuses should be ascertained where dual statuses actually occurred. Thus, the person might be working within his own household for much of the time without monetary payment but have occasional incursions into the monetary sector for profit or wages.

It was realized that in some cultures religious functionaries are quite numerous and complicate efforts to measure the work force. It is proposed that religious functionaries be included as item III-5 (a new subgroup in Category III), "persons not in the work force"; or in a Category V; or that they might be included in Categories I, II, or III according to the type of work actually performed. That is, a monk who engaged in teaching activities could be included in Category III-1 if he conducted such activities inside a monastery without monetary payment. Or he could be placed in Category II as a separate grouping if he worked outside the monastery for payment in kind, or in Category IA if he performed his duties in return for monetary payment. It was recognized that decisions on this matter, which among other things involved value determination as to whether the religious functionary was or was not in the work force must be left to the discretion of each culture or country. But, in any case, it was proposed that members of religious orders be differentiated in tabulations so as to make comparisons across countries possible.

Finally, it was recognized that military personnel might not fit readily into the functional classifications outlined and proper allocation would vary with their values in various countries. The data obtained on occupation and industry to supplement the functional approach however would permit identification of military personnel for purposes of international comparability.

Proposed Schedule. A tentative schedule was also drafted to serve as an instrument for experimental purposes. It was recognized the schedule was too detailed and complex for actual continued use, but it was felt that experimental work with the schedule would indicate the best way to condense it so as to make it a more practical instrument.

To begin with, it was decided it was very important to develop an opening question, with meaning in the culture in which the questionnaire was to be employed, that would orient the respondent to what was desired. This could take the form of indicating that inquiry was being made on the way in which the person obtained "his means of livelihood"; or to ascertain what the person does most during the day. The working group agreed that a meaningful opening question was highly important in both establishing rapport and obtaining the type of response that was desired. After such a start a tentative question was formulated, which includes, in addition to inquiries designed to sort the population into the desired functional categories, supplementary information on occupation, industry, and other items; and, also, an initial effort to obtain information about unemployment and underemployment.

Comparability with Labor Force. Although the new approach to the measurement of the work force in the developing countries was designed primarily to meet their needs, it was recognized that it would be desirable to effect comparability with information obtained through the labor force approach to the extent that this might be possible. It was recognized also that the actual task of translating the desiderata into language meaningful in each culture was in itself a formidable task—a task that would be made even more complex in efforts to design bridges between the labor force approach and the proposed new approach.

An effort was nevertheless made to develop at least a first approximation to a basis for comparability between the labor force and the proposed new functional approach. As has already been indicated, the new approach and the labor force approach should produce essentially the same results for persons in the monetary sector. Comparability of Categories II and III, however, would depend at least in part on cut-offs on actual hours of input as ascertained in the new approach

Major functional category	*Total*	*Looking for work*[a]	*Hours of work or input*[b]
I. Work for wages or profit (monetary)	X		
II. Work outside household (nonmonetary)		X	X
III. Work inside household (nonmonetary)		X	X
IV. Other			X

X indicates comparability with labor force concept.
[a] Looking for work to be ascertained from questions in schedule.
[b] Above given number of hours.

so as not to include in the work force persons who would be omitted in the labor force approach because of inadequate input. Although persons in Categories II and III seeking work should, in general, be comparable with those seeking work in the labor force approach, it is doubtful that strict comparability could be obtained. Similarly, it is doubtful that the total work force figure in the new approach would match that obtained through the labor force approach, even if the time periods were identical. The basic differences in conceptual framework and techniques of measurement would probably preclude identical results. In any case it was agreed that an effort would be made in as many countries as possible to try to tabulate 1970 census results in such a manner as to permit maximum comparability with the categories of the new functional approach.

CONCLUDING OBSERVATIONS

The workshop group recognized that its proposal constitutes but a first step in the development of an approach to the measurement of work force in developing areas. Provision was made for the actual testing of the proposal in surveys in Thailand and Japan. Hopefully the results of such experimentation will provide the group with the necessary information for appropriate modification of the proposal. There is consensus, however, on the inadequacy of either the gainful worker or the labor force approach to provide the kinds of information required in developing countries about their human resources; and on the need to develop an approach better approximating the reality of the situation in the developing countries.

NOTES

1. Carrol D. Wright and William C. Hunt, *History and Growth of the United States Census, 1790–1890* (Washington: Government Printing Office, 1933), p. 29.

2. *Ibid.*, p. 19.

3. For example, see *Fifteenth Census of the United States: Population,* Vol. V, *General Report on Occupations* (Washington: Government Printing Office, 1933), p. 29.

4. *Ibid.*, p. 29.

5. Alba M. Edwards, *Comparative Occupational Statistics for the U.S., 1870–1940* (Washington: Government Printing Office, 1943), ch. 8.

6. *Ibid.*, Part II.

7. See, for example, Charles E. Persons, "Census Reports on Unemployment in April, 1930," *Annals of the American Academy of Political and Social Science,* CLIV (March 1931), 12–16; Mary Van Kleeck, "The Federal Unemployment Census of 1930," *Journal of the American Statistical Association* (*Suppl.*), XXVI (March 1931), 189–200; George B. L. Arner, "The Census of Unemployment," *Journal of the American Statistical Association* (*Suppl.*), XXXVIII (March 1933), 48–53; Howard B. Myers and George M. Webb, "Another Census of Unemployment?" *American Journal of Sociology,* LXII (January 1937), 521–33.

8. For employment indexes and unemployment estimates, by industry, for 1933, see (1) American Federation of Labor, *American Federalist,* 40, 7 (July 1933), 700 and 40, 7 (October 1933), 1080–1; (2) National Industrial Conference Board, *The Service Letter on Industrial Relations,* VI, 10 (October 30, 1933), 80; (3) Federal Reserve Board and (4) Bureau of Labor Statistics, Department of Labor estimates in U. S. Department of Commerce, Bureau of Foreign and Domestic Commerce, *Statistical Abstract of the United States,* 1934 (Washington: Government Printing Office), Tables 335–9, 342. Methods for obtaining data given in (1) and (2) are described in the references given. For methods used in (3) and (4) see Federal Reserve Board, *Federal Reserve Bulletin* (November 1929), pp. 706–716, and November 1930; and U.S. Bureau of Labor Statistics, Department of Labor, *Bulletin 610, Revised Indexes of Factory Employment and Payrolls, 1919–1933.*

9. For an analysis of the methods used in forty surveys of unemployment conducted between 1929 and 1937, see John N. Webb, "Concepts Used in Employment Surveys," *Journal of the American Statistical Association*, XXXIV (March 1939), 49–59.

10. And a fuller memorandum on the same subject under the same title prepared for the Urban Section of the Division of Social Research, Works Progress Administration (mimeographed). See also Calvert L. Dedrick and Morris H. Hansen, *Census of Unemployment .1937*, Final Report, Vol. IV: *The Enumerative Check Census, Census of Partial Employment, Unemployment and Occupations: 1937* (Washington: Government Printing Office, 1938). See also Philip M. Hauser, "The Labor Force and Gainful Workers —Concept, Measurement, and Comparability," *American Journal of Sociology*, 54 (January 1949), 338–55.

11. *Sixteenth Census of the United States, 1940: Population*, "Estimates of Labor Force, Employment and Unemployment in the United States, 1940 and 1930" (Washington: Government Printing Office, 1944).

12. See *Concepts and Methods Used in Manpower Statistics from the Current Population Survey*, Bureau of Labor Statistics, Report No. 313; Bureau of Census *Current Population Reports*, Series P–23, No. 22 (Washington; June 1967), pp. 3–7.

13. *Ibid.*, pp. 15–19.

14. International Labour Organization, *The International Standardization of Labour Statistics* (Geneva, 1959); see also United Nations, *Principles and Recommendations for the 1970 Population Censuses* (New York; United Nations, 1969), pp. 26–27.

15. Gunnar Myrdal, *Asian Drama* (New York: Pantheon, 1968), II, 994 ff.

16. *Ibid.*

SUNE CARLSON

FOREIGN SUBSIDIARIES AND THE DYNAMICS OF INTERNATIONAL ECONOMIC INTEGRATION

THE establishment of foreign subsidiaries has been a major subject of study in our international business research program at the Institute of Business Studies at Uppsala.[1] As long as these studies were of an exploratory nature, the lack of a theoretical foundation for our research did not worry us very much. But as our work proceeds, and as we approach such problems as the adaptation of Swedish industry to changing market conditions in Europe, or the dynamic aspects of Scandinavian economic integration, the need for some kind of theoretical framework becomes more and more obvious. This preliminary theoretical effort should be viewed against this background.

THE KNOWLEDGE FACTORS

One of our most recurrent research findings has been the importance of "knowledge factors" in international business operations, not only in connection with the establishment of subsidiaries but of international business in general.[2] That knowledge factors are among the important inputs of most business firms has been evident for some time. But they are, in addition, becoming an increasing part of these firms' outputs, which contain more and more "software" in the form of marketing and service activities.

In this paper I shall be concerned with the knowledge factors only in their relations with subsidiary establishments, and, among the knowledge factors, mainly with those which relate to a firm's input. I shall distinguish, on one hand, between *market knowledge* and *technical knowledge* and, on the other, between *external knowledge* and *internal knowledge*.

Market knowledge is related to a particular market, e.g., the German market for ball bearings. It consists of information regarding present and future demand, competition, intermediaries, advertising media, etc. Technical knowledge is related to the development, construction, production, and use of individual products and of the processes connected with all these. Roughly speaking, technical knowledge is everything—except the knowledge of particular markets—which a firm needs in order to carry out its activities. An important part of technical knowledge is managerial know-how.

External knowledge is knowledge that can be obtained from the outside, e.g., from suppliers of machinery, research institutes, and various consultants. It is a part of a firm's cultural environment—of its external economies—and it varies considerably from one locality to another. Internal knowledge, in contrast, consists of all the information over which the firm has exclusive possession, and which it tries to protect by patents, copyrights, contracts, and other means. It is a kind of monopoly power.

Investment in knowledge is in many ways similar to other kinds of investments. But some of its characteristics are of particular importance in the present context. First, since the knowledge required for the development, manufacturing, or marketing of a product generally is difficult to specify and to measure quantitatively, the amount of money needed for investment in knowledge is hard to foresee. However, required investments in knowledge certainly tend to increase with the advancement of technology. Such investments are, for example, higher for television than for radio and higher, in turn, for color than for black-and-white television. Since knowledge is difficult to specify, it is also difficult to buy and sell. A firm cannot always be sure about the availability of external knowledge, and may have to develop a good deal of its own technical and market knowledge.

Second, investment in knowledge has to a large extent the character of "sunk cost." In most cases it is specifically related to a certain product, process, or market, and cannot be used so effectively in any other connection. Furthermore, knowledge investments generally have a high rate of obsolescence, while the depreciation rate is often nil or even negative. Most knowledge increases in value the more it is used. Also, the obsolescence rate tends to increase with the advancement of technology. For these reasons, a firm wants to utilize these investments as quickly as possible. The impetus for rapid utilization is particularly noticeable in technology-intensive industries.

Third, as with most investments, certain economies of scale occur in connection with knowledge investments. Thus, a large firm which, for example, can carry on large-scale product development generally has an advantage over a small firm. In order to improve its situation, the small firm may try to purchase external knowledge, or it may try to join other firms in various types of cooperative ventures.

FOREIGN SUBSIDIARIES

For the time being I shall disregard these difficulties of specifying and measuring quantitatively various types of knowledge, postponing the discussion of this problem to the next section. Here I shall merely assume that the firm's output (o) represents a mix of hardware (h) and software (s), which can be regarded as a set

$$o = [h, s] \qquad [1]$$

Similarly the firm's input (I) may be regarded as another set

$$I = [m_e, m_i, t_e, t_i, v_1, \ldots, v_n] \qquad [2]$$

where the knowledge factors are denoted by

	External knowledge	Internal knowledge
Market knowledge	m_e	m_i
Technical knowledge	t_e	t_i

and the other productive services by $v_1, \ldots, v_n$. When the firm sells its output on several markets $A, B, C, \ldots$ etc., there will be a pair of knowledge factors for each market $m_{eA}, m_{iA}, m_{eB}, m_{iB}$. But let us start the analysis with the production for a single market.

Production for a Single Market. Assume a firm which under a certain tariff protection is producing for the home market A. When in connection with the establishment of a free-trade area or a custom union, the tariff barriers are lowered or disappear, there will be an incentive to increase the imports from another member country, B, which has lower unit costs of the productive factors $v_{l'}, \ldots, v_n$. This is what might be called a static effect of the economic integration.

One way our firm in *A* may counterbalance this new competition is to subcontract parts of its production to firms in country *B*. If it can achieve sufficient economies of scale, the firm may instead establish its own subsidiary unit in *B* for expert production to the *A* market. In this latter case it combines its internal market knowledge (m_{iA}) and technical knowledge (t_{iA}) from the home base with external technical knowledge (t_{eB}) and other productive services from *B* into a new input set

$$I_B = [m_{eA}, m_{iA}, t_{iA}, t_{iB}, v_{lB}, \ldots, v_{nB}] \qquad [3]$$

Compared with its indigenous competitors *i B*, a firm which has headquarters in *A* and merely a production unit in *B* will lack knowledge of local conditions, and it will probably have to pay more for its productive services.[3] It will also have longer and more expensive communication lines for instruction and control. On the other hand, it will have the advantage of better knowledge of the market (m_{iA}) and of better facilities for coordination of its market and technical knowledge.

What effect an international economic integration will have on the establishment of foreign subsidiaries will depend on the relative strength of these different factors. When successful operations depend on superior market knowledge or on the facilities to develop custom-oriented combinations of software and hardware, we may expect an increasing number of subsidiary production units to be established. When, on the other hand, the market knowledge is of less importance, or when the software part of the output is insignificant, subcontracting will probably take the place of subsidiary establishments. For example, in the case of textiles, we may expect one type of development for ready-made fashion clothing, and another for standardized piece-goods. Similarly, the technology-intensive sectors of the mechanical engineering industry may show a different pattern of development from other sectors.

Production for Several Markets. Leaving the assumption of a single market, I shall consider next a firm which sells its output on several markets. One of these is the country *C*, where the firm has an agent which provides it with the necessary external market knowledge (m_{eC}).

When *A* and *C* become members of the same integrated area the tariffs between them disappear. This static effect of integration will in itself make *C* a more attractive market than before. In addition, there are dynamic effects: faster economic growth, accelerated technological progress, new marketing development, etc. For these reasons the firm in question may decide to increase its investments in internal market knowledge (m_{iC}) by the establishment of a sales subsidiary. Like the first case discussed such an action will be the more necessary, the more the sales volume depends on market knowledge and on efficient coordination of market and technical knowledge. Again, the establishment of subsidiaries will be particularly important in connection with highly processed and technology-intensive goods.

There is also another reason: When the tariffs disappear, the nontariff barriers become more important, and these barriers specially affect these types of goods. In order to find out all the intricate implementations of nontariff barriers, the firm may find it necessary to have its own people on the spot. More information about tariff conditions can easily be obtained by an agent.

When software is an important element of the output, the establishment of a sales subsidiary may not be enough. To be able to give the customers the technical service required, various kinds of service operations may have to be added. When the scale factors are not too forbidding, perhaps a local production of some part of the hardware may also be necessary. Thus, we get a subsidiary with its own output set

$$o_C = [h_C, s_C] \qquad [4]$$

and with an input set which combines internal technical knowledge from the mother plant with its own knowledge and other local input factors

$$I_C = [t_{iA}, m_{eC}, m_{iC}, t_{eC}, t_{iC}, v_{lC}, \ldots, v_{nC}] \qquad [5]$$

Once this process has started, it may seem natural that the subsidiary should produce some hardware parts not only for its own market, but for other markets as well. In this way the international economic integration may gradually lead to a multinational organization operating throughout the integrated area, in which each national unit becomes specialized in certain parts of the total output. A network of intercompany deliveries will result. If the firm already has production plants in other member countries, which had been built in order to get around local tariffs, this specialization may be accelerated. With the integration these plants have lost their original *raison d'être,* but they may still have some knowledge about local production conditions, the cost of which probably would be sunk if they had to be shut down or sold to outsiders.

Production for Another Integrated Area. The question of sunk cost is relevant also in the case when the firm has been exporting to a country, *D,* which enters into another integrated area than country *A.* But here it is the sunk cost for market knowledge rather than technical knowledge that matters. The more the firm in question has invested in internal market knowledge (m_io), the less willing it will probably be to give up its market share because of discriminatory tariff treatment. Since the firm particularly will feel the discrimination on the hardware part of its output, it may try to substitute at least a part of its imported hardware by local purchases, or it may start its own local production. In both cases there will be a need for a subsidiary unit in country *D*—in the former case for assembly and service, in the latter also for production. When this production unit can also function as supplier to other countries in the integrated area, it may even achieve certain economies of scale. The output and input sets of such a subsidiary in *D* will be similar to those of the subsidiary in *C*, discussed above. Again, the internal technical knowledge will come mainly from the mother company, the internal market knowledge from the subsidiary, and the other input factors from the country of the subsidiary.

This type of establishment may be said to be a result of the static integration effects. Thus, the present case is at least partially similar to the import case discussed at the beginning of the section. The choice between buying or producing will, for example, be influenced by the same kind of considerations. But the dynamic effects must also be taken into account. Also, with respect to an integrated area to which the mother country of the company does not belong, we may expect that such integration effects as accelerated economic growth or technological development may influence the establishment decisions. This is specially true when the location of a subsidiary in country *D* will facilitate the gathering of knowledge also about the other countries in the area.

Production for Area with More Facilities. Since foreign trade means much more for a small country than for a large one, the various effects of an international economic integration are also more significant. This is true for the effects on the establishment of foreign subsidiaries as well.

When the acquisition of internal knowledge is very expensive, the proceeds from the production also of a relatively large plant in a small country may not suffice to finance the knowledge investments. The production capacity—and particularly the labor force—is often not large enough. If a firm cannot get sufficient funds from the sale of finished products, it can, of course, try to finance its knowledge. But, as has already been mentioned, this is not a simple matter. Patent rights and technical licenses are seldom easily negotiable. Furthermore, if the firm succeeds in finding someone who wants to purchase the production rights for a particular market, such a deal may be quite risky. As soon as the firm stops selling on the market in question, its market knowledge will soon become obsolete and it will be at the mercy of the license holder.

When the production facilities are limited at home, the establishment of fully controlled subsidiaries in markets where such facilities are available is, of course, a much more attractive solution to the problem of knowledge finance. It is also such a development, which, for example, explains much of the present structure of present Swedish industry. Without the establishment of a large number of subsidiaries abroad the country could not support the technology-intensive industries it has today. It is clear that international economic integration in Europe has played a decisive role.

HYPOTHESIS AND MEASUREMENTS

Thus far I have tried only to show how decisions to establsih foreign subsidiaries might be influenced by certain knowledge factors. The analysis has been kept strictly at the micro level. Examples have been given of how the existence of internal market and technical knowledge might lead to the setting up of production units in other countries, or how the need for improved market knowledge might cause a firm to establish sales subsidiaries. It has also been suggested that the development might be different for different goods depending on their varying combinations of hardware and software, and their varying technology-intensity and marketing requirements.

The next step is to translate these rather vague ideas to definite hypotheses which can be verified empirically. These hypotheses may deal with the static situation—how different branches of industry are organized internationally under different trade block arrangements at a particular point in time —or with the more dynamic problem—how the different organizational structures are changed over time during the integration process. But as soon as I proceed to this step, I am immediately faced with all the difficult problems of measurement which I ignored in the previous section. To get operational definitions which permit direct quantitative measurements on such concepts as technical and market knowledge, software, or technology-intensity is probably impossible. To get measurements of the relevant sizes of subsidiaries is difficult enough. I shall be satisfied if I can find some substitute variables which I can define operationally and which can be used as indicators of the phenomena I am interested in. Two examples may illustrate my attempts.

Several reasons have been given why foreign production subsidiaries should be of special importance in the case of technology-intensive industries. The necessary software can be produced locally; market and technical knowledge can be coordinated more easily; the subsidiary operations can contribute to the knowledge investments, etc. In order to test this hypothesis empirically, I need some kind of indicator both of what I mean by "importance" and of what I have called "technology-intensity." In Figures 1 and 2, which relate to foreign production subsidiaries in Sweden and Swedish production subsidiaries abroad, my measurement of "importance" has been in both cases the number of people employed by the subsidiaries as percentages of the total number of employees in the respective branch of industry in Sweden. I could also have used investment values, which would have given much the same results, but since my focus was on organizational structures, I used the employment figures.

FIGURES 1 AND 2

THE ESTABLISHMENT OF FOREIGN SUBSIDIARIES IN INDUSTRIES WITH VARIOUS DEGREES OF TECHNOLOGY INTENSITY

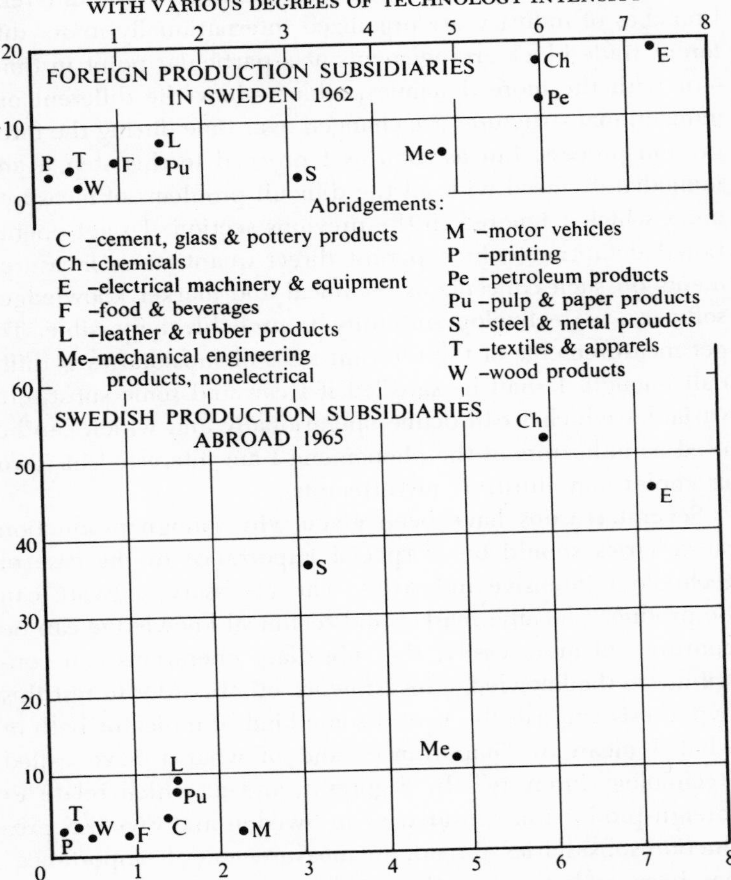

Verticle scale: number of employees in percent of total labor force in Sweden. Sources: H. Johansson, *Utländskt företagande i Sverige* (Uddevalla: Studieforbundet Naringsliv och Samhalle) and H. Lund, *Svenska företags investeringar i utlandet* (Katrineholm: 1967), Table D, p. 138.

Horizontal scale: number of scientists and engineers in percent of the total labor force in the U.S. Source: D. B. Keesing, "Labor Skills and the Structure of the Trade in Manufactures," *The Open Economy* (New York: 1968), Table 1, p. 12.

As an indicator of "technological intensity" I have used the number of scientists and engineers as percentages of the total labor force in the respective branch in the United States, mainly because these figures were easily available. My assumption is that industries in Sweden and the United States have more or less the same technological structure, which may lead to some erroneous conclusions. The Swedish subsidiaries abroad in the chemical industry, for example, have to a large extent a lower technology-intensity than the chemical industry on the average. Still the two figures indicate quite conclusively a concentration of production subsidiaries to such technolgoy-heavy products as chemicals, electrical machinery and equipment, and petroleum products. I hope to check these findings later against Swedish employment data and data on research and development expenditures, but I do not expect the results to be much different.

Another proposition advanced was that different goods have different requirements as regards market knowledge, which might influence the establishment of sales subsidiaries in particular. To test such an hypothesis is even more difficult. First of all, the only Swedish sales figures on subsidiaries available is their total number in various branches of industry,[4] and that does not say very much about their importance. One would need at least branch data on the sales of the subsidiaries in a particular market area as percentages of the total export to the area. But such data are generally hard to obtain. Second, to find an indicator of the need for market knowledge for various kinds of goods is not easy. In Sweden we have just obtained preliminary figures on the "cost of personal selling" as a percentage of total sales for various industrial branches,[5] but even if our knowledge factor correlates with the selling costs, which is far from certain, the breakdown of the figures is not detailed enough regarding the metal and mechanical engineering industries which have the largest number of subsidiaries.

These examples both relate to the static problem of industrial structures. Much more interesting are the dynamic problems of subsidiary establishment and international economic integration. It is my hope that the kind of theoretical fragments presented here will also help in building models regarding the timing of various kinds of subsidiary establishments and of their changes in their respective output and input sets. But for the empirical testing of such models, even more data will be needed from individual firms, some of which might be difficult to obtain.

NOTES

1. See, e.g., Harry Johansson, *Utländsk företagsetablering i Sverige,* (Uddevalla: Studieforbundet Naringsliv och Samhalle, 1968); S. Shivanna Ramu, *Foreign Ventures in India. The Swedish Case* (Stockholm: Ejnar Munksgaard, 1968); and E. Hörnell and J.E. Vahlne "Svenska dotterbolag i utlandet," *Industriforbundets Tidskrift* (September 1970).

2. See, for example, Sune Carlson, "Some Notes on the Dynamics of International Economic Integration," *The Swedish Journal of Economics,* No. 1 (1970). The importance of the knowledge factors in connection with direct foreign investments has been emphasized, among others, by Kindelberger and by Södersten. Cf. Charles P. Kindelberger, *American Business Abroad* (New Haven and London: Yale University Press, 1969), pp. 14 ff; and Bo Södersten, *International Economics* (New York: Harper and Row, 1970), ch. 23.

3. Because of their better credit rating large American companies which are establishing production units in Europe, are sometimes able to pay less for borrowed money than their local competitors. Scandinavian firms, which generally are smaller and less well known internationally, often have to pay more.

4. Cf. Hörnell and Vahlne, Table 4.

5. "Preliminär redovisning av reklamkestnadernas storlek i Sverige 1965–1967," mimeographed memorandum published jointly by Statistiska Centralbyrän and Industrins Utredningsinstitut (Stockholm: 1970), Table 3.

PART THREE

THEODORE LIDZ, M.D.

THE FAMILY: THE SOURCE OF HUMAN RESOURCES

EVEN amidst the battle for Guadalcanal in World War II, probably the most devastating and terrifying campaign ever fought by United States troops, it became apparent that our meagre manpower was being diminished by family influences. The sources of emotional incapacitation seemed obvious—the point-blank shellings by the 15-inch rifles of the Japanese battleships, the incessant bombings, the hairbreadth escapes, the isolation, and the ravages of disease. But for some marines the critical missile arrived in the mail. The letter with news of a mother's death, the infidelity of a wife, the marriage of a fiancée left the marine making friends with death, no longer determined to survive amidst the terror and despite the overwhelming odds.

Perhaps even more important was the evidence that the instability of the home in which the marine had been raised increased his vulnerability to incapacitating anxiety or depression. Eighty percent of those who suffered from repetitive combat nightmares and overwhelming anxiety came from homes broken by the death of a parent, divorce, or severe incompatibility in contrast to less than 20 percent of patients hospitalized for treatment of malaria; and two-thirds of all those suffering from combat neuroses came from broken or severely disturbed families.[1]

My attention had been drawn to such factors because just prior to that war, we had noted what has now become so apparent that it is virtually axiomatic—that those severe casualties of life we term "schizophrenics" and who fill a quarter of the hospital beds in the country had virtually always grown up in seriously disturbed homes; but our study had been disrupted by the war. Over the past two decades attention has focused increasingly on the relationships between various types of disturbances in the family of origin to various types of mental incapacitation, emotional illness, and psychosomatic disorders. Mental retardations, delinquency, addictions, suicide, homosexuality, schizophrenia, depressive psychoses, as well as obesity, anorexia nervosa, thyroid disease, peptic ulcer have been related to differing varieties of intrafamilial problems.

I can here only attempt to indicate the importance of the family to several such conditions to illustrate the reasons for the growing interest in the family. In 1952, Bradley Buell and his associates [2] published their finding that 6 percent of the families in St. Paul, Minnesota, pre-empted 46 percent of the health services and 55 percent of all "adjustment services, including psychiatric service, casework, and protective supervision," statistics later found valid for other cities. Two recent studies have examined such multiproblem families in detail. Minuchin and his co-workers (1967) studied disorganized, low socioeconomic families that had each produced more than one delinquent child, predominantly black and Puerto Rican families living in New York.[3] Malone, Pavenstedt, and their colleagues [4] studied the families and the young children of disorganized families from the North Point area of Boston, predominantly white. Their findings are surprisingly similar, despite the ethnic differences.

The nursery school children studied in the Boston project were seriously impaired in various ways. Despite a pseudo precocity concerning autonomy, they were markedly delayed in their perceptual development; their language was impoverished, and the inability to generalize from one experience to another and even to name an object hidden from view was striking. Impulsivity and inability to delay gratification were obvious; and they could be almost paralyzed by anxiety, though careless about injuring themselves. They were distrustful of adults and impaired in their ability to differentiate between adults, frustrating their teachers' efforts to establish meaningful relationships. Such children were very difficult to teach or correct, and clearly were unprepared for a regular kindergarten. The children in the New York study were older and had already been in serious trouble.

The families were not simply poor and could not be considered representative of the "culture of poverty." It would be difficult to say they were Irish, Puerto Rican, Haitian, or Negro culturally for they were without cultural tradition. It was also difficult to discuss the family structure or organization for they were essentially disorganized. However, Minuchin and his colleagues properly could differentiate between several types of disorganization, such as disengaged families in which members were essentially disconnected; the enmeshed family in which the mother overcontrols without affection and provokes rebellion; families in which the unmarried mother is still living as her mother's daughter; families with juvenile parents whose predominant interests are in peer groups rather than in the spouse and children, etc.

The parents in their childhoods had few experiences that foster maturity, inadequate models for identification, and marked learning defects. They bring to their families of procreation "all the deprivations, dangers springing from uncontrolled impulses, excesses leading to aggressive acts and asocial acting out, inconsistencies of every sort, and a general passivity toward actively changing things." [5] These are families of children in which parents are rivalrous with offspring and do not give the needs of young children precedence over their own impulses and drives. The households lack any routines and the training and care of children are markedly erratic. The parents are incapable of that irreducible minimal capacity for childrearing—a recognition that "children are undifferentiated, impulsive beings who have to be nursed and coerced into differentiated growth." [6] The boundary between the generations which is essential for a child's development is virtually absent in these families.

Such disorganized families are not limited to the urban slum. Similar families that give rise to anomic and highly deviant offspring can be encountered on the periphery of society anywhere, and occasionally even among the well-to-do, floating upon inherited wealth for a generation or two. In poverty areas they shade into families which are better organized but improperly prepare their offspring to use language and think properly because of the paucity of verbal communication in the family, and its use to order and reprimand rather than to discuss,[7] or fail to transmit the ethical code because the culture of poverty uses different moral values than the larger society. The disorganized family of the slum clearly presents a serious and difficult challenge to poverty programs. Economic aid is unlikely to help these families or their children appreciably, and more far-reaching measures of socialization and enculturation seem essential to halt the perpetuation of such individuals and families from generation to generation.

Hendin's thought-provoking study [8] of the high suicide rate among young American blacks, which concomitantly illuminates the high homicide rate in this population, directs attention to another problem that requires understanding of the total family in its social setting. Hendin finds these men who have made serious suicidal attempts to be possessed by overwhelming rage and impulsions to violence of homicidal proportions. Although growing up amidst racial prejudice in brutalizing surroundings and with severe economic deprivations appearing to contribute to the seething hostile feelings, the central characterologic problems seem to derive from maternal deprivation, rejection, and cruelty. For most of these men, the capacity for love, tenderness, and friendship had been crushed in childhood, leaving rage and self-hatred as dominant emotions leading them on a self-destructive course—"whether by way of drugs, crime, homicide or suicide."[9]

The rejection of a black son by his mother is commonly accompanied by maternal domination that adds to the boy's loss of self-esteem as well as to his hostility toward women. Such problems cannot be understood in terms of mother-son relationships alone, for they involve a situation common among lower-class black families—that of the matriarchal home in which the mother gains little if any support in maintaining the family and raising the children from an adult male who is a secondary if not only a transitory figure in the home. The boy has no stable male model with whom to identify and follow into adulthood but only the model of a male intruder whom he resents. All too early, he follows the directives of peer groups, unchecked by a father he would like to emulate but only by the admonitions and punishments of a mother.

Black nationalists, including the psychiatrists Grier and Cobb, would like to believe that black mothers purposefully reject and emasculate sons to prepare them for their menial place in a white world. This is not what one hears from such mothers who gain little gratification from sons because they are going to get into trouble and be burdensome, and because the mother as a child had no consistent father who gave her affection, nor as a woman a spouse who gave love and support that would lead her to love his child. The origins of the family dilemma in the slavery that required a matriarchal family and in a social system that has denied the black male status and a living wage does not negate the importance of the family dynamics and the psychodynamics involved.

The origins and focus of my own interest in the family has been the study of schizophrenic patients whose number is legion. It is now apparent that whatever else may enter into the causation of these gross failures of integration, these patients have always grown up in seriously disturbed or distorted families. My colleagues and I have studied mainly upper and upper-middle class families with schizophrenic offspring (and more recently families with delinquent children) in order to avoid the complexities introduced by socioeconomic deprivations and untoward extrafamilial environments.[10] This is not the place to attempt to describe the involved findings of our studies and those of others. Stated in the simplest terms, many of these families, in particular those of female patients, are split by a pervasive schism between the parents, with each undermining the worth of the other to the children, and setting mutually contradictory expectations, while the mother's overprotectiveness has an inimical quality. In the remaining families the patterns of childrearing and the family way of life were distorted or skewed because the eccentric and deviant ways of the dominant parent, usually the mother, are not countered by the other parent who goes along with the spouse's peculiar and distorting influence. Here the mother is not only overprotective but seeks completion from the child and is unable to differentiate her needs and wishes from his. In all of these families there are serious disturbances in the parents' ways of communicating and thinking which prevents the child from gaining a firm grounding in the meaning system and logic of his culture.

Having noted and verified that schizophrenic patients always originated in seriously disturbed families, we originally sought some factor within the radius of the family circle that had specific pertinence to the etiology of the condition. However, whatever aspect of the family or its transactions we examined we found something seriously amiss: the parents as individuals, as a marital couple, as parents, as role and identification models for their children; the marital interaction, the communication within the family, the relatedness to the larger community, etc.

In seeking to comprehend the findings, we turned to ask some fundamental questions that had rarely been asked and even less frequently answered adequately. Why is the family a universal phenomenon? What are the essential functions of the family? How does it carry them out? What is the role of language in human adaptation, and what is the family's role in inculcating language? Then, in uncovering what our patients had lacked in their families of origin, we began to grasp what seemed to be requisite in family life for assuring the development of reasonably integrated offspring.[11]

FUNCTIONS OF THE FAMILY

The family is ubiquitous because it is an essential correlate of man's biological structure which requires that he develop in a social system and assimilate a culture. The human, like all other animals, is equipped physiologically to survive within a relatively narrow range of environments. His essential adaptive techniques, however, are not inborn but permitted by his unique brain that enables him to acquire language, and thereby to communicate verbally, think abstractly, and have foresight. To understand man, we must appreciate that he has two endowments: a genetic inheritance, and a cultural heritage without which he is no more human than his pre-Stone-age progenitors. The family is the basic social system that mediates between the child's genetic and cultural endowments and which instills the basic societal techniques while providing for his biological needs.

Because the child is immature and dependent for many years even in simple societies, he requires nurture and protection from persons to whom his welfare is as important as their own. His prolonged attachments to those who raise him and his identifications with them provide major motivations and directives for his development. The family ways are long the only way of life for the child, and these ways and the child's patterns of reacting to them become so thoroughly ingrained in his personality that they can be considered part of his constitutional make-up, and are confused with inborn factors with which they interact.

Most theories of child development, whether behaviorist or psychoanalytic in orientation, have markedly oversimplified the process. A child does not develop a workable and integrated personality simply through proper nurturance of his inborn potential and the avoidance of undue emotional trauma, nor by conditioning processes, but requires positive direction and guidance in a suitable interpersonal environment and social system. Any attempt to study the child's personality development or maldevelopment independently of the family matrix distorts as much as it simplifies; and is bound to err, for such abstractions eliminate the essentials in the process. Many of the complex molding influences have been overlooked because they are built into the family which everywhere, even without being aware of it, is responsible for fostering the child's development by carrying out a number of interrelated functions. As children everywhere are very similar biologically and have similar physiological needs but must be prepared to adapt to different social and physical environments, the family must fill certain requisites everywhere but differs in how it meets them according to ethnic and environmental differences.

The various interrelated functions which the family must carry out to foster and direct their children's development can be considered under four headings. These are: (1) the parental nurturant functions, which must meet the child's needs and supplement his immature capacities in a different manner at each phase of his development; (2) the dynamic organization of the family, which forms the framework for the structuring of the child's personality, or, perhaps stated more correctly, channels and directs the child into becoming an integrated individual; (3) the family as the primary social system in which the child learns the basic social roles, the value of social institutions, and the basic mores of the society; (4) the task of the parents and the family they create of transmitting to the child the essential instrumental techniques of the culture, including its language.[12]

Parental Nurturant Function. The parental nurturant function is the one requisite of the family that has been specifically recognized by most developmental theories, and as it has been the focus of intensive study does not require careful elaboration here. We are concerned with the nature of the nurturance provided from the total care given to the helpless neonate to how the parents foster an adolescent's movement toward independence from them. It concerns more than filling the child's physical needs, it involves his emotional needs for love, affection, and a sense of security; it includes providing opportunity for the utilization of new capacities as the child matures. Proper nurture requires parents to have the capacities, knowledge, and empathy to alter their ways of relating and their attitudes to the child in accord with his changing needs. Although the mother is the primary nurturant figure, her relationship with her child does not transpire in isolation. Her capacities to nurture are obviously affected profoundly by her relationship with her husband, the demands of other children, the security and the emotional input she receives from others.

The quality and nature of the parental nurturance that a child receives will profoundly influence his emotional development—his vulnerability to frustration; and the anger, aggressivity, anxiety, hopelessness, helplessness he experiences under various conditions. It affects the quality of basic trust he develops; influences his sense of autonomy as an individual, contributes to the child's developing self-esteem as a boy or girl. It lays the foundations for trust in the usefulness of collaboration with others and of language as an aid in solving problems. Physiological functioning is permanently influenced by how parental figures have responded to physiological needs. It is apparent even from these brief comments why so much attention has properly been directed to the parental nurturant functions and how profoundly they influence personality development; but, they are only one aspect of what a child requires from his parents and family.

Integration of the Personality. To consider the structural requisites of the family we must appreciate some of the special characteristics of the family as an entity. The family is a true small group in that the action of any member affects all, and its members must find reciprocally interrelating roles to minimize conflict. As a group it requires unity of directives and leadership in pursuing them. These characteristics are heightened by the intense and prolonged interdependency of the members. The nuclear family, further, is a very special type of small group because it is specifically composed of two generations and two sexes; and because it must simultaneously carry out three cardinal functions: to stabilize and provide completion to the spouses who married to form the nuclear family; to nurture and enculture their offspring; and to serve as the basic social unit of society.

The family provides a shelter for its members within the larger society, and its members, at least theoretically, receive affection and status by ascription rather than because of achievement which provides a source of emotional security in face of the demands of the outside world. The family must, however, reflect and transmit the ways of the society to assure that the children will be able to function when they emerge from the shelter of the family.

The two generations have different needs, prerogatives, and obligations. The parents seek to merge themselves and their dissimilar backgrounds into a new and permanent union that satisfies the needs and completes the personalities of each. They are properly dependent on one another, and serve as guides, educators, and models for their children, giving of themselves so that the children can develop; but they may not properly be dependent upon immature children. The children, in contrast, obtain their primary socialization within the family, remain dependent for many years and form intense emotional bonds to the parents, and yet must so develop that they can leave their family of origin and function independently of it, if not form families of their own. The parents are not only permitted but expected to have sexual relations to help give permanence to their union, but all direct sexual relationships within the family are prohibited to children lest their intrafamilial ties become too firm.

The two genders have differing but complementary functions and role allocations: the female role derives from woman's biological make-up and her initial union with her children, her nurturance of them, and her need to maintain a home for that purpose, leading to an interest in the emotional needs of others and interpersonal relationships—an expressive-affectional role. The male role, also originally related to man's physical structure, is concerned with the protection and support of the family, and its relationships with the larger society—an instrumental-adaptive role.[13]

Taking these characteristics into account, which I have presented only sketchily, for the spouses to fill their parental rather than their marital functions adequately, they must *form a coalition as parents while maintaining the essential boundaries between the generations and adhering to their respective gender-linked roles.* These requisites, which sound very simple, have far-reaching consequences which I can only touch upon here.

A parental coalition is necessary to provide unity of leadership for the family has two leaders, an instrumental and an expressive leader; unity is possible even though difficult because the two are complementary. The coalition is also important to provide each parent and parental role with the required support. The wife, for example, can better delimit her erotic investment in a child when her sexual needs are satisfied by her husband; and she can provide emotional security more readily when the husband provides economic security. The child properly requires two parents, one of the same sex with whom to identify and whose model can be followed into adulthood; and a parent of the opposite sex who becomes a basic love object whose love can be gained by identifying with the parent of the same sex. But, a parent can effectively fill neither role for the child if belittled, despised, or treated as an enemy by the spouse. When serious failures of the parental coalition occur, the child may invest his energies in supporting one or the other parent or in seeking to preserve their marriage rather than in his own development. He may also be caught in the precarious situation where behavior that pleases one parent brings rebuff from the other; or he may take on the role of a scapegoat, becoming a major cause of parental dissent to mask their discord and thus retain the two parents he needs. The child's tendency to possess one or the other parent for himself alone, the essence of the oedipal situation, is overcome when the parental coalition is firm requiring repression of such wishes. In brief, when the parental coalition fails, the child readily becomes subject to conflicting motivations and directives that interfere with harmonious development.

Maintaining a proper separation between the generations permits the child the security of dependency to utilize his energies in his own development, free from rivalry with a parent or the need to support a parent emotionally. He can find his place in the childhood generation where he belongs while gradually learning adult roles by observing and experiencing the parents. Parents can inappropriately breach the generation boundaries in various ways such as: utilizing a child to fill needs unsatisfied by a spouse; by acting as a rivalrous child; by the mother failing to differentiate between her own needs and feelings and those of a son. The most obvious infractions are incestuous and near-incestuous relationships in which a parent overtly or covertly gains sexual gratification from a child. The child not only can widen the gap between parents and insert himself into it but need not—and perhaps cannot—then turn to the extrafamilial world for completion. Further, the child's fears of retaliation and retribution that are part of the oedipal situation are then apt to have a real basis in the actual jealousy and hostility of the displaced parent. With confused generation boundaries, aggressive and libidinal impulses toward parents become heightened rather than undergoing repression and gradual resolution, and can be controlled only through strongly guarded defense mechanisms.

The parents' adherence to their respective gender-linked roles in forming the parental coalition plays a major role in guiding the child's development as a boy or girl. Of all factors entering into the formation of personality characteristics, the sex of the child is most decisive. Confusions and dissatisfactions concerning sexual identity contribute to the etiology of many neuroses and character defects as well as perversions, and probably all schizophrenic patients are seriously confused concerning their gender identity. Being born a boy or girl simply directs but does not assure achievement of proper gender-linked attributes which depend largely upon gender role allocations in infancy and through proper role assumptions and identifications as the child grows older. Clear-cut role reversals in parents can obviously distort the child's development, as when the father does the cooking and housekeeping, leading the child to aberrant concepts of masculinity and femininity. A mother who is rivalous with all men unwittingly teaches a son that masculinity will evoke rebuff from her, and he must feel and act castrated to be acceptable to her. A homosexual father who is hostile to his wife simply because she is a woman directs his daughter to nonfeminine ways of gaining his approval.

A more common problem arises when the mother is unable to fill an expressive-affectional role or the father cannot provide instrumental leadership for the family. A cold and aloof mother will be particularly detrimental to a daughter who requires experience in childhood with a nurturant mother to attain feminine and maternal characteristics; and an ineffectual father will be especially deleterious to a son who must overcome his initial identification with his mother by internalizing characteristics of a father. Although sharing of role tasks by parents has become necessary in most contemporary families and has led to some blurring of gender-linked roles, parents still need to maintain their gender roles and support one another in them.

Such consideration of the relationship between family structure and the integration of the children's personality opens a field that has scarcely been explored but holds much promise for advancing our understanding of human behavior and its deviations.

The Family as a Social System. The form and functions of the family evolve with the culture and subserve the needs of the society of which it is a subsystem. It is the first social system that the child knows and into which he grows, and from it he must gain familiarity with the basic roles as they are carried out in the society in which he lives: the roles of parents and child, of boy and girl, of man and women, of husband and wife, and how these roles impinge upon the broader society and how the roles of others impinge upon the family and its members. Although roles can be considered as units of a social system, they also become part of the personality through directing behavior to fit into roles and by giving cohesion to personality functioning. Individuals do not learn patterns of living entirely from scratch but in many situations learn roles and then modify them to the specific individual needs.

Within the family the child also learns about basic institutions and their values, such as the institutions of the family, marriage, extended family systems, institutions of economic exchange, etc.; and values are inculcated by identification, superego formation, teaching, and interaction. The wish to participate in or avoid participation in such institutions is a major motivating force and directive in personality development. It is the function of the family to transmit to the offspring the prescribed, permitted, and proscribed values of the society. The family value systems, role definitions, patterns of interrelating with one another, enter into the child through the family behavior far more than through what he is taught or even what is consciously appreciated by the parents.

The Family and Enculturation. The major techniques of adaptation that man requires are not inherited genetically as part of his physical make-up but are transmitted through the cultural heritage that is a filtrate of the collective experiences of his forebears. I am considering the process of enculturation separately from the process of socialization. It concerns that which is transmitted symbolically from generation to generation rather than through societal organizations, but there is obviously considerable overlap between these two processes.

Enculturation depends to a very great extent upon language, and one of the most crucial tasks of the family is to inculcate into its offspring a solid foundation in the language of the society, which includes its ways of categorizing experience, its system of meanings and its logic. After the first year of life the acquisition of almost all other instrumental techniques depends upon language; and cooperation with others, so critical to human adaptation, depends upon a shared system of meanings and values. Indeed, the capacity to direct the self depends upon having words with which one constructs an internalized symbolic version of the world which one can manipulate in imaginative trial and error before committing oneself to irrevocable action.

The topic has received increasing attention in antipoverty programs where it has become evident that cultural deprivation of the children is no less important than their economic and social deprivation. Many disadvantaged children cannot learn adequately in school because they have not acquired the wherewithal for abstract thinking and sufficient breadth of experience to reason adequately. Further, even when the stimulation in the family for learning language is adequate, the meanings and logic learned can be, and often are, aberrant. Schizophrenic disorders, for example, are increasingly being related to the patient having acquired a faulty foundation of reasoning and categorizing experiences because of the peculiar transactions in his parental home. Similarly, parents' use of language to gloss over transgressions and to maintain appearances may be an important element in the genesis of delinquency. Such problems merge into the family's task of inculcating the ethical values of the culture upon which much social collaboration rests.

THE FUTURE OF THE FAMILY

The recognition of the importance of the family as a unit to proper childrearing has particular importance at this time, because of the various pressure groups belittling the family —some seeking to rid society of this source of so much unhappiness, and others seeking to change it radically but with little awareness of the potential consequences. Segments of the New Left as well as some of the Women's Liberation Movement again embrace Engel's ideas that marriage is a bourgeois device to enslave women,[14] ignorant of or ignoring the devastating consequences of the Soviet attempts to weaken marital bonds and parental authority,[15] as well as disregarding the importance of marriage and the family in noncapitalist societies. Some youth would replace the family with group living, seeking togetherness without individual responsibility.

The liberating feminist advocates the abolition of differing roles for men and women, believing that fathers can nurture children as well as mothers. They deny women have any greater inherent maternal capacities, and neglect the maternal feelings that arise through pregnancy and giving birth to the infant. The elimination of gender-linked roles would also eliminate major directives to the child's personality development. Such practices could lead to an outcome that some feminists desire, one uniform intersex gender in which males and females were distinct only in anatomy, but perhaps also to the elimination of the difference that "makes the world go round." It is not clear why "feminist" movements seek to make women more masculine and less feminine. Harmonious family life, or group functioning in any form, is not fostered by members having identical or even similar roles and functions, but by the need of each for the reciprocal capabilities and qualities of the other that lessen rivalries and foster a unity.

Currently, too, some black militants refuse to consider the significance of the fatherless family to the problems of many inner-city black children, insisting that the notion that a child should have two parents is only a white, middle-class "hang-up." They ignore the fact that virtually all societies, regardless of race or whether literate or preliterate, have institutionalized nuclear families containing two parents; and they are not willing to examine how the matriarchal fatherless family has created serious difficulties for the children who grow up in them. The boy lacks a masculine figure with whom to identify, and rebels against the domination of the mother who often undermines her son's self-esteem by her lack of regard for males. The girl tends to learn that women are only sexual objects to men and has no childhood "love object" in a father to increase her self-esteem.

The family is, however, in difficulty. Its worth is doubted because it so often fails to carry out its primary functions adequately, neither fulfilling the needs of spouses nor producing properly integrated offspring. Some sources of its impaired capabilities are apparent. With the migrations and urbanization that have accompanied industrialization, the extended family has been disrupted.[16] Parents and their children are apt to live relatively isolated from kin, and numerous tasks that formerly were shared by relatives fall upon the parents alone. Parents raised in isolated units have little experience in rearing children, particularly when the mother has been raised and educated to pursue a career. Marriages now frequently cross ethnic, religious, and social class lines, and the parents who grew up with divergent customs, belief systems, and role allocations must fuse them into a new entity. Such family systems have not evolved over generations to assure continuity of the cultural pattern and raising children suited to life in the society. Indeed, whether or not a given family forms a suitable training ground rests largely upon the personalities of the two parents and how they fit together.

The scientific era has with increasing rapidity required changes in techniques of adaptation, and parents usually are more capable of raising children as they themselves were raised rather than for contemporary or future needs. Further, the reliance on science rather than tradition has undermined the unconscious assurance that the traditional ways and the traditional beliefs were correct guides to living. The parents, insecure in their own belief systems, and ignorant of many things that their children need to know, are less certain in directing their children's behavior, in setting limits for them, and in inculcating belief systems.

As it becomes clear that the family cannot be discarded and that the integrity of the society rests upon the foundation of the family, it is essential that means be found to provide support for the family and to augment it with institutions that can help it raise children suited for life in our rapidly changing world. Some of the cardinal tasks of the family can be shared by other institutions as has been demonstrated by the Israeli kibbutz. At present, efforts notably to improve child-rearing require attention to means of strengthening and modifying the family, and providing support for the parents more than continued emphasis upon techniques that primarily seek to foster maternal love and improve nurturant care.

Thus, the establishment of day care centers in suburbs as well as inner cities can serve as important means of relieving the mother of spending virtually all of her time caring for children by herself. They can provide places where mothers socialize with other mothers and learn about child care from trained workers, as well as permit some mothers to continue in their occupational or educational activities. Such centers are essential to overcoming some of the critical problems of the disorganized family of the inner city. In these families, as has now been amply documented, the mothers frequently lack the emotional stability and interest to rear children properly and are simply ignorant of adequate childrearing techniques. The lack of warm nurturance and the poverty of cognitive stimulation permanently cripples the child even prior to nursery school age. The idea that a mother should spend most of her time with her small children because they need love and maternal warmth to gain a sense of security is misplaced when the mother is incapable of providing such nurturance. Release from the confinement with small children and help with the unfamiliar responsibilities of child care would appreciably diminish women's dissatisfactions with their roles.

We can consider various other measures for supporting the family. The importance of the proximity of relatives should be given more weight in considering moves for economic and career opportunities. High schools and colleges need to supplement youths' inadequate preparation within the parental family for properly rearing the next generation. Male teachers in grade schools as well as male workers in day care centers could help offset the paucity of fathers in inner-city families. However, the first step in seeking to strengthen the family may well be increasing people's awareness of the central and critical importance of the family to the couple who marry, to the children they raise and to the continuity of a coherent society. It is important to counter ideas that the family has outlived its usefulness; that people can be truly content with less permanent relationships; that marriage serves only to legitimatize sex; or that children can be raised properly by the mother alone, or without parents. As we study the family's functions and how it carries them out, we begin to realize that we have neglected the influence of the family as a unit upon the child. We have sought to raise happier and emotionally healthier children by promoting natural childbirth, rooming-in, breast feeding, proper feeding techniques and bowel training, etc. Such measures have helped even though we sometimes have doubts of what has come of it all, but we have, at times, lost the forest for the trees. Perhaps it is so obvious that it has been taken for granted and then often forgotten—that who the parents are; how they behave; how they relate to one another; and what sort of a family they create, including the intangible atmosphere of the home—are what count most in the long run.

NOTES

1. T. Lidz, "Nightmares and the Combat Neuroses," *Psychiatry*, 9 (1946), 37–49.

2. Bradley Buell et al., *Community Planning for Human Services* (New York: Columbia University Press, 1952).

3. S. Minuchin et al., *Families of the Slums* (New York: Basic Books, 1967).

4. E. Pavenstedt ed., *The Drifters: Children of Disorganized Lower-Class Families* (Boston: Little, Brown, 1967).

5. *Ibid*, p. 249.

6. *Ibid*., p. 313.

7. B. Bernstein, "Language and Social Class," *British Journal of Sociology*, 11 (1960), 271–76; B. Bernstein "Social Class and Linguistic Development: A Theory of Social Learning," in *Education, Economy and Society*, A. Halsey, J. Floud, and C. Anderson, eds. (New York: Free Press of Glencoe, 1961) pp. 288–314.

8. H. Hendin, *Black Suicide* (New York: Basic Books, 1969).

9. H. Hendin, "Black Suicide," *Columbia Forum*, XII, 3, (Fall, 1969) 15.

10. T. Lidz, S. Fleck and A. Cornelison *Schizophrenia and the Family*, (New York: International University Press, 1965).

11. T. Lidz, *The Family and Human Adaptation* (New York: International University Press, 1963).

12. T. Lidz, "Psychoanalytic Theories of Development and Maldevelopment: Some Reconceptualizations" *American Journal Psychoanalysis*, 27 (1967), 115–26.

13. T. Parsons and R. Bales, *Family, Socialization and Interaction Process* (Glencoe, Ill.: Free Press, 1955).

14. F. Engel, *The Origins of the Family, Private Property and the State* (Chicago: Kerr, 1902).

15. N. Timasheff, *The Great Retreat* (New York: Dutton, 1946).

16. E. Bott, *Family and Social Network* (London: Tavistock, 1957).

ANNE ROE

WOMANPOWER: HOW IS IT DIFFERENT?

IF a separate chapter in this book, and many millions of words in other publications, are devoted to an examination of "womanpower" as distinct from "manpower," there is a very good reason for it: In this, as in almost every facet of life, sex differences are pervasive. The first question asked about a newborn child is always: "Is it a boy or a girl?" The answer is a good indication of the way the child will be treated by its parents, teachers, and peers, and of the numerous ways in which work will enter into its life.

My attempt in this chapter will be not only to review some of the many ways in which sex has affected and now affects working life in the United States, but also to offer some suggestions as to the causes, some reasonable and some ridiculous, for these differences. I cannot subscribe to the thesis of some of the current women's liberation movements that sex differentials are always oppressive to females and entirely due to a variety of selfish male motives. This does not, of course, deny that the whole situation should be examined in some depth. I shall not attempt, meantime, to discuss differences between white and nonwhite women. Although these are marked, it is generally true that in any way in which white women are disadvantaged, nonwhite women suffer more.

The evidence with regard to differences, whether discriminative or not, is very clear. At any one age working women do not comprise as large a percentage of the total working population as do men; and the pattern of their working lives is more often than not markedly different from that of men. There are great differences in the effect of marriage and children on their occupational lives, in the kinds of work they do, in the pay they receive, in the ease of entry into and advancement in occupations, in occupational group memberships and activities, and in numerous, often unnoticed, minor ways. In spite of all the recent legal provisions supposedly assuring women equal pay for equal work, it is clear that they are still not equal in most things.

Certainly there have been some improvements, and more were hoped for. Title VII of the Civil Rights Act of 1964, which is administered by the Equal Employment Opportunity Commission, prohibits discrimination in private employment based on sex, as well as on race, color, religion, and national origin.[1] In 1967, over one-third of the complaints heard by the commission were for sex discrimination.[2] Unfortunately, as this is written, we are in the throes of a serious economic situation; and as usual, women, minority members, and the young (although not necessarily in that order) have been the first and most affected in terms of unemployment, layoffs, and the other correlates of economic recession. Ginzberg's studies of well-educated women, published in 1966,[3] led him to state that they then had not only an increasing number of options, but that their options were increasing more rapidly than those of men. At the present time, this is probably not true, and even in the recent past it was not clear to what extent women were aware of and taking advantage of their options.

HOW MANY WOMEN WORK AND WHEN DO THEY WORK?

The latest comprehensive report on women's employment is the 1969 *Handbook on Women Workers* issued by the Women's Bureau of the U.S. Department of Labor, from which the following data are taken. In 1968 42 percent of all women of working age (16 and over) were in the labor force, as compared to 81 percent of men, with an additional 5.4 percent of men in the armed forces. In 1968, 37 percent of the labor force were women; in 1940 the figure was 25 percent, and in 1920, 20 percent. Except for a sharper and unsustained increase during World War II, and a slower rise in the mid 1950s, the increase has run about 2 percent per year. Only 1.2 percent of women and 2.2 percent of men were recorded as unable to work. This is a small difference in percentages, but it applies to about 839,000 women and 1.5 million men. Is this one way in which women are advantaged? They have fewer and later disabilities, along with a longer life span.

Not only has the percentage of working women changed; there have also been great changes in the percentages of married women working, of working mothers, and in the ages at which women are working. These changes are shown in Table 1. It should be added that there are also considerable age-related differences associated with marriage (and probably child-rearing) as shown in Table 2.

Interesting as are these statistics about participation by age, they have one serious shortcoming. We cannot tell from these data which of the women in the labor force in the early years are those that return to it later. A few suggestive stud-

TABLE 1

LABOR FORCE PARTICIPATION RATES OF WOMEN, BY AGE, SELECTED YEARS, 1940–68[a]

Age	*1968*	*1960*	*1950*	*1940*
Total	41.0	37.4	33.0	28.9
16 and 17	25.8	23.7	25.2	13.8
18 and 19	48.3	48.0	45.6	42.7
20–24	53.2	45.4	44.6	48.0
25–34	42.8	35.9	33.6	35.5
35–44	48.7	44.3	38.2	29.4
45–54	52.6	49.5	37.1	24.5
55–64	42.6	37.4	27.6	18.0
65 and over	9.5	10.8	9.7	6.9

Source: U.S. Department of Labor, *Handbook of Women Workers*, 1969.

[a]Data are for civilian noninstitutional population in March 1940 and in April of other years.

TABLE 2

LABOR FORCE PARTICIPATION RATES OF WOMEN AGED 16 AND OVER, BY MARITAL STATUS, SELECTED YEARS, 1940–67[a]

Marital status	*1967*	*1960*[b]	*1950*[b]	*1940*[b]
Total	39.7	34.8	31.4	27.4
Single	50.7	44.1	50.5	48.1
Married	37.8	31.7	24.8	16.7
Husband present	36.8	30.5	23.8	14.7
Husband absent	53.2	51.8	47.4	53.4
Widowed	27.0	29.8 }	36.0[c]	32.0
Divorced	71.2	71.6 }		

Source: See Table 1.

[a]Data are for March of each year.

[b]Surveys made prior to 1967 also included data for girls 14 and 15 years of age.

[c]Not reported separately in 1940 and 1950.

ies, such as those of Ginzberg et al,[4] Mulvey,[5] and Baruch,[6] have tried to examine development of individual careers over time among particular groups of women, but we need many more studies of this sort. Only through such studies, whether retrospective, or continuing, or of overlapping groups (such as Cooley [7]) will we be able to understand how adult lives develop. In contrast with the numbers of studies of development of infants, children, and adolescents, adults are almost "forgotten" men and women. That such studies would be revealing is clear. Thus, there have been some suggestions that women who return to the labor force after a period out for marriage and childbearing and for other than economic reasons, are more likely to be those whose earlier work experience was satisfying than otherwise.

In short, the pattern of women's working lives has changed drastically. Increasing numbers of women now follow a two-phase working life: working for a time when first finished with education, marrying and raising children, and then returning to work. (The working lives of single women are quite like those of men, entering the labor force when formal education is completed and remaining there until retirement.) Some attempts have been made to explain why these changes have come about, but there is much that has not been examined, let alone explained.

One important question arising out of these dramatic changes relates to the considerable lag between the development of the two-phase pattern of women's working lives, on the one hand, and concerted efforts on the part of industry, government, or education to adjust to this, on the other. A few changes have been made in industry and the professions, in terms of part-time work and changes in hours, and there has been a slight increase in daycare centers, but the adjustments have been ridiculously few. Education, except for a very few "continuing education" programs for women, has been equally backward despite the clear need for a systematic reconsideration of all aspects of the education of women. Why? Apathy, stupidity, resistance to change? One may hope that the general ferment in education will eventually precipitate a productive discussion of the issue of womens' education.

Nye and Hoffman have suggested that "new labor-saving machinery in the home and new inventions and distributive techniques in industry and trade which permitted the mother's economic tasks to be performed more efficiently outside the home; smaller families; and the spread of equalitarian family ideology" are among the social factors that have facilitated womens' participation in the labor force.[8] Doubtless all of these have had some influence, but there is still great pressure on women in favor of "Kinder and Küche" if not for "Kirchen," as any reader of popular magazines must note, and these pressures may be mirrored in the faulty accomodations of employers and educators.

Women are themselves very ambivalent about what they "should" be and do. The Kenistons remark that "definitions of family, conceptions of womanliness and images of work left over from an era when they were necessary for social survival and congruent with family functions have persisted into an era in which they are no longer viable," and that "most young women in this country still cherish the fantasy of a marriage that will totally and automatically fulfill all emotional and intellectual needs, a fantasy that sets the stage for collosal disappointment, guilt and self-castigation when, as increasingly happens, marriage alone is not enough."[9] They advise that more models of women who have satisfactorily combined work and marriage are needed.

In fact there is some scattered evidence that women whose mothers have accomplished this are more likely to be committed to do the same; as more and more women accomplish it, there will be more and more role models available. And, the Kenistons add, "Could we but make work more humane and challenging for men, asking less of their patience and more of their imagination, it would be less necessary for women to compensate for what is missing on the job by being positively 'feminine' in the home." [10]

Baruch, dissatisfied with such analyses as that of Nye and Hoffman, examined theories of the nature of women in detail, but found little that gave "an adequate basis for a theory of career development for women, or even a good rationale for the higher education of women." [11] She looked for more psychological interpretations through an examination of the achievement motive in women as it was related to age, family situation, education, and work. A sample of 137 Radcliffe graduates gave evidence of a suspension of striving for achievement, between the fifth and tenth year after college. On the level of fantasy, this motive returned in some women fifteen years out of college, although it may not yet have been acted upon, but by the time twenty years had elapsed since college, women with the highest achievement motive had returned to paid employment. Other studies have also found that women fifteen years after college were dissatisfied with the limitations of women's role activities and eager to resume careers.[12]

Baruch then examined a nationally representative sample of 763 women who had participated in a study conducted by the Survey Research Center.[13] For the college women in the sample the temporal pattern of achievement motive resembled somewhat that found in the Radcliffe sample, but not for women with other educational backgrounds. The major effect observed was the decline of achievement motive with age, particularly after 55.

When these studies failed to satisfy her fully, she turned to a consideration of the effect on women of the mass media and of old age insurance benefits. Her extensive analyses cannot be reported in detail, but her summary is as follows:

> The conclusions are only inferences but consistent with the data. The social security old age and retirement benefits are such as to encourage women to reenter the labor force and work to earn maximum coverage under this insurance plan. Achievement motivation seems to have less to do with the trend of changing patterns of employment in the population in general, although it is associated with strong career patterns in one highly selected sample of women, for whom the career is still often an achievement-relevant situation. For the majority of the population, women with high achievement motivation may have been persuaded by the mass media and advertising to seek gratification in women's role instead of in long-term career commitment outside the home. The data suggest that once achievement motivation has returned to regnancy, the seeking of careers some years later may follow. More time and longitudinal studies can provide answers which are less speculative than these last conclusions. The trend of more women entering paid employment, accruing old age insurance benefits, will very likely continue, as more women understand the benefits, and as the number of required quarters of employment increases. Whether success in woman's role will remain achievement relevant for large numbers of American women remains for the future to reveal.[14]

This summary is surely a provocative one and should suggest many further investigations.

MARRIAGE AND WORK

The proportion of working married women with and without children and with husbands present has shown an even sharper increase than that reported for women in general—from 30 percent in 1940 to 57 percent in 1967. I do not have corresponding figures for married men with wives present, but it seems reasonable to assume that most men who can be are in the labor force and that this has not changed in this period.

The effect of marriage on work experience is very different

for men and for women. With men, the fact of marriage has little relation to whether or not they are working, although it may sometimes affect what kinds of work they do or where they do it. Marriage, and particularly the presence of children, may be a major cause for moonlighting for men; but age, at least between the beginning of the work life and retirement, is relatively unimportant. The effect of marriage on work experience for women, however, is very different. The extent and nature of the effect varies with age and the presence of children. These are of course correlated, but the probability of a woman's working is influenced more by marital status than by age. Full details on these differences are readily available, and the statistics are in general about what one would expect, given some knowledge of current social situations.

Of more interest here is whether or not marriage has been a help or a hindrance in the work of women who work chiefly because they wish to, and not for purely or mainly economic reasons. These probably amount to about 20 percent of working women. Few studies have examined this question, and most of the data refer to well-educated women who had fairly well-defined career goals.

Bryan and Boring [15] compared 245 women Ph.D. psychologists with a matched group of 247 men. Some of their data are presented in Table 3. Only one hundred and thirty-nine (57 percent) of these women had married, of whom thirteen were divorced, and eleven widowed. Of the men, all but thirteen had married (95 percent), four had been divorced and one widowed. These data are particularly interesting because on the whole psychology has seemed in some ways to have offered women a rather better situation than other professions. (For example, women constitute about a third of the membership of the American Psychological Association, but are fewer than 3 percent in law and 7 percent in medicine.) From combining the two halves of Table 3, it

TABLE 3

EFFECT OF MARRIAGE ON PROFESSIONAL CAREERS OF MEN AND WOMEN

	Full-Time Employment		*Less than Full-Time Employment*	
Response	*married women*	*married men*	*married women*	*married men*
Indispensable factor in professional achievement	5.1	13.4	4.0	8.8
Definitely an asset	33.8	59.8	17.3	57.3
Advantages balanced disadvantages	15.2	6.7	16.0	5.9
Little or no effect	20.3	15.9	4.0	26.5
Made pursuit of career more difficult	27.0	6.1	31.9	1.5
Chief factor in the abandonment of career	—	—	23.9	—
Other	8.5	1.8	22.6	5.9
N	59	163	75	68

Source: A. I. Bryan and E. G. Boring, "Women in American Psychology: Factors Affecting Their Professional Careers," *American Psychologist,* 2 (1947), 3–20.

can be seen that 72 percent of the married men found marriage a professional asset, and only 5 percent found it a hindrance. But for the women, only 28 percent found it an asset, and 34 percent found it a hindrance or even a cause for abandoning a career. It is probably also true that the reason for the much greater percentages of women than of men in part-time employment is a conflict between marriage and career. As to satisfaction with professional work and other interests, 37.5 percent of the women but 51.1 percent of the men reported that professional work contributed more than anything else to their satisfactions.

The study by Ginzberg of 311 women who had pursued graduate study at Columbia included fewer who had never married (28 percent) but even this is very high; in the general population only about 6 percent of women remain unmarried, and most of those who married did so later than is usual. In this group also, only a third of the women had doctorates although about 9 percent more were well along, with only the thesis remaining.[16] It is not clear whether there were fewer married women among those with doctorates.

As to various satisfactions, these women seem to have found their greatest satisfactions in personal relations either at home, at work, or in volunteer activities, but paid employment and volunteer work offered the most in terms of self-realization. There is, however, no analysis of possible differences between the married and the unmarried in these respects.

Mulvey carried out a study of 475 women, aged thirty-seven to forty-seven, who were graduates of the public high schools of Providence, R.I., investigating by questionnaire their current level of adjustment and career orientation as productive or non-productive, their aspirations and satisfactions. Relatively few of them had higher education. She found high contentment to be associated with satisfaction with career pattern and job, particularly with the traditionally feminine jobs and/or active participation in volunteer activities. Low morale was associated with discontinuities in marital state, widowhood, divorce, low-level job, and little or no participation in volunteer activities. Finally, "the married state, unbroken and continuous, irrespective of family and/or employment status, is the greatest single contributor to the highest level of adjustment".[17]

Something, however, should be said about the option of marriage as it is available to women. Ginzberg et al. stated that "It was largely up to them (the women) to determine whether they wanted to marry, when and whom."[18] Surely men still have more freedom in this respect than women. It is probably true that many men are still reluctant to marry women who are openly intelligent and competent, but I suspect that this may be changing, among modern college youths at least. But this is an almost unstudied area, and one of considerable significance. It would be important to learn not only what men's attitudes are but also what women think they are. Women who prefer (non-defensively) not to marry are certainly in a very small minority. Since general attitudes towards marriage are changing with great rapidity, perhaps it should be put now that women who prefer not to have a close and reasonably enduring relationship with any man are in a small minority.

Certainly there are many unexamined issues about the relations among marriage, self-fulfillment, work, and other satisfactions in life. Although very great cultural changes in these respects are taking place, particularly among the young in our society, it is probable that a cultural lag will continue. There is a question as to whether or not research can keep up with the changes. By the time we learn more about the past it may have become not only irrelevant but also misleading for the future.

The issue of the effect on the children of working mothers is not touched on here. It is far from an unexamined issue, and there are excellent summaries available. No general statement can be made other than that it differs under different circumstances, but is by no means usually or even frequently deleterious. Rossi, in a comprehensive and thoughtful essay, has covered these issues fully.[19]

KINDS OF WORK

Although there have been some changes in the kinds of work which women do, these have been considerably less in extent and degree than the changes just discussed. Table 4 gives the major occupational groupings of employed women for 1940,

TABLE 4

MAJOR OCCUPATION GROUPS OF EMPLOYED WOMEN AGED 14 AND OVER, 1940, 1950 AND 1968[a]

	Percentage Distribution			*As Percent of Total Employed*		
Major Occupation Group	*1968*	*1950*	*1940*	*1968*	*1950*	*1940*
Total	100.0	100.0	100.0	36.6	29.3	25.9
Professional, technical workers	14.4	10.8	13.2	38.6	41.8	45.4
Managers, officials, proprietors (except farm)	4.3	5.5	3.8	15.7	14.8	11.7
Clerical workers	33.3	26.4	21.2	72.6	59.3	52.6
Sales workers	6.8	8.8	7.0	39.7	39.0	27.9
Craftsmen, foremen	1.1	1.1	.9	3.3	2.4	2.1
Operatives	14.8	18.7	18.4	29.9	26.9	25.7
Nonfarm laborers	.4	.4	.8	3.5	2.2	3.2
Private household workers	7.2	10.3	17.6	97.6	92.1	93.8
Service workers (except private household)	15.6	12.6	11.3	57.0	45.4	40.1
Farmers, farm managers	.3	1.5	[b]5.8	4.1	5.5	[b]8.0
Farm laborers, formen	1.7	3.9		28.0	27.4	

Source: See Table 1.
[a]Data are for April of each year.
[b]Not reported separately in 1940.

1950, and 1968. As percentages of total employed, women in professional and technical work have actually decreased in this period; there has been some rise at the managerial level, and a very large rise among clerical workers and service workers. Other changes seem to reflect primarily the general shift away from farms. Decrease in household workers in percentage of women so employed is noticeable, although one also notes that there has been a relatively greater decrease among men. Table 5 lists the occupations in which women were three-fourths or more of the total employed. About two-

TABLE 5

OCCUPATIONS IN WHICH WOMEN WERE THREE-FOURTHS OR MORE OF TOTAL EMPLOYED, 1960

Occupations with 100,000 or More Women	*Occupations with Fewer than 100,000 Women*
90 Percent or More	
Housekeepers (private household)	Nurses (student)
Nurses (professional)	Laundresses (private household)
Receptionists	Attendants (physicians' and dentists' offices)
Babysitters	Dietitians and nutritionists
Chambermaids and maids (except private household)	Demonstrators
Secretaries	Milliners
Dressmakers and seamstresses (except factory)	Boarding and lodging
Private household workers (not elsewhere classified)	
Telephone operators	
Stenographers	
Practical nurses	
Typists	
Sewers and stitchers (mfg.)	
80 to 89 Percent	
Hairdressers and cosmetologists	Boarding and lodging
Waitresses	Librarians
Teachers (elementary school)	
File clerks	
Bookkeepers	
Housekeepers and stewardesses (except private household)	
75 to 79 Percent	
Cashiers	Spinners (textile)
Operatives (apparel and accessories)	Dancers and dancing teachers
	Attendants and assistants (library)
	Operatives (knitting mills)
	Midwives

Source: See Table 1.

fifths of these were white-collar (secretaries, retail sales) about one-fourth were manual, and the remainder were service occupations.

Is this sort of occupational distribution entirely irrational? (Discussion of this point is hampered by the limited census categories, which obscure some important difference.) Here one must consider the questions not only of women's competencies but also of their interests and values.

There has been a good deal of research on sex differences, and there is really very little argument about their nature and extent. The degree to which they are biological or cultural is still argued, and this is of some importance in this context. We are beginning to appreciate the intimate interrelationship between genetic potential and experience in the ultimate expression of that potential. If, for example, society needs more persons with mechanical skills and interests, and development of these is more strongly affected by early experience than by sex-linked genetic endowment, a solution seems obvious. So far, however, no social group has given any evidence of enough foresight to make use of such information even if it were available. It may be just as well. In getting more mechanics, e.g., we might lose some other interests of greater importance. The results of tampering with limited aspects of the environment have had too many unforeseen and appalling results.

Mean differences have been demonstrated in many intellectual abilities but their significance for us is reduced by the fact that overlap of distributions is almost complete. In fact, females at almost all ages, including doctorate holders, have somewhat greater verbal abilities than their male counterparts.[20] Differences in temperament, interests, and values are probably of more importance, and here there seems to be considerably less overlap. The most relevant of these for this discussion are such differences as the generally broader and deeper interests of women in persons and the generally higher interests of men in scientific and mechanical activities; the considerably lesser aggressive drives and the greater dependency in women, and the very different pattern of values. Such differences have been prevalent in our society for a long time. Campbell [21] and Campbell and Soliman,[22] for example, have reported a number of studies of changes in patterns of interest over time in different occupational groups, as well as what seem to be general cultural changes. These suggest a shift to more emphasis on interpersonal interactions and verbal activities and away from blue-collar and outdoor activities, but discussion of these provocative studies would take us too far afield.

In a recent conversation, L.S.B. Leakey reported that Dian Fosse is now achieving with wild gorillas the kind of study that Jane Goodall did with chimpanzees. Both women have not only made extensive close and continuing observations, but have been able to make physical contact with the animals in grooming and being groomed. Dr. Leakey believes that this would be impossible for any man to achieve—apparently none has—and also that women are better observers than men. This reminded me that many years ago, the Director of the Sydney Zoo told me that during the war they had necessarily engaged women keepers, and that since then they had continued to do so, because the women turned out to be much better than men with the small mammals in particular —they mothered them.

Given the fact that these *average* differences between men and women do exist, the sex balance in the occupational structure reflects them with some accuracy. In fact, some of the latest changes in the occupational structure seem to reflect more change in men's interests than in women's. For example, women were in the majority among secondary school teachers in 1950, but now constitute less than half of them.

There has also been a decline in the proportion of women among teachers at the college and university level but this reflects a decline of women professionals rather than a change in men's interests.

These average differences are, of course, just that—average differences. There are men whose abilities, interests, and values are in some respects more like women's than like most other men's; and the reverse is also true. However, men who go into nursing, social work, elementary school teaching, enter and advance in these fields with comparative ease. But women with strong scientific and mechanical interests and high executive ability do not enter appropriate fields easily, if at all, and they do not advance easily. The position of women in medicine and to a somewhat lesser extent in law, is particularly anomalous. Nurturance, caring for persons, which is so characteristic of the lives of women, and of their interests generally should find expression in law and in medicine as well as in nursing, and some other modern societies do not restrain them so greatly in these fields. (For example, in the USSR there are more women physicians than men.) Why does ours? Do the American Bar Association and the American Medical Association have an answer?

There is one group of women who are working, in any meaningful sense of the word, but who probably do not get into the census counts, because most of them do not receive regular wages or salary. These are the wives who assist their husbands on a more or less regular basis. They include women working at professional levels as assistants to professional husbands, watching experiments, cataloguing data, etc., as well as the wives of men running small businesses from their homes, such as electricians and builders, who answer the phone, keep the books, send out the bills. So far as I know they remain unstudied, but their contributions may well be essential to their husbands' work, and they deserve some sort of public recognition, if only in the census figures!

WORK HISTORIES

It now remains to take a look at what happens to women in the attempt to get a job, on the job after they are in it, and the kinds of group recognition that may come to them. To sum up briefly, women are disadvantaged in the first place in getting a job, in any situation for which both men and women are equally qualified. Except in a relatively few instances (federal civil service employment, some industries under union pressures, etc.) women are paid less for the same work than men. They advance less rapidly, if at all. Fewer of them belong to unions or professional associations, and in these they do not hold offices or policy-making positions proportional to their memberships.

To look at entry jobs, some of the most striking data come from information about college graduates, men and women who have presumably received at least approximately the same training. Expected salaries for June 1970 college graduates by sex and selected fields are shown in Table 6. Offers to women are notably lower, and oddly enough, most firms seem to prefer to hire a man at the higher salary. Of course some companies argue that women are not expected to stay as long in the job and therefore are a poor investment because of the cost of in-service training. For some positions there is some sense to the argument, but for many others it is irrelevant. Few companies have kept sufficiently accurate records to be sure, or looked at them if they have them. It is also very likely the case that women who are well-treated, even if they take a few years out for childbearing, are more likely to return to work, and to the same firms than other women, another point that needs more research.

There is further information in a paper by Fidell.[23] She sent one of two forms describing the professional behavior of

TABLE 6

EXPECTED SALARIES FOR JUNE 1970
COLLEGE GRADUATES,
BY SEX AND SELECTED FIELD

	Average Monthly Salary	
Field	*women*	*men*
Accounting	$746	$832
Chemistry	765	806
Economics, finance	700	718
Engineering	844	872
Liberal arts	631	688
Mathematics, statistics	746	773

Source: U.S. Department of Labor, *Fact Sheet on the Earnings Gap* (Washington: Women's Bureau, 1970.)

ten young Ph.D. psychologists to chairmen of 228 colleges and universities offering graduate degrees in psychology. The chairmen were asked to indicate the desirability of the candidate described in each paragraph on a scale from "totally unacceptable" to "highly desirable" and to indicate at what level the candidate should be offered a position, and then to rank order the ten. The paragraphs were carefully drawn to cover different degrees of relevant variables. The forms differed only in that feminine first names and pronouns were attached to four paragraphs on Form A and to a different four paragraphs on Form B. Sixty-eight percent of the forms were returned. Although the difference was not statistically significant, less desirable mean ratings were made for six of the eight comparison paragraphs when the description applied to women; higher levels of employment were indicated for males on all but one paragraph and the paragraphs describing men had a slightly higher mean rank order than these supposedly describing women.

Once at work, the salary and advancement differentials continue. They vary with kind of work, as seen in Table 7,

TABLE 7

MEDIAN WAGE OR SALARY INCOME
OF FULL-TIME YEAR-ROUND WORKERS, BY SEX AND SELECTED
MAJOR OCCUPATION GROUP, 1968

	Median Wage or Salary Income		
Major Occupation Group	women	men	*Median Wage or Salary Income as Percent of Men's*
Professional and technical workers	$6,691	$10,151	65.9
Nonfarm managers, officials, and proprietors	5,635	10,340	54.5
Clerical workers	4,789	7,351	65.1
Sales workers	3,461	8,549	40.5
Operatives	3,991	6,738	59.2
Service workers (except private household)	3,332	6,058	55.0

Source: See Table 6.

and the distributions of earnings by earnings intervals also differ. Sixty percent of the women, but only 20 percent of the men, earned less than $5,000 in 1968; 3 percent of the women, but 28 percent of the men, earned more than $10,000. Much, but by no means all, of these differences indicate that women are more likely than men to be employed in low-skilled, low-paying jobs. Part of this is the advancement problem, but in most occupations at the same jobs men are better paid. This is true from the professional level to the unskilled level. For college professors, there is a difference of over $1,100 in favor of the men; the weekly salary differential between the earnings of women and men class A accounting clerks ranged from $2.00 to $45.50. The greatest gap of all is for sales workers, where women earn only 40 percent of what men earn. These gaps have not been decreasing over time. In 1955 the median wage or salary incomes of women who worked full-time year-round was 63.9 percent of men's; in 1966 it was 58.0 percent.

In the sciences there have been a number of analyses of these differences. I have taken data from the National Science Foundation's *Summary of American Science Manpower* (1968), which does not give breakdowns by sex, and combined it with data from a forthcoming report which were kindly supplied me by Milton Levine. These do not give figures for men and women separately, but for all scientists in each group and for women, which, of course, dilutes the difference. These are given as medians. Assuming that the medians are roughly equivalent to means in these groups (a risky assumption in view of the probable differences in distributions, but these would just increase the differences shown in the table) I have computed Table 8 for fields of science having over 1,000 women reporting.

TABLE 8

COMPARISON OF MEAN SALARIES FOR MALE AND FEMALE SCIENTISTS IN FIELDS WITH MORE THAN 1,000 WOMEN

	N		*Mean Salary*		
Field	*male*	*female*	*male*	*female*	*Difference*
Chemistry	86,302	7,486	13,867	9,000	4,867
Biology	40,276	5,907	13,456	9,900	3,556
Psychology	17,758	5,319	13,709	11,500	2,209
Mathematics	21,741	2,736	13,453	9,400	4,053
Sociology	5,171	1,467	12,567	10,000	2,567

Source: National Science Foundation, *Summary of American Science Manpower, 1968* (Washington: National Register of Scientific and Technical Personnel, 1970); other data supplied by Milton Levine.

To some extent, these mean differences reflect the generally lower rank of women, but within the same rank women are paid less. Why?

The evidence on rank is as consistent as that on salaries. Women do not achieve the rank that men do as often or as soon, and this is true in industry, in government service, in universities, wherever the issue has been studied. Only a few studies will be mentioned. There has been some increase in the percentage of women in the federal civil service in higher level positions, but this in only a beginning.

A report published by the National Academy of Sciences, after an analysis of the careers of women Ph.D.'s, concludes, "Women progress less rapidly up the academic ladder than do men and receive less support for research than do men. Many more of them depend on a single source of support. They do correspondingly less research and much more teaching than do men, even in nonacademic positions. Salaries received by married women are in general about 70 percent to 75 percent of those received by men at the same time interval after receipt of the doctorate. Salaries of single women are more variable, but on the average they are somewhat higher than those of the married women though still markedly lower than men's salaries." [24]

Rossi found that women in academic sociology departments are more likely to teach undergraduate courses, to hold part-time positions, and to hold fewer positions at advanced levels or at prestigious institutions.[25]

Harvard has begun looking into this situation, and a preliminary report is shown in Table 9. None of the few women who are Associate or Full Professors is in the faculty of Arts and Sciences; some are in the Graduate School of Education and some in the Medical School. Harvard and Radcliffe undergraduate schools are thoroughly integrated and all the graduate schools admit women; in the Graduate School of Arts and Sciences about one-fourth of the students admitted in 1968–69 were women.

Studies of social workers and engineers [26] reflected the same situation: Among social workers, the men (relatively latecomers to the field and not in the majority) went into administrative posts earlier and more often; among engineers, the women said without exception that you had to be better than a man to get as good a job, and even then you might not get it.

TABLE 9

HARVARD UNIVERSITY OFFICERS, 1968–69

Title	*Total*	*Women*	*Percent Women*
Corporation	5	0	0.0
Board of Overseers	30	0	0.0
Regular faculty			
University professors	5	0	0.0
Full professors	580	3	0.5
Associate professors	151	8	5.3
Assistant professors	401	17	4.2
Research professors and assistant research professors	3	0	0.0
Clinical professors, associate and assistant clinical professors and clinical associates	357	17	4.8
Lecturers	406	50	12.3
Visiting faculty	158	9	5.7
Associates	235	24	10.2
Instructors	791	69	8.7
Tutors	75	4	5.3
Teaching fellows	1296	205	15.8
Research associates, fellows and assistants	1530	244	15.9
Totals	6023	650	10.7

Source: Harvard University Gazette, 65, 32 (1970), 2.

I have given some emphasis to the situation of professional women because so many of the various reasons advanced for these differences, when any are offered, simply do not hold. Married or single, these women are as committed to their work as their male counterparts.

So far as I can find, there has been no general examination of the numbers of women in elective or appointive policy-making positions in unions or professional organizations. I have secured a few data from labor unions with large percentages of women members (personal communications). I offer some of this information in Table 10, which suggests that it would be of considerable interest to collect similar data from many unions. Several of the union research directors suggested that there are so few women in the governance structure because there are relatively few women who could or wish to meet the extreme demands of extended travel and near total absorption required in the work of the upper level officials. This could well be true, especially for those with children, but there are many unmarried women to whom this consideration is probably irrelevant.

The same situation apparently holds in most professional organizations. When women do attain recognition, it is usually as secretaries, not as presidents, editors, committee chairmen, or others of the most prestigious positions. I can attest from my own rather considerable experience with psychological organizations that women, married or single, are as hard-working, dependable, and reasonable in general as men.

What one would most like to know is how many women would like to hold executive positions in these organizations. It has been made very evident in psychology, for example, that women resent the current situation strongly. One rebuttal is that to a considerable extent professionwide visibility depends upon publications.

Some comment must be made about the research and publication issue. In many universities the "publish or perish" edict rules (sometimes only when convenient). Apart from this issue in universities, publication is a major item in achieving the kind of intraprofessional visibility that leads to election to positions in professional societies. Do women publish fewer, or less competent papers than men do? There are very few data on this, and some suggestion that it is true only at higher academic ranks. It should be examined more carefully—not only in terms of research publications, but also in terms of patents granted in proportion to the women working in such fields, and in administrative innovations, etc. The

TABLE 10

PARTICIPATION OF WOMEN IN UNION ACTIVITIES, 1966

Union	Approx. No. of Women	Percent Women	Officers and Board Members: men	Officers and Board Members: women	Comments
ILGWU	364,000	80	22	1	Women admitted from start in 1900. Many women hold elective or appointive positions. Most shop chairmen and local union officers and business agents are women. Women head 121 of 465 locals (26%). Equal pay for equal work taken for granted; rates established regardless of sex. No differences in benefits.
CWA	177,000	55		0	Some locals all-male or all-female, but over-all on local level 40–50% women officers in elected positions. In mixed locals usual to have 1 or 2 women, although rarely as president.
RCIA	300,000	50		0	First vice-pres. a woman. Many thousands of women are executive officers of local unions, delegates to conventions and shop stewards. Women field representatives employed both for International Union and locals.
HRE	202,500	45	13	2	Founded 1891; first waitresses local 1900; equal wage rates 1937. All-women locals have all women executives. Mixed locals have many women officers. Have had paid women organizers for many years.

IBEW	300,000	30	Founded 1891; women admitted in 1892; in 1896 their second paid organizer a women. Constitution guarantees equal rights for women and contract agreements require equal pay. Women receive some special benefits such as maternity leave.
SEIU	97,580	28	Founded 1921, women admitted from beginning and one of charter signers a woman who later became an International Trustee. Negotiations carried on by local unions only; attempts to negotiate equal pay have had varying success.

Source: Data from U.S. Department of Labor, and personal communications from union headquarters.

matter of publications raises the general issue of differences in creative production.

An interesting sidelight—in the past lists of references generally gave the full first name of a woman author, but only initials of male authors. Why? Some publication manuals, and some publishers have now dropped this practice e.g., this was the rule given in the APA publication manual for 1957, but the 1967 revision prescribes initials only for both. Although a cursory examination of a number of recent books suggests that most publishers now treat both the same, apparently New York University Press does not and dissertations at Harvard follow the old style.

WOMEN AND CREATIVITY

Creativity is an area in which almost everything remains to be done. In all the spate of researches on this subject in recent years, there has been very little on sex differences.[27] In all fields, there have been fewer contributions from women than from men, although women among the artists and writers have merited and achieved recognition in higher proportions than among scientists. Are there any other reasons for the lesser number of contributions of women and the differences among fields? Certainly the whole pattern of Western culture has discouraged, and still discourages women here, if only because it has so fully discouraged their intensive involvement in anything outside the home.

Creative men are more like women in some respects than are other men chiefly, perhaps, in having greater sensitivity than the average man. Creative women are more like men in some respects, chiefly in higher autonomy, self-sufficiency, and greater reserve and coolness in interpersonal relations. Taylor and Barron list thirteen traits deliniating the productive scientist, and most of these have a more "masculine" tone to them than "feminine," although in intelligence and ego strength, for example, there seem to be no differences.[28] Since, however, we do not know whether or to what extent these characteristics are genetically or culturally controlled, we cannot ascribe the paucity of creative women to genetic factors. Even if we could, the distribution of such traits is so wide that there are clearly more women (and doubtless more men) who could be creative on that basis than are presently demonstrating it. Apart from that, it is probable that a major factor is the degree to which the productive artist or scientist is involved with the work, and the need for long periods of uninterrupted time to pursue it. In both of these aspects a woman may be seriously disadvantaged in such pursuits if she is married, and indeed almost certainly is if she has children.

Whether, in the long run, the combination of the satisfactions of marriage and children plus such professional satisfactions as may be achieved in spite of them outweigh for women the professional satisfactions which might be attained with less divided attention is surely an individual matter. For any individual, man or woman, there is also the matter of the balance of work with "fun" and other aspects of life. As to what counts as "fun," the sexes seem to be agreed. I may cite two eminent lyricists as authorities: Dorothy Parker, "And I think if my memory serve me, there was nothing more fun than a man"; and Oscar Hammerstein, "There is nothing like a dame." A psychologist might note that although the sentiments are similar, there are dissimilarities in succinctness and tone which may be suggestive of certain sex differences.

Surely we have now reached the stage at which it is no longer necessary to prove that some women can do most things that men can do and vice versa. Let us shift our goals to ignoring sex where it is irrelevant and even more important, to learning more about sex differences that are relevant and how to use them.

NOTES

1. U.S. Department of Labor, Laws on Sex Discrimination in Employment. Federal Civil Rights Act, Title VII; State Fair Employment Practices Laws; Executive Orders. Women's Bureau Wage and Labor Standards Administration (Washington: 1970).

2. A. Rossi, "Job Discrimination," *Atlantic Monthly*, (March 1970), pp. 99–102.

3. E. Ginzberg and Associates, *Life Styles of Educated Women* (New York: Columbia University Press, 1966).

4. *Ibid.*

5. M. C. Mulvey, *Psychological and Sociological Factors in Prediction of Career Patterns of Women* (Cambridge: Harvard University, Graduate School of Education, Ed.D. dissertation, 1961).

6. R. W. Baruch, *The Achievement Motive in Women: A study of the Implications For Career Development* (Cambridge: Harvard University, Graduate School of Education, Ed.D. dissertation, 1966); *The Interruption and Resumption of Women's Careers,* Harvard Studies in Career Development No. 50 (Cambridge: Harvard University, Graduate School of Education, 1966).

7. W. W. Cooley, *Career Development of Scientists: An Overlapping Longitudinal Study,* Cooperative Research Project No. 436, Office of Education, U. S. Dept. of Health, Education and Welfare (Cambridge: Harvard University Graduate School of Education, 1963).

8. F. I. Nye and L. W. Hoffman, "The Socio-Cultural Setting" in F. I. Nye and L. W. Hoffman, *The Employed Mother in America* (Chicago: Rand, McNally, 1963).

9. E. Keniston and K. Keniston, "An American Anachronism: The Image of Women and Work," *American Scholar*, 33 (1964), 355–75.

10. *Ibid.*

11. Baruch, *The Achievement Motive in Women,* p. 1.

12. U. S. Department of Labor, *Fifteen Years After College: A Study of Alumnae of the Class of 1945*, Women's Bureau Bulletin 283 (Washington: 1962); Betty Friedan, *The Feminine Mystique* (New York: Dell, 1963); M. Dawson, *Graduate and Married* (Syd-

ney: The Department of Adult Education in the University of Sydney, 1965); "The Minnesota Plan for the Continuing Education of Women," *University of Minnesota Newsletter* (February 1963).

13. G. Gurin, J. Veroff and S. Feld, *Americans View Their Mental Health* (New York: Basic Books, 1960).

14. Baruch, *The Achievement Motive in Women,* p. 182.

15. A. I. Bryan and E. G. Boring, "Women in American Psychology: Factors Affecting Their Professional Careers" *American Psychologist* (1947), No. 2, pp. 3–20.

16. Ginzberg, *Life Styles of Educated Women.*

17. Mulvey, *Psychological and Sociological Factors.*

18. Ginzberg, *Life Styles of Educated Women.*

19. A. Rossi, "Equality Between the Sexes: An Immodest Proposal" *Daedalus,* 93 (1964), 607–52.

20. National Research Council, *Careers of Ph.D.'s: Career Patterns Report Number* 2. (Washington: National Academy of Sciences, 1968).

21. D. P. Campbell, "Stability of Interests Within an Occupation Over Thirty Years," *Journal of Applied Psychology* (1966), pp. 50, 51–56.

22. D. P. Campbell and A. M. Soliman, "The Vocational Interests of Women in Psychology: 1942–1966," *American Psychologist,* 23 (1968), 158–63.

23. L. S. Fidell, "Empirical Verification of Sex Discrimination in Hiring Practices," Paper read at the meeting of the California State Psychological Association, January, 1970.

24. National Research Council, *Careers of Ph.D's,* p. 98.

25. A. Rossi, "Status of Women in Graduate Departments of Sociology: 1968–69," *American Journal of Sociology,* (1970) , 75, pp. 1–12.

26. A. Roe and M. Siegelman, *The Origin of Interests.* APGA Inquiry Studies No. 1 (Washington: American Personnel and Guidance Association, 1964).

27. See, for example, C. W. Taylor and F. Barron, eds., *Scientific Creativity: Its Recognition and Development* (New York: Wiley, 1963); H. J. Walberg, "Physics, Femininity, and Creativity," *Developmental Psychology,* 1 (1969), 47–54; R. B. Catell and H. W. Eber, *Supplement of Norms for Forms A and B of the Sixteen Personality Factor Questionnaire* (Champaign, [1]: Institute

for Personality and Ability Testing, 1964); Institute for Personality and Ability Testing, "Data for Psychologists Selecting Students for Creativity and Research Potential," Information Bulletin #10, 1963.

28. Taylor and Barron, pp. 385–86.

RALPH W. TYLER

MORE EFFECTIVE EDUCATION FOR THE PROFESSIONS

THE increasing complexity of our modern industrial society, the burgeoning demand for professional services, such as medicine, law, nursing, and engineering, and the rapidly growing knowledge relevant to these professions, are exerting strong contradictory pressures on professional schools. Many within their faculties are urging that the initial preparation be lengthened and involve greater specialization. Others in the faculties plead for interdisciplinary training and the development of a program designed to educate general practitioners. From the interested public comes demands for educating larger numbers, shortening the time of initial preparation and developing programs designed to educate professionals to meet the needs of the people who have not been served in the past. As these conflicting demands are being made, the professional schools are also experiencing increased difficulties in financing their current operations.

Clearly, this is a time for re-examination of objectives in professional education and of the effectiveness and efficiency of the means by which professional manpower needs are being met.

The educational objectives of a professional program are commonly assumed to be the development on the part of the student of the knowledge, skills, and attitudes required for him to perform the professional tasks in which he will be engaged. But in times of rapid social change the demands on the profession are also changing, so that a student who is prepared to perform the tasks of the past is not equipped to deal with some of the major ones he encounters on graduation. For example, most medical services in the past have been furnished to middle-class patients who suffered acute illnesses. Most of them were able to get well if the infection in their bodies were reduced or eliminated, or if an offending organ were removed.

Now a much larger proportion of potential patients are from working classes and many more suffer from chronic rather than acute diseases. Often their diet, their personal regimen, their anxieties over the financial problems created by their inability to work complicate their illness; many do not respond to the treatment. To help these patients secure and maintain health, the physician needs new procedures. Lawyers, too, find the practices appropriate for counseling clients who are business executives are not adequate to aid poor people who seek protection from unjust attacks upon their persons or property. Engineers trained to design specific mechanical or electrical systems for industry or commerce find new problems when asked to design devices to reduce health hazards and increase individual controls in homes and community centers for the poor.

Educational objectives are not only influenced by new tasks but also by the organizational structure (delivery system) in which the tasks are performed. The role of the physician differs when his services are delivered from an office to which the patient comes, when delivered in the supporting context of a hospital for acute diseases, when delivered in a community health center, or in some other structure. His role is not the same when his working team includes only a nurse and a record clerk as when he is part of a much larger and more complex organization. Similar differences in organizational structures are developing in other professions. Learning to operate in these different contexts is part of the education of the professional, a part which has rarely been given explicit attention.

The central tasks of a profession are not performed by routine practice of accepted procedures. The problems the professional is expected to solve are complex and involve variations in conditions that make specific rules too rigid to be effective. The professional is presumed to operate on the basis of artistic adaptations of general principles relevant to the problem faced. In the case of medicine, principles developed by anatomists, physiologists, biochemists, and clinical researchers have served to guide the physician in his understanding of the medical problems encountered and in the treatment he devises. With the development of new roles for the physician, there is also need to review all the possibly relevant fields of scholarship to identify concepts and principles from whatever discipline they may have been formulated that can help the physician understand his problems more fully and guide his designing of treatments. The so-called basic sciences of medicine may not be the same as those in the past when problems and roles are changing. The same need for reviewing basic principles is found in the other professions. These reviews are necessary in identifying the knowledge resources on which to build education for a profession.

A careful examination of the organizational structure in which the professional operates usually indicates that the educational goal of producing "the professional" is unrealistic.

There is division of labor in most professions such that persons with different interests and abilities are effectively contributing to the work. In the past professional schools have often talked about "the ideal physician" or teacher or lawyer or nurse or engineer, who represented the model the school sought to produce. Often the faculty analyzed this "ideal practitioner," listing the competencies attributed to him. This list then became their educational objectives. It is clear now that most professions have become so complex that delivery systems have been developed utilizing a variety of persons working together to perform the complete functions of the profession.

In such cases, it is necessary for the professional school to analyze the several roles performed by different individuals and to consider how to devise educational programs that will prepare each one. The question should also be raised as to the extent to which it is feasible to prepare an individual to perform several or all of these roles. This feasibility seems to be dependent upon: (1) the adaptability and breadth of preparation of the potential students: (2) the overlapping of training requirements for the different roles: and (3) the time needed to prepare a student for several roles. In essence, the question is, "Can the students that we have or could get acquire the knowledge, skills, and attitudes for several of these roles within the time limits that an efficient educational program will allow?" It is likely that there will be few cases where individuals can expect to learn what is required for performing all the tasks of the profession. Hence, several different occupational programs will need to be designed. In nursing, for example, it has been proposed that differentiated programs be provided for those preparing for acute clinical nursing, for those preparing for the nursing of chronic and long-term illnesses—and that additional education be developed for those who take responsibility for intensive care cases, for nursing service administration, and for nursing education. This illustrates the desirability of identifying different roles that can productively employ persons with different interests and abilities and then to design appropriate educational programs.

The mention of the differences in interests and abilities of students leads to a further comment. The day when every profession could fish for the most talented young people from a large pool of human resources has largely passed. The demand for professionals has increased tenfold in the past fifty years. Instead of searching for a very small number of candidates most of the professions now need to recruit a very much larger number. Furthermore, other occupations have gained attractiveness to young people. The recruiting task for some fields is not to set highly restrictive criteria that will admit only a few, but to identify among young people promising capabilities of many sorts and to design educational programs that can build on these talents.

Formulating educational objectives for a professional program involves not only what is to be taught to whom, but also when. Part of the reason for assigning a long period of time to the initial period of professional education was the desire to see that the student was fully prepared before he embarked upon his career. This effort utilizes a considerable amount of time in what the psychologist calls "overlearning," that is, carrying the learning and practice exercises to the point where very little forgetting or other learning losses are likely to occur. A more efficient use of time carries the learner through a phase at a time and as soon as he demonstrates initial competence in the performance of that phase, he is employed in work where this can be practiced as a regular part of his professional activity until he is a master of what he has learned. Then he engages in the next phase of his professional education. By distributing the learning periods throughout his professional life and capitalizing on special learning environments furnished both by the work situation and the environment of the school, professional education can be both more effective and more efficient. Furthermore, a larger part of the student's learning time is also contributing needed services to the profession.

The re-examination of the question of when a student should learn to be a professional leads to a review of what is becoming known about student learning in a professional school, knowledge that has important potential for increasing the efficiency of education. A typical layman's view of an ideal learning situation for a university student is that of Mark Hopkins on one end of a log and a student on the other. This notion is not well supported by research studies of learning in professional schools. Hughes, Becker, and Greer's study of a medical school called *Boys in White* gave quite a different picture. The faculty members appeared to have little knowledge of the total demands made on students in their various lesson assignments. The students, faced by what seemed to them to be an impossibly heavy load, decided what was important to do, and what was not, how much to do, and how much time to spend on their various courses. The student peer group became the source of decisions about educational objectives and the amount of time to be used in learning efforts. The lack of coordinated faculty planning of the actual learning experiences that students will find helpful in achieving objectives makes the typical professional program a collection of unrelated and often ineffective assignments. Most professional school faculties have not utilized what is known about the general nature of human learning in the planning and conduct of the educational program.

Conscious human learning can be briefly described as follows. One observes the behavior of a person or persons that appears attractive and he seeks to emulate it. The term "behavior" is used here in the psychological sense to include ways of thinking, feeling, and acting. If his efforts to practice this behavior seem to him to be successful, he gains satisfaction from it. He continues to practice until it becomes part of his repertoire, on which he draws in situations in which he thinks it appropriate. This simplified description can be analyzed into several phases or conditions for effective learning. The first is *motivation,* that is, a desire or urge to acquire some behavior that he has not previously carried on. The second is *perception of the behavior he wishes to acquire* that will guide his efforts to practice it. The third is the *actual effort to carry on the behavior*. The fourth is a *reward system* that enables him to gain satisfaction when he carries on the behavior successfully and informs him when he has not done so. Another helpful condition is a "*feedback system*" that helps him perceive the respects in which his effort was unsuccessful in order to guide further attempts to acquire the behavior. He also needs opportunities for sufficient practice of the behavior for it to be within his power to use it when he wishes. In professional programs, practice is commonly furnished as he engages in the work of the profession as well as practice provided within the school program.

In the acquisition of highly complex behavior such as problem-solving or difficult surgical skills, a hierarchy of behavior may need to be devised such that the initial understanding and skills are simple enough for the beginner to carry out, and each subsequent phase or step builds on the preceding knowledge and skills until the student can carry out relatively complex and difficult behavior patterns.

These several conditions are widely recognized, but they are rarely used to guide systematic planning of programs for the education of professional personnel. This may be due partly to the fact that many students have been able to establish these conditions for learning as they went on with their training in the professional schools. Some students perceive what are essential skills to learn and helpful knowledge to employ in their work even though their lectures, textbooks, laboratory exercises, and other school activities are not selectively focused in these terms. Then, too, some students complete the requirements of the faculty by doing the assignments but without actually acquiring the essential intellectual, emotional, and physical equipment required for professional work. Some students drop out or fail, but rarely are these cases perceived by the faculty as a failure of the educational program but rather they are treated as errors made in selecting a "poor student."

Reviewing the programs of many professional schools in the United States, one can identify certain conditions for learning that are generally met and others that seem to be neglected. Most professional students have sufficient motivation that they will make efforts to learn. However, in many programs, the student is not clear about what behaviors he needs to carry on to be a competent professional. In engineering, the freshman student often spends most of his first year in courses taught by mathematicians and scientists. He sees something of what they do, but he observes few engineers closely enough to see what they do, and particularly to distinguish what an engineer does with mathematics or physics in contrast to what a mathematician or physicist does. The freshman medical student often gets little help in clarifying the role of modern physicians. His time is devoted to working with anatomists, physiologists, and biochemists. He may get a better understanding of what one needs to learn to be one of these scientists than he does of the learning required of a physician. In these circumstances the student may think these courses are hurdles to test his staying power rather than furnishing a chance to learn behavior essential to his chosen profession. When a student is not clear about what he is trying to learn, his efforts are often misdirected and the "feedback system" does not guide him in improving his attempts.

This misperception of what one needs to learn is particularly common when the professional role is one of identifying problems and solving them rather than following an established set of procedures. Students often think that they have come to the professional school to get "answers" that they will use as professionals, rather than realizing that they are to learn how to identify problems and then work out their own answers.

Present programs differ widely in the extent to which the learner is stimulated to carry on various parts of professional behavior so that he may learn them. The use of lectures and textbooks often minimizes problem-solving behavior and overemphasizes memorization and the practice of specific skills. Rarely have faculties as a whole undertaken the analyzing of the major components of professional roles and providing realistically for the student to practice in context these components until he has mastered them and can use them in professional work. Some departments or other partial areas of professional activity are likely to have made such an analysis and have developed relevant learning experiences for students that enable them to acquire parts of the professional role thus identified.

Reward and feedback systems to reinforce learning and to direct the student's improvement are also spotty, taking professional programs as a group. Tests and examinations are often designed to stimulate the student to study or to separate students on a grading scale rather than to furnish the learner with an indication of the things he is learning successfully and those where his efforts have not been fruitful. Even less frequently are feedback systems used to help guide the student's learning efforts when his behavior has not been adequate.

Attention to the sequential arrangement of learning experiences to enable the student to master step by step the elements of a complex behavior such as diagnosis and prescription in medicine, or the design of a complex system in engineering could improve many professional curricula that are reported in the current professional literature. Again, some areas within a profession seem to have given thought to the problem while others have not.

The same situation applies to the distribution of practice between the school and the work situation outside the school. Some engineering programs employ cooperative education in which the student alternates work on a job and learning in college. The work experience is designed and coordinated so as to be part of his professional education. This permits a better distribution of practice than a program in which the student is not able to use his professional education on the "real job" until he graduates. A growing number of professional schools in various fields are exploring ways to utilize a more efficient distribution of learning experiences. Nursing, teaching, social work, business administration are illustrations of fields in which cooperative education is being developed. In medicine a number of schools have arranged for first- and second-year students to spend a half day or so each week in a setting where they can work with physicians or other professionals in the health sciences. These experiences serve both to clarify what it is that physicians need to learn and also to furnish practice for some of the concepts and attitudes that are given attention in the school program.

Consideration of the problem of distributing practice more efficiently in the education of professional personnel leads to the problem of helping a professional person maintain and if possible improve his professional performance after graduation. Studies of the graduates of professional schools show that two kinds of circumstances are important in determining whether or not the graduate maintains a high level of professional performance.

One of these relates to the attitudes and practices of colleagues with whom he is in continuing contact in his work. For example, if a young physician goes into a community where the older, respected physicians use short-cuts in lieu of careful diagnoses and are scornful of the "impractical theories" of the medical schools, he is likely to lose much of his drive to become a master diagnostician and problem-solver. Instead, he is greatly tempted to emulate the short-cuts used by the older, seemingly successful colleagues. As another example, Becker studied the induction of new teachers into a large city school system. He found that the older teachers laughed at the new ideas that new teachers talked about. The neophytes were told not to make a big job out of teaching. If they maintained discipline in the class, gave textbook assignments, they would succeed as teachers. Don't take wild-eyed ideas seriously.

If the graduates of professional schools are to maintain the quality of their professional work, their initial jobs should be in settings where they will be in contact with several other congenial colleagues who share their views of professional standards.

A second influence bears upon the availability of continuing education or its equivalent. Thus it is revealed in studies of graduates that professional performance tends to deteriorate after a period of experience of from seven to ten years. Not all graduates show less adequate performance after these years, but more than half do. Interviews with graduates indicate that when they do not participate in some form of continuing education or other external stimulus to go on learning, they find their work routine or boring after a while. As one doctor said, "Now I can handle my work so easily, I put my effort into golf where I find fresh challenges." Situations like this suggest the responsibility of professional schools to work with graduates to help them find their work a continuing challenge and to obtain new and fresh illumination of their professional problems and activities.

Professional schools are encountering new problems, they are feeling conflicting pressures, and they find their resources all too limited to do the things they want to do. This is a time for careful re-examination of the educational objectives of the profession in order to identify what is now important to teach, to whom and when. A systematic effort to furnish the conditions of learning that have been shown to be characteristic of complex human learning can increase the effectiveness and the efficiency of professional schools. This is a way of meeting the growing demands for competent professionals.

MARGARET MEAD

FROM PLIGHT TO POWER

AT the White House Conference of 1960, Eli Ginzberg provided the principal organizing theme that the position of American youth was changing from a group which was talked about, analyzed, lectured to, lamented, and worried about to a state in which they were emerging as a possible political influence in the American scene. There had been a foretaste in the early 1930s with the abortive attempt to organize the American Youth Congress, an attempt blunted in Washington, when Mrs. Roosevelt listened to them, the press attacked them, and they went home. For the rest of the Depression years, the elders of the society talked about Youth, now spelling it with a capital Y (after attempting to deal with the problems of a collective plural, "seven youth boarded a bus"). Special studies were made for the Youth Authority, The Adolescent Study of the Progressive Education Association, and the NYA, which provided jobs for indigent young people in the same tone of voice that the WPA provided jobs for the unemployed older people.

The problems of youth were assimilated to: problems of unemployment (where they were grouped with other problems of unemployment); problems of education, with an emphasis on studies of their hopes, aspirations, and faults in the current education system. These were combined with attempts to deal with the large high school populations which had emerged after World War I, and with the emerging sense of democracy, a conscious element in the late 1930s and early 1940s which included a feeling that Youth, who were being talked about, legislated for, inveighed against, should have some voice of their own. In the period of coordination of Youth-serving agencies, long serious discussions were held at meetings, at which no single youth was present, on whether young people being serviced by the agencies could somehow be represented in the deliberations of the bodies devoted to their interests. But most of these efforts were made in the same tone of voice that had developed student councils in high schools and colleges; by adult fiat, bodies were brought into being in which limited expressions of opinion were permitted or even solicited from the young, but they were always within an adult framework of control and budget.

Young people were benevolently permitted to exercise such authority as was delegated to them only when it did not clash with the interests of the powers that had given it to them in the first place. Those familiar with the way in which English schools operated commented on the difference between American and English schools in this respect. In English schools, authority to discipline was given to a student group and could not be capriciously withdrawn. Possibly this was based on a medieval view of a community of self-governing scholars, which even secondary schools might mildly approximate.

But the American model of authority was specifically a

matter of delegation by a higher level to a lower one. When dealing with dependent groups, whether students, the poor, women, or ethnic minorities, authority came down by fiat from above.

Significantly, in the period at the beginning of World War II, the principal diatribe directed against youth, at a period when they were joining their seniors in marching for peace, or reflecting teaching which had made them suspicious of all news, was that they lacked the moral fibre that would be necessary if they were to defend this country. In the early 1940s I wrote two responses to this attack (*Harpers*, 1941; *National Parent-Teacher*, 1941), pointing out that when young people asked such questions as, "Ought one to have a conscience?", they were still profoundly concerned with ethical issues. During World War II itself, young people were so enmeshed in the war effort that the sense of possible conflict between generations disappeared.

Meanwhile, new questions were raised, even as the United States began enthusiastically building for greatly extended free higher education, with California leading the way. A careful scrutiny of elementary school education revealed grave discrepancies between stated goals and actual achievements. The tremendous amount of illiteracy found in the United States, especially in the southeast and among black, Mexican, Puerto Rican, and Indian groups, all of whom had nominally had schooling, revealed the weaknesses of educational systems where minority children were conceived as inherently incapable of learning the culture which their teachers made a half-hearted attempt to teach them, succeeding only in teaching them their inability to learn.

During and immediately after World War II, there was a rash of adolescent dissident movements, whose followers dressed extravagantly, practiced various forms of socially disapproved behavior, who were, in fact, the adolescent failures, the drop-outs and cop-outs before the words were invented, from a system that had never seriously tried to educate them. The zoot suiters, the *eidelweis,* the teddy boys, the weegies and bodgies of Australia, were distinguished not by ethnocentricity but merely by uneducated lower-class status, coupled with discrepant, unsuccessful education. Almost forgotten today, in the turmoil of much more determined demonstrations against the present system, these youth groups were an early sign that the system was not working. Apprenticeship was dying; in rural areas children had no time nor taste for the manual tasks their fathers performed. The great exodus to the cities accelerated; and the overloaded city schools groaned under the weight of young people who could never be absorbed into the labor market.

Meanwhile there were other warning voices. The most gifted children of the American intelligentsia began to drop out of universities, finding somehow that the universities failed to give them what they wanted—what a decade or so later began to be called "relevance." And the speed of technological change made it abundantly clear that if the bulk of our population were to continue to work remuneratively within the present type of industrial system, whether that was capitalist or socialist, it would be necessary to retrain, if not reeducate, vast numbers of people two or three times during their lifetimes. This estimate was still associated with remunerative work, that is, with the expectation which had ruled our thinking since the industrial revolution, that those who could not find remunerative work would be denied full status as human beings.

This emphasis on expected need for re-education to counter technological change was accompanied by the recognition that in technological societies, to be human one had to be literate. The ability to read and write was added to the abilities to walk and talk, which for a hundred thousand years had been the major requirements for rudimentary humanity. We looked at the illiteracy in the world, at the waste of manpower in the United States, revealed in Ginzberg's studies of the draft, at the vast uneducated masses of India and China, and were aghast. We counted up the needs in the United States for engineers, physicians, physicists, and enormously increased the investment in graduate schools. A vast educational machine, deeply deficient at the base, eroded by faulty and unwilling extensions of diluted educational methods to the entire population, and top-heavy with institutions of higher education modeled upon the past education of a handful of elite, came into being.

California began to reflect not only the demand for free education for all, but also the new demands for education after childbearing for married women, an educational second chance for those who had failed at lower levels, a return for more higher education after several years out of school, and the delights of education purely for itself, for the retired but still curious. The movement toward more and more publicly supported colleges, accessible to all, was spreading, and is still spreading from state to state as New York, Florida, and Virginia join the procession, even as student revolts from Berkeley to Tokyo to France have challenged and threatened the entire system. The revolts are so widespread, the complaints so diverse but so ubiquitous, the opponents and proponents of change use such contradictory arguments that we may well suspect that the causes lie deeper than we have guessed.

We have had in fact a growing clash between those who conceived education as contributing to the individual, to human development and fulfillment on the one hand, and those who conceived of education as serving the needs of what has come to be called the Establishment, that is, of established institutions—the state, the school, the church, industry, those institutions which represent only a part of the community life. Where there was as yet no distinction between community and government, or community and church, and no industry in the modern sense, the education of children simply served to perpetuate the maintenance skills of the small society; boys learned to hunt and fish, and a few learned special esoteric skills like garden magic or divination; girls learned to prepare food, care for babies, gather roots, or later, plant and weed and harvest; or both sexes shared the care of herbs or domestic animals. The development of each individual to be a full member of that society, however limited its skills and its viewpoint, was coincident with the educational system. Such are the educational systems of those isolated primitive peoples who still live a primitive life today.

Educational systems as institutions only came into being when there was a higher degree of division of labor and special training was needed for the sons of the ruling class, for military officers, for clerks and scribes and accountants, for priests and seers and keepers of mysteries, for specialists in the knowledge of the past, and additionally when children needed to be educated differently from the way their parents had been, either because the specialist occupations needed more recruits or because the children of conquered, annexed populations or immigrants had to learn the language and customs of the dominant culture. But the overriding goals of education were still the training of specialists, including hereditary rulers and gentry, and the recruitment of more members for some special skill. It was primarily some change of status, as from the country to the city, from slavery to manumission, from subjects of one state to subjects of another, which triggered the need for schools for those who were to be the majority of undifferentiated workers for any society. Apprenticeship, either within or outside the family, the learning by the young of what the old knew, in a face-to-face, one-to-one, situation, remained a dominant mode for the children of the elite who were tutored, and the skilled, who learned from parents or master workmen.

Our present situation in which we separate children at a younger and younger age from any relationship to the work activities of their parents, sort them by age, ability, past social status, and future occupational designations, and keep them shut up together, learning at a snail's pace what each could learn individually much faster, may be seen as the product of industrialization at a period when technology had not yet made machines that could free men from both manual and tedious mental labor, and synthesis had replaced the search for raw materials. The demand for the extension of education to females, to the poor, to the previously enslaved, to the colonial peoples, has been a combination of the rising demand for democratic participation in the activities of society, and the rising demand of industrialized states for suitably trained workers, disciplined, literate, accustomed to the rhythm of the clock and the machine.

As increased earning power and increased mobility outside the confines of the home neighborhood were associated with freedom—freedom for women from the dependence on male relatives, freedom for the poor from the dependency on sharecropping and agricultural serfdom, freedom of ethnic groups from stigmatized menial service tasks, freedom of colonial peoples from the hard labor associated with the production of primary crops—rubber, ore, cotton, sugar. First literacy, then higher education, then freedom to work at more remunerative tasks in a society with a rising GNP, based upon the consumer power (or, in socialist society on the consumer share) of those who had the more remunerative tasks—this was the ideal toward which the world has been moving. Because of the close association between access to education and access to work which was assumed to give freedom, it has not been sufficiently remarked how deeply exploitative these demands for more and more education were. The very concept of manpower is a society-based, not an individual-based concept, however humanely it be interpreted by Eli Ginzberg in his exposition of the successes of educated women. The assumption has been that the society's need for educated manpower and the individual's need for education in order to acquire greater mobility and hence greater freedom within an economic system postulated on scarcity of men, skills, and resources, would produce benefits for the individual has been in many ways illusory.

One of the principal undesirable side effects of these demands for more widespread and ever higher education has been the increasing segregation of the young during their period of highest learning capacity, ages 5 to 10, from the productivity and creativity of their culture, and the infantilizing of adolescents and young adults as long as they are classified as students, a separate segment of society, unfit for full responsibility and full respect. This tendency toward infantilization of students resulted in the extension of dependency, and virtual political and economic disenfranchisement, and the withholding of full adult rights up into the '30s for those who were learning special skills like social work or psychiatry, where supervision continued almost indefinitely.

The whole process of the extension of pupil-status into adulthood has been based on the egalitarian belief in education and the fear that once education is interrupted society will withdraw the privileges which it has reluctantly accorded further education. All the gains that have been made in universal education have been accomplished by extending a single schooling period, down into kindergarten, nursery school, and today into day care centers, up into high school, junior college, college, graduate school, and postdoctoral education. The concept that there is a schooling period to which all human beings are entitled, paralleling the needs of an industrial society, has been the dynamic underlying the idealistic part of our changing educational system.

As long as the needs of the economy and this idealistic educational ethic coincided, this continuing extension of the schooling period was possible, and continued to be viewed, for the most part, as an advantage and a privilege. In the United States, in the 1930s and well into the 1940s, Negro sharecropper parents, and poor parents in Harlem, worked hard to send their children through high school and to college. First-generation European immigrants saved to put their children through high school, and second-generation parents saved to put their children through college, now regarded as a prerequisite to everything worth having in the society. Education was both a right and a privilege, and stood against the early exploitation of children in the cotton fields, among migratory laborers, and the later exploitation of young people in blind alley jobs.

In 1954 when I suggested to the National Conference of Parents and Teachers that we consider letting children leave school at the age of 14 and return at any period in the course of their lives if they felt they could use more education, I was denounced as an advocate of child labor. It took only a few more years however, for diatribes against child labor to give way to schemes for youth employment, as it became increasingly clear that our present school system was coming under fire. The long, long years of compulsory school, the need to stay in school under threat, first of legal penalties, later of no worthwhile jobs, later still of being drafted, have all contributed their share to changing attitudes toward the infinite desirability of an increasing single stretch of education. But this disillusionment with our present-day schooling has continued to be complemented with the belief that a better type of schooling was all that was needed, a belief that better science education, readers suited to different economic groups, better schools in ghettos, provision for the children of migrants, etc. would remedy the present defects. Meanwhile the need for more highly educated manpower continued—and campaigns began to keep pupils in school who were capable of doing college level work—pupils whom we had never expected to keep in school before were now described as "drop-outs" and committees formed in every state to keep them in. Women were told that the life of homemaking to which society's arrangements had condemned them, living in isolated suburbs far from help of any kind, was not fulfilling, after all, and a nationwide campaign to get women back for more education and training for the cheap educated labor market was underway.

The state of California represented the highest achievement of these new ideals. A statewide system of free education made it possible for young people to move from job to college and back again. Women could pick up their discontinued education and "complete" it (the old idea of one lump of education to which every citizen was legally entitled, remained). Retired colonels could study philosophy side by side with sixteen-year-old girls; students who had done badly in high school had a second chance. Students worked, married, fathered children, and went on to college. There were community colleges for those who would be motor mechanics and those who would go on to be automobile salesmen. Parents who wanted to educate their children themselves were prosecuted. Attempts were made to see that the children of migrant laborers went to school while at the same time excluding from the country the low-paid migrant Mexican laborers. Automation of services were everywhere speeded up, and drive-ins of all sorts superseded both restaurants and waitresses.

And then, in the mid-1960s the whole California system, so carefully and imaginatively built, a system that other states were beginning to copy, came under attack—first at Berkeley, then at college after college. The very principle of free higher education was called in question and has now been rescinded. Students burn down college buildings. Students in the National Guard attack their fellow students who are demonstrating for peace. The police maim and kill. Higher education for all who can benefit by it is so disturbed and disliked by the majority of the less educated populace—and note that with a continual system of upgrading there will always be a less well-educated older generation—that they will vote to keep in power the declared enemy of education, and all other forms of enlightened community behavior.

Nor is this all. In England students barricade themselves in buildings and private eyes with police dogs are brought in to deal with them; in France a political regime was brought down by student revolt; in Japan the major universities were closed for over a year with no one studying for the professions that are essential to maintain the state. The Soviet Union made one abortive attempt to introduce work into the plan of continuous education, and has just begun to feel the pinch as youth begin leaving school and find themselves unemployed.

So we may well ask, what has happened to this structure which appeared so desirable that it was only a matter of extending it all over the world to produce, in fact, a much more satisfactory world? Why are the school system and the colleges coming under attack today where a generation ago it was the industrial system, as it employed those with little or no schooling, that was the principal target of reform movement? One explanation may, of course, be that the attack is the same, that it is merely the battleground that has shifted, as Marxists or anarchists denounce "the system," or a new group of advocates of natural man or primitivism rebel against industry and the way in which modern industrialization exploits and despoils the whole living world. These are the answers that are given on all sides by student rebels and armchair dissidents, and revolutionaries suckled on an outworn creed. Whether they see the present system as one stage in an inevitable set of stages which will in the end set man free by subduing the forces of evil, capitalism, nature, and human intractability—or as a perversion of man's true destiny of freedom and beautiful accord with a nature which he neither violates nor exploits, as he pursues his individual, or small cult group, salvation—both theories are bound to old styles of thinking, where salvation could be found either in straight-line progress, in pendulum swings against abuses, or in straight-line regression to earlier periods of human history.

But I believe that the educational system is bearing the brunt of the present attack for other reasons. It is, of course, partly because of the unique generation gap that separates those born during and after World War II, everywhere in the world, from those born before. This meant a period in which the oldest members of the post-World War II generation—a generation who never knew the world without a bomb, the population explosion, transistor radio and tv, space exploration and the threat of environmental pollution—were all still within the educational establishment, classified as too young for power. So our campuses erupted when these eldest members of the new generation were in college, and they gave leadership which extended down into secondary schools. Now the circle is beginning to round, as they become teachers, supporting the revolts of the young against the outworn and archaic systems of education which they are now entering as the youngest members of the establishment. This is one of the mechanisms by which the attack is spreading.

There is also no doubt a reflection of the moment when the United States and to a lesser extent the other older industrialized countries are shifting from a producer society that needs all its labor, to a consumer society where the problems are those of equitable distribution of the products of an increasingly automated industry, and a fantastically productive mechanized, commercialized, and officially engineered agriculture. Training for jobs for the groups who have become unemployable as no longer needed unskilled labor, is a thinly disguised way of turning them into consumers, under the heading of created employment. It is part of a desperate attempt to make an educational system which transforms a manageable agricultural and industrial proletariat into either higher level employees or more contented consumers. And yet at the same time we are faced with the fact that it will be quite impossible under the present system to make every member of society into a happy consumer. The level of life which mass advertising has taught him to desire—and this is true in the center of New Guinea where a page of *Life* magazine advertising is pinned to the door, as it is in Harlem, rural Mississippi, or on an American Indian reservation—is unobtainable without irreversibly wrecking the natural environment upon which the future well-being of mankind depends.

Since World War II we have gone through a rapid series of versions of the "good life," shared in depth by the United States, the Soviet Union, and Peoples' Republic of China. The spread of heavy industry was expected to guarantee a healthy and contented populace, but the realization that heavy industry at the expense of agricultural development was spreading a malignant and premature growth of cities, as well as the recognition that countries that produced raw materials for industry could not both improve their standard of living and continue to sell their products which could be outpriced by synthetic materials, led to the perception of the widening gap between the "rich" and "poor" countries. And beyond this there was the still more dismaying recognition that if any country of any size, and particularly the United States, where 6 percent of the population consumes half of the earth's irreplaceable natural resources, continued to develop and spread its present style of life, it would strangle in its own waste and destruction, and pull the rest of the world down with it. But as poorly diffused and poorly understood as these new findings are, they are having a profound effect on the young, on the one hand, and on the adult expectations and hopes for the young, and fear and hatred of the young on the other.

We are witnessing the breakdown of a system of belief that was essentially linear in nature: more inventions, more progress, higher demands, more education to produce those who could participate as producers and consumers in the results of this endless progression toward a growing GNP. The words that were used were borrowed from biology; we talked of economic "growth," "maturing" nations. But the true metaphor came from a mechanical and irreversible sequence in which a linear process of factory-like production took raw materials and turned them into products: cars and washing machines and fertilizer, in factories; educated citizens in schools. As our faith in such a continuingly improving system, more heavy industry, more automation, more objects of consumption, a higher standard of living, all hitched to what was conceived of as an inexhaustible supply of raw materials and synthetic possibilities, there comes a demand for recycling. Children are no longer to be seen as future manpower, just as water is no longer seen as inexhaustible and wasteable, and the earth as inexhaustibly life-supporting.

As respect for life and its limitations, of the planet and its limited resources, are forced upon us by the evidence of pollution and population explosion and the risks of an annihilating war, we now face a renewed challenge as to what is meant by education. No longer are children to be pushed through a system of education which sorted them into different tracks, finished them off at later and later stages, and after a brief period of productivity and consumership were thrown on a compost heap, to be reluctantly and minimally supported until death relieved society of the burden. No longer was education to be simply a required stage in the life cycle, enforced, sometimes under the guise of privilege, on all the young, so that they might participate in this never-ending expansion of GNP.

The California type of universal higher education available at all ages becomes, at once, the last gasp of a system and the precursor of a new one. So we have the peculiar spectacle of one group of people weeping with tenderness as they see the young and the not so young of the poor and deprived, dressed in caps, gowns, and newly designed hoods, graduating from community colleges—given a second chance and a new skill or a new enjoyment and understanding of life—while the students at our most venerable institutions refuse to wear caps and gowns or threaten to come naked beneath them and throw them off to disrupt the ceremonies.

The community colleges in which the linear process is in part disallowed and the old are permitted to learn, or relearn, or simply learn to enjoy, suggest a new form of education, even as the angry taxpayers of an earlier concept of a pioneer society devoted to rewards for hard exploitive labor and mindless consumption, send police and National Guardsmen to attack the students in the parent universities. They anticipate the new kind of recycling of education that must follow our recognition that our relationship within the natural world must return to biological model, in which all of life—and death—are of one process where no part is unessential, no part final, and no part irreversibly exploitive. When the day care center and the nursery school are added to the community college, and the university is close by, and when everyone, at different periods of life, both learns and teaches, we will begin to have a system of education which will not be seen as part of a factory process of shaping the young, into dispensable parts of a linear process, but instead as an indispensable part of life for every age.

With this new emphasis there can be provided a new emphasis upon nonmaterial consumption, to take the pressure off the kind of material consumption which is destroying our environment. This is one of the things that youth are stressing, in their delight in song, the least exploitive and the freest of all the arts, and in flowers renewable each spring. Granted that they have very little comprehension of the extraordinary changes that will need to be made in the whole structure of the industrialized and industrializing world, to stem the destruction of the planet's resources and save it as a habitat for future generations of men, they show, in the speed with which adaption, for example, is replacing the demand for enormous self-replication, a prevision of what the wisest and best informed economic and social prophets realize must come.

If consumption must be simplified, if the standard of living can no longer be based on every home being like a power plant, and on an ever-rising GNP, education becomes in great part a preparation for new kinds of joy, of being, of participating, rather than of producing. The skills necessary to a simplified but nevertheless highly automated artificial environment, can be developed as special norms of delight, labor made light enough so that no backs are broken, can become part of being. Education, or schools, or the teaching learning centers of the community—whatever we call them—can become a part of society instead of a form of compulsory segregation away from it, where teachers are wardens and children and youth are prisoners, as it is becoming today, in these last stages in which the older system is being called in question and the newer systems have not evolved.

And meanwhile, we have the clash of values, as those who have just emerged from deprivation clamor for a voice and a place, and see education as the focus of their desires. So the militant black groups demand that credentials no longer be the criterion for entering college, and poets demand that the soul-destroying routines of the overburdened, over-routined, out-of-date city schools no longer determine the curriculum for Head Start. Older people, prematurely retired by a rapidly changing industrial system, demand that they be allowed to learn, and to teach what they have newly learned. And there is hope—an ingredient which Eli Ginzberg always manages to inject, if necessarily by rigorous selectivity, into what he writes—hope, that the changing values of youth represent the changing recognition of the adults who still control our outmoded and dangerous social and economic forms.

PART FOUR

BRINLEY THOMAS

"GRASS ON THE SLAG HEAPS" REVISITED

IN 1942 Eli Ginzberg published a remarkable book, *Grass on the Slag Heaps: The Story of the Welsh Miners,* the fruit of an on-the-spot investigation during the year before war broke out. He had come to Britain to carry out a scientific study of labor mobility, and South Wales was regarded as best suited for the analysis. Seldom has any author shown such profound understanding of the complex human problems of coal-mining communities undergoing the agony of prolonged mass unemployment. Ginzberg not only mastered the official and unofficial sources but he had the extraordinary gift of getting under the skin of Welsh society. He lived among the unemployed and migrants and shared their experiences; he interviewed people in all walks of life; and he used this first-hand knowledge to paint an astringent picture of a sick society. As Dr. Thomas Jones said in his Foreword, Ginzberg ". . . came to us equipped with unusual eyes and ears and with a mind trained to detect and record what was most significant in our social life. The result is a volume of permanent worth."[1]

Rereading *Grass on the Slag Heaps* today, one is again staggered by the incredible fact that governments allowed a whole generation to waste away in enforced idleness. The unemployment rate in Wales as a whole in the 1930s varied between 30 and 38 percent, and in some of the coal mining valleys up to 60 percent. "It is difficult to read without resentment that in the late nineteen-thirties the second richest nation in the world prided itself on providing one-third of a pint of milk per day for the children of the unemployed in the valleys of South Wales, children who were suffering many insufficiencies."[2] In a trenchant section of his concluding chapter Ginzberg wonders what a visitor from Mars would make of it all.

> The visitor from Mars would have expected that once the facts had been brought to the public's attention there would have been speedy action, for all sensible people realize that it is both wicked and stupid to permit men to rot in idleness and breed children in despair. But the man from Mars might have overlooked the fact that the wealthy were worried about taxes, that the trades-unions were intent upon guarding their monopolies, that churchmen were bogged down in doctrinal disputes, that army officers were pre-occupied with tactics, that physicians discussed the relative importance of psychic and somatic factors, and that ordinary people were just too busy with their own problems and their own pleasures to concern themselves with the plight of men, women and children whom they had never seen and probably never would. The man from Mars would have returned to his planet greatly confused.[3]

In his summing up, Ginzberg distributes his strictures all round. "The miserliness of the wealthy, the incompetence of the reformers, and the stodginess of the bureaucrats go far to explain the victimization of South Wales."[4] There is a great deal of truth in this, but it does not explicitly go for the main target—the absurd Treasury dogma, expressed in the Chancellor of the Exchequer's budget speech in 1929, ". . . that whatever might be the political or social advantages, very little additional employment and no permanent additional employment can, in fact, and as a general rule, be created by State borrowing and State expenditure."

What is most surprising is that Ginzberg paid no attention to the thunderings of the great Cassandra who could never influence the course of events in time. There is not one reference to Keynes throughout the book. The Treasury dogma had been demolished by Keynes in his Programme of Expansion (General Election, May 1929) and The Means to Prosperity in the Spring of 1933, one of the worst years of unemployment. The basic cause of the tragedy of the depressed areas was the fact that the statesmen and bankers of the 1920s and 1930s were purblind prisoners of false doctrine. This is how Keynes put it in May 1929.

> The suggestion that a policy of capital expenditure, if it does not take capital away from ordinary industry, will spell Inflation, would be true enough if we were dealing with boom conditions. And it would become true if the policy of capital expenditure were pushed unduly far, so that the demand for savings began to exceed the supply. But we are far, indeed, from such a position at the present time. A large amount of deflationary slack has first to be taken up before there can be the smallest danger of a development policy leading to Inflation. To bring up the bogy of Inflation as an objection to capital expenditure at the present time is like warning a patient who is wasting away from emaciation of the dangers of excessive corpulence.[5]

It is fantastic to recall that the obvious truth of these words was rejected as nonsense by the Government and the Bank of England: Lloyd George was the only leader who campaigned on a Keynesian platform. By 1933, 34 percent of Britain's coal miners, 42 percent of the iron and steel workers, and 62 percent of the shipbuilding workers were unemployed.

In the history of nations certain crises burn themselves into the consciousness of the people and leave a permanent spiritual scar. Such was the great depression of the interwar years in Wales. In *Grass on the Slag Heaps* Eli Ginzberg captured the agony, despair, and futility of that experience. Unemployment on that scale will never occur again, and yet the memory of it is still only just below the surface in Wales, Scotland, and the North East of England. As I write, the Upper Clyde Shipbuilding Company, employing 7,800 men directly, with another 21,000 indirectly dependent on it, has gone into liquidation. These are the shipyards where the famous Cunard Queens were built. A wave of anxiety has swept over the whole of Scotland and people are once again troubled by the spectre of the black 1930s.

Looking back at this distance, we need to place Ginzberg's sombre picture in its true perspective by viewing it in the context of long-run economic growth. When we survey the course of the Welsh economy over the last century, the striking fact is that it has been expanding more or less rapidly for eight decades out of ten: the colossal reaction between 1921 and 1938 was a temporary lapse.

At the time of the Great Exhibition of 1851, when England was celebrating the triumphs of her leadership in the Industrial Revolution, Wales had a population of just over one million, with two-thirds of it in rural areas.[6] The largest town was Merthyr Tydfil, the center of the iron industry; Cardiff was a mere township of only 20,000. Between 1851 and 1911 the population of Cardiff grew ninefold—from 20,000 to 182,000; and her annual coal exports rose fourteenfold—from 708,000 tons to nearly 10 million tons. Few areas in the kingdom could rival the rate of expansion in the Rhondda valleys. Their population in 1851 was less than 1000; in 1921 it was 163,000. Before coal began to be mined these valleys were famous for their natural beauty; the hillsides were covered with thick woods and the rivers were rich in salmon and trout. After two generations of mining most of the trees had disappeared, the rivers were black with pollution, and the density of human habitation was as high as 24,000 persons per square mile of area built on. In addition to the growth of mining in the South Wales valleys, there was substantial investment in the making of steel, using the Bessemer and the Siemens processes. By the end of the nineteenth century almost the entire output of British tinplate was produced in South Wales. In the north the slate industry had expanded until at the end of the 1890s the annual output reached 500,000 tons of slates. In 1911 the population of Wales was 2,241,000; it had doubled in sixty years and two-thirds of it was now in urban areas. In the half-century ending in 1913 the average real wages of workers doubled.

One way of comparing the development of different countries is to ask to what extent they were able to provide a living within their own borders for the natural increase in their populations, i.e., the annual excess of births over deaths. Taking the period 1881-1911, the record for the four parts of the United Kingdom was as follows. By far the worst was Northern Ireland, which suffered net emigration equivalent to 125 percent of its natural increase, so that its population actually fell by 4 percent. Scotland lost through emigration a third of its natural increase and England lost a tenth, but Wales kept the whole of its natural increase and added to it by immigration an amount equal to 7 percent of its natural increase.

The momentum of industrial advance in Wales in the Victorian period was stronger than in any other part of the United Kingdom. It did not, however, keep going at an even pace. There was an interesting fluctuation which was inverse to the course of events in England. This comes out clearly when we compare the phases of development in the English and Welsh coalfields. In the 1860s and 1870s progress in South Wales was comparatively slow: the big advance in coal mining took place in Durham, Wigan, Chesterfield, and Barnsley. During those years the rural exodus from Wales was absorbed for the most part across the border. In the 1880s the center of gravity in British coal mining was in South Wales where an enormous expansion occurred; and in that decade the net inflow into Glamorgan and Monmouthshire colliery areas from the Welsh countryside was seven times greater than in the 1870s. The English coalfields took the lead in the 1890s and the net absorption of immigrants by Glamorgan and Monmouthshire fell to half of what it had been in the 1880s. The climax came in the fabulous decade of 1901–11 when the South Wales coalfield completely dominated the scene by attracting a net total of 129,000 people, most of whom came from England. In the first ten years of this century Wales was one of the leading countries of new settlement; it was absorbing immigrants at a rate almost as high as the United States (an annual rate of 4.5 per 1,000 as against 6.3 per 1,000).

The long cycle in the growth of industrial towns in Wales was inverse to the corresponding cycle in England.[7] The reason was that the economy of Wales was governed by the export trade in coal. When activity in the export trade in Wales was relatively depressed, activity in capital construction in England was relatively buoyant, and vice versa. Thus, the people who had to leave the land in Wales were absorbed in one phase by the towns depending on the export trade in Wales and in the next phase by the towns profiting from the upswing in capital construction in England. The only annual statistical record of Welsh emigration overseas is to be found in the Annual Reports of the Commissioner General of Immigration in the United States from 1875. As we would expect from the industrial expansion in Wales in the period up to 1913, the number who went overseas was negligible. If we take the decade 1881–90 when America was absorbing immigrants at a record rate, the annual rates of emigration of workers (per 10,000 population) from the four countries of the United Kingdom were as follows: Ireland, 77; Scotland, 20;

England, 12; Wales, 3. Thus, in proportion to the population English emigrants to America were four times as numerous as the Welsh, the Scots seven times, and the Irish twenty-six times.

What effect did urban development have on the nation's language and traditions? It is usually taken for granted—it is certainly a commonplace of the standard textbook—that industrialization was an anglicizing force which swept over the country leaving the rural areas of the north and west as the last strongholds of the Welsh-speaking tradition. Is it really true that industrialization and the accompanying flight from the land undermined the language and culture of Wales in the period 1850–1913? The truth of the matter, which historians do not seem to have noticed, is that the Welsh language was really saved by the growth of industrial towns which enabled most of the people uprooted from the Welsh countryside to be absorbed within the boundaries of Wales.

In 1911 there were in the three coal mining counties of Glamorgan, Monmouthshire, and Carmarthenshire 556,000 people who could speak Welsh; this was 57 percent of the total number of Welsh speakers in Wales at that time. The vast majority of these people would simply not have been there but for the pull of industry. If Wales had remained completely agricultural like Ireland, the whole of her surplus rural population which was Welsh to the core (400,000 people in the sixty years up to 1911) would have had to go to England or overseas; these people together with their descendants would have been lost to the land of their birth forever. This loss would have been a grievous blow to the Welsh language, and it was prevented by the growth of industrial areas in Wales. Industrial development was on such a scale that Wales was able to provide a good living for the great majority of the native stock displaced from the countryside. The farm laborers from all parts who flocked into the Rhondda took the Welsh way of life with them and brought up their children to speak the mother tongue. Describing the Rhondda valley in 1896 the Report of the Welsh Land Commission said: " . . . speaking broadly, the characteristics of Welsh life, its Nonconformist development, the habitual use of the Welsh language, and the prevalence of a Welsh type of character, are as marked as in the rural districts of Wales." In 1905, there were in the Rhondda no less than 151 Nonconformist churches with a seating capacity of 85,105; these churches alone could accommodate three-quarters of the entire population of the Rhondda Urban District. Indeed in the whole of Wales in 1905 the seating capacity of Nonconformist churches was equal to 74 percent of the total population. The mining townships were so Welsh in character that many of the English immigrants—not to mention Italian shopkeepers—were rapidly assimilated. And it is worth noting that even in 1951, 54 percent of the 715,000 recorded as Welsh-speaking were in the South Wales industrial areas.

No doubt the romantic nationalist will reply that the Welsh heritage would have been much safer in the hands of a small nation of monoglot peasants. But what would have been its fate in the great agricultural crisis which hit the whole of Europe in the 1880s? Given a miracle, Wales—like Denmark—might have found her Grundvig; but it is much more likely, when we remember the physical disabilities of Welsh agriculture, that she would have been caught, like Ireland, in the vicious circle of mass emigration. Instead of having a population of over 2½ million, modern Wales would have been just a handful of impoverished peasants scratching a meagre subsistence and eking it out with remittances from their kinsmen who had been lucky enough to go to America. It would have been a tiny and much more depressed version of Ireland—without the stimulus which the rise of the House of Guinness meant to the Emerald Isle. It was the massive growth of coal mining which saved Wales from that fate. Instead of bemoaning the rural exodus, the Welsh nationalist should sing the praises of industrial development which gave the Welsh language a new lease on life and Welsh Nonconformity a glorious high noon.

The depression of the interwar years completely reversed the trend. The net overflow from the Welsh countryside continued on the pre-1913 scale, but to it was now added an enormous movement of 421,000 people out of the distressed industrial areas. The only redeeming feature was the net inflow into the nonindustrial towns, mostly in North Wales. Between 1921 and 1939 Wales lost on balance 450,000 people through emigration; her natural increase was 259,000, so that her population fell by 191,000.

One of the immediate consequences of World War II was an increase in the economic importance of Wales. Severe air attacks made it essential to disperse industrial production, and many plants were transferred to western locations from the more vulnerable areas in England. It was ironical that the redistribution of industry, which should have taken place before the war, was now rapidly carried out for strategic reasons. For example, between 1939 and 1944 there was an increase in the number employed in Wales in chemicals from 4,000 to 69,000; in engineering, from 11,000 to 48,000; in vehicle construction, from 7,000 to 30,000; and even in agriculture from 23,000 to 29,000. Although this was due to wartime exigencies, it proved to be a valuable springboard for postwar expansion. New techniques and grades of skill were introduced, and the advantages of locations away from congested areas were realized.

Production for the war effort also had the effect of greatly increasing the number of women gainfully employed in Wales where hitherto there had been no tradition of this kind. The record here was remarkable. By 1946 the number of females in employment in Wales was 83 percent greater than in 1939. They were distributed over various branches of activity as follows: manufacturing 31 percent; distributive trades, 23 percent; miscellaneous services, 17 percent; and national and local government, 16 percent. Since so many men had been recruited into the armed forces, four out of every ten persons employed in manufacturing were women. At the peak of the war effort in 1944, female employment in Wales was 134 percent larger than it had been in 1939, whereas in Great Britain as a whole the corresponding increase was only 36 percent.

As a result of the war manufacturing in Wales expanded by four-fifths; it accounted for one-fifth of total employment in 1946 as against one-ninth before the war. Some of this was of course of a purely temporary character, such as the making of explosives, which in the last year of the war employed 48,000 people. Meanwhile the labor force in coal mining declined from 144,000 to 116,000 and in tinplate manufacture from 23,000 to 12,600. A surprising sequel was the ease with which the transition to peacetime production was effected as soon as the war was over. The pessimists who expected Wales to slip back to the pre-1939 stagnation were proved wrong. The new potentialities revealed during the war became substantial realities; and they were given a further impetus by the Distribution of Industry Act of 1946, which gave expression to the principle that it was in the public interest that new factories should be located in the Development Areas. New trading estates became the centers of light engineering and the production of a wide variety of consumers' goods. Even within two years from 1945 most of the government-owned space provided during the war had been rapidly transformed for use by private firms.

Wales was now firmly embarked on a new trend which has made its economy far more diversified and efficient than it was before the war. The record shows that it has recaptured something of the dynamic element it had between 1860 and 1913 without the extreme specialization on one line of exports which was its main characteristic in that period. In the last twenty years a virtually new manufacturing sector using the latest technology has developed in Wales, and it employs 35 percent of the working population. Coal mining, which before World War II accounted for 25 percent of the labor force, has been reduced to 6 percent. The economy is much more diversified, including chemicals, oil refining, man-made fibers, motor car components, electrical engineering, aluminum, and a wide range of consumer goods. Plenty of labor was available from the surplus released by mining and other declining industries and through the recruitment of the previously untapped supply of women workers. Among the American companies which have established plants in Wales are Hoover, Minnesota Mining and Manufacturing, Ford, Revlon, Johnson and Johnson, Monsanto, Standard Oil, Texaco, Standard Telephone and Cables, Uni-carbide, Dow Chemical, Jefferson Chemical, Firestone, Borg-Warner, and General Electric.

There are, of course, Jeremiahs in Wales whose motto seems to be: Look back in anger and look forward in blinkers. Whatever our purveyors of gloom may say, the economic prospects for the 1970s are distinctly favorable. The signs are that we are about to enter a period of rapid economic growth. This is not to say that we are by any means out of the wood. The last two years have been particularly difficult, and unemployment in some areas is very serious. The relentless program of pit closures has been far more drastic than was anticipated, but this phase may now be over. Britain is in the throes of turning from coal to new sources of energy—oil, natural gas, and nuclear power. This is going to mean a considerable increase in the efficiency of the British economy as a whole, but unfortunately in the meantime a heavy price has to be paid in areas which specialized on coal, especially Wales. The Government's Development Area policy has been of immense help in enabling Wales to weather this structural crisis, and it is essential that it should be maintained in full for several years yet. The crucial problem has been to build up a strong manufacturing sector which will more than fill the inevitable gap left by the declining industries.

By a handsome margin Wales is top of the regional manufacturing league table. Between 1959 and 1968 employment in Welsh manufacturing industries grew by 18.7 percent, five times higher than the rate for Britain as a whole. Wales's nearest rival was the South West with a growth rate of 12.9 percent. The decline of 3.8 percent in the North West is a sharp reminder of the obsolete manufacturing units with which this region was saddled. In total working population Wales is only a little over one-tenth the size of London and Eastern England, and yet in the 1960s Wales's increase in manufacturing employment was 40 percent of what took place in London and the East. If the 1960s are anything to go by, South Wales and the South West are set to be one of the most bouyant manufacturing growth areas of Britain in the 1970s.

If, through reorganization, there is a rundown in skilled labor in steel in the 1970s, it should be easy, with retraining, for these men to go into other science-based industries. Indeed, the very fact that such labor will be available together with a wide choice of first-class industrial sites is a bull point for incoming firms. Air travel will enter a dramatic new phase in the next decade. Even when the third London airport is ready, the metropolis will still be wallowing in congestion. The answer lies in Wales and the West. There could be a fine international airport on the Welsh side of the Severn estuary, taking millions of American visitors who will tour Wales and the West and Stratford-on-Avon, before going on to London. We have hardly begun to tap the immense potential of the Welsh tourist trade. With imagination and enterprise rural mid-Wales, where depopulation has been a serious problem, could be made into an attractive tourist area similar to what has been achieved at its best in countries like Bavaria.

The record of the 1960s shows that Wales is now part of

the buoyant manufacturing growth zone of the South. Its manufacturing sector is a brand new creation of the postwar period, technologically advanced and forward-looking, and growing faster than in any other region of Britain. If the United Kingdom enters the European Common Market, Wales will give a good account of itself.

If Eli Ginzberg were to return to his old haunts in the mining valleys of South Wales (and there would be a hearty Welsh welcome for him), he would rejoice to see many an old slag heap covered with a green blanket of young trees, and he would be surprised to find that fish can now be caught in many an old stream. Pits are few and far between: they have given way to modern industrial estates within easy distance of the valleys. The accent is on the clearing of derelict land and urban renewal.

There are still serious problems of adjustment, and the recent recession has been the worst for many years, with unemployment in some areas as high as 10 percent. Nevertheless, the present young generation, unlike that of the 1930s, is not despondent about the future. The moral of the tragedy which Eli Ginzberg portrayed so unforgettably has been well understood.

NOTES

1. In Eli Ginzberg, *Grass on the Slag Heaps* (New York: Harpers, 1942), p. xiii.
2. *Ibid.*, p. 201.
3. *Ibid.*, pp. 193–94.
4. *Ibid.*, p. 222.
5. J. M. Keynes, *Essays in Persuasion* (New York: Macmillan, 1931), pp. 124–25.
6. The following paragraphs draw on material from the author's paper "The Growth of Industrial Towns," in A. J. Roderick, ed., *Wales Through the Ages*, Vol. II (Llandybie: C. Davis, 1959).
7. This is part of a larger theme developed in a work in progress.

WILLIAM FOOTE WHYTE

THE BEHAVIORAL SCIENCES AND MANPOWER RESEARCH

MANPOWER research has traditionally been the province of labor economists. It is now well recognized that the solution of manpower problems requires knowledge drawn from the behavioral sciences as well as economics, but this recognition does not lead automatically to any effective action.

Even when economists are receptive—as many of them are—to the development of behavioral science research, they may be puzzled as to what these disciplines have to offer and how their research may be applied to manpower problems. There are also problems of understanding and communication on the other side. Since few behavioral scientists have been working on manpower problems—or at least on what economists define as manpower problems—behavioral scientists have difficulty in explaining to economists what they might contribute to manpower research.

As Chairman of the National Manpower Advisory Committee of the Department of Labor and as an ex officio member of its Sub-Committee on Research, Eli Ginzberg has made great efforts to bring behavioral scientists into the manpower research field and to promote an interdisciplinary development of that field. My invitation to join the Sub-Committee was part of the Ginzberg program. When he was Director of Research for the Office of Manpower Policy Evaluation and Research, Curtis Aller pursued the same objective vigorously, and it was in response to his request that I wrote the first draft of the present paper for a meeting of the Sub-Committee on Research in 1966.

The purpose of this paper is to seek to propose answers to the following two questions:

1. What do the behavioral sciences have to offer to manpower research?

2. How may the findings of research (particularly behavioral science research) be more effectively applied toward the solution of practical manpower problems?

ON ECONOMICS AND THE BEHAVIORAL SCIENCES

I shall begin my answer to the first question by placing it in the context of the evolution of the social sciences. I shall point to certain trends in the social sciences, including economics, and then undertake to focus more sharply on the limited area I know best.

As economics has developed in the United States, we now find two competing tendencies: abstract theoretical and mathematical economics on the one hand, and developmental economics on the other. In recent years, the high-prestige branch of economics has been abstract, mathematical theory. In fact, J. K. Galbraith [1] claims that there is a correlation in the

United States between the prestige of the branch of economics and its distance away from the practical problems of the society—the farther away, the higher the prestige.

It seems to me that high-level, abstract economic theory and developmental economics are moving in two quite different directions. Abstract economic theory is moving toward increasing refinement and specialization within the field of economics. Developmental economics is moving toward closer interrelations with other social sciences.

Let me illustrate my point by citing the case of Everett C. Hagen, a distinguished economist who published *On the Theory of Social Change.*[2] While this is a controversial book that has been attacked as well as praised, it is coming to be recognized as an important contribution to the literature of economic development.

In preparing to write this book, Hagen read widely in the literature of psychology, anthropology, and sociology. He submitted the manuscript to Richard C. Irwin and Company for consideration in their economics series. The editor of the series, Lloyd G. Reynolds, thought well of the book and recommended its publication. In view of the range of ideas and materials covered in the book, the publisher decided to submit the manuscript also to anthropologist Allan R. Holmberg. Not only did Holmberg give an enthusiastic endorsement to the book, he also reported that he would plan to use it as a textbook for his course in Culture Change in the Department of Anthropology.

This raised a question in Hagen's mind. While Reynolds had recommended the book for publication in the economics series, he had not mentioned any possibility of its being used as a textbook in any course in economics. If Holmberg had seen this possibility in an anthropology course, maybe it would be better to have the book published in the sociology and anthropology series of the same publisher. With the permission of Reynolds, the book was submitted to sociologists Robin Williams and William F. Whyte, who were then co-editors of the sociology and anthropology series. When we responded with an enthusiastic endorsement of the book, the publisher proceeded to bring it out in the sociology and anthropology series.

I suggest that developmental economics has much to offer to manpower research today. While the field has grown up particularly out of research on the developing countries, it has necessarily had to focus upon phenomena such as social class and cultural differences which are importantly involved in research in depressed areas of our own country. The economist who seeks to do research or to direct action among the poor in the United States must learn to deal with what anthropologist Oscar Lewis has called "the culture of poverty."

That is simply another way of saying that the economist of development needs to add a behavioral science orientation to his intellectual equipment. This need is being increasingly recognized, but all too often today we find economists plunging into research with assumptions regarding motivation, attitude change, and other social and psychological phenomena that the behavioral scientist would regard as either naive and oversimplified or demonstrably false.

A word of caution: in this area of research, the economist necessarily must make certain assumptions regarding motivation, attitudes, and behavior, but let him fortify himself by taking these two steps. Let him first seek to make his own assumptions about behavior explicit—for we sometimes find a failure to recognize what assumptions are actually being made. Second, let him seek out behavioral science colleagues for criticism and advice regarding the relation of his assumptions to the findings of behavioral science research. (Of course, the same sort of advice is appropriate for the behavioral scientist whose work takes him into economics.)

ON THE NATURE AND EVOLUTION OF THE BEHAVIORAL SCIENCES

Anthropology, psychology, and sociology are often grouped together as the behavioral sciences. If we look beneath those three disciplinary labels, we find a great variety of subunits, only a few of which can be fitted together in terms of any logically coherent pattern. Furthermore, within some branches of these disciplines, specialization has proceeded so far that an integration of knowledge across the branches of a single discipline is next to impossible to achieve.

Anthropology, today, really consists of four separate fields: archaeology, physical anthropology, linguistics, and social anthropology. I see them as separate and distinct because the theories and methods used in one of these fields, with very occasional exceptions, are not used in the others.

There is a similar separation among the fields of psychology. When we hear social psychologists refer to physiological psychologists as "the brass instrument boys," we see the extent of separation between the two fields. Nor does there seem to be much in common in the theories and methods used among the fields of clinical psychology, psychological testing, and social psychology. Furthermore, specialization has proceeded very far in some of these fields. Recently, one university had been considering employing a sensory psychologist, but there was considerable debate within the psychology department as to which of the senses the man should represent.

Apparently, there is no such thing as a man who is reasonably competent in all the senses. An authority on the eyes will not be thoroughly conversant with all the literature on the ears, and the man who specializes in touch cannot be expected to be thoroughly conversant with eyes and ears. There seems to be only one sensory area where psychologists have not been able to reach the ultimate in specialization: taste and smell. Since these senses are in fact linked together in nature, it has been impossible for the psychologist to separate them.

Sociology developed out of two quite different sources: social philosophies involving the nature of society itself, and a concern with the social problems of the day. To some extent, this division is still seen in sociology; on the one hand Talcott Parsons, the leading theorist, is clearly in the grand tradition of his predecessors who tried to devise theories about societies as a whole; and, on the other hand, other sociologists are concerned with social problems such as delinquency and crime, family instability, and social disorganization.

In recent years in sociology, we have witnessed a rapid growth of activities that stem neither from social philosophy nor from reformist concentration on social problems. More and more sociologists are deciding by their work that sociology consists essentially of the study of organization: of the community, of the institutions of economic and political life, and of the groups that make up larger organizations. These fields have been variously named: social organization, industrial sociology, bureaucratic organizations, the community, the small group, and so on. They fit together in that they concentrate on the interactions and activities of men as they live and work together in groups. Let us call this field by the most inclusive term—social organization. The constitution of the field has clearly been influenced by two outside sources. From social anthropology has come the interest in culture and the concern with communities as functioning wholes. From social psychology has come the emphasis upon the small group as the essential building block for larger structures.

By now it should be evident that anthropology, sociology, and psychology have overlapping interests. Why should these fields be separate? History provides an explanation but no justification. As we trace the history, we find even the explanation breaking down. Social anthropology had its origin in the study of nonliterate and rural communities, whereas social organization grew out of urban and industrial studies in the advanced industrialized nations. No such dividing line can be drawn today. Sociologists have for many years been carrying on studies in rural communities in their own industrialized countries. More recently, they have extended such studies into villages in other lands and have become increasingly concerned with the anthropological problem of intercultural comparisons. On the other hand, more than forty years ago, social anthropologist W. Lloyd Warner brought his anthropological methods and theories to bear upon the study of a small industrial city in New England. Since that time, anthropologists in increasing numbers have turned to the study of literate societies and urban communities and institutions.

There remains just one generalization about the differences among these three fields: with few exceptions, students within each field follow their own favorite research method. Thus, students of social anthropology pursue knowledge with the personal interview and observation. Students of sociology tend to rely upon the questionnaire survey. Social psychologists practice small group experiments (though they also use the classical sociological method of the questionnaire).

If students of social anthropology, social organization, and social psychology share an interest in many of the same problems and are coming increasingly to depend upon a common body of theory, should they remain separate simply because the research they carry on is done by different methods? It is my thesis that this very separation of methods among the fields is holding back the advance of knowledge in the United States.

These methods should not be seen as competitive with each other, but rather as complementary. The anthropological methods of interviewing and observation are well suited to the study of social structure and to the flow of interpersonal events or social processes. They enable us to probe deeply into the thoughts and feelings of individual men, but they are not well suited to the quantitative study of the attitudes, beliefs, and values of groups or organizations. The questionnaire survey is the method of choice for quantitative studies of attitudes, beliefs, and values, but it is poorly adapted to the study of social structure and social processes.

Ideally, the small groups experimenter uses anthropological and survey methods along with his experiment. He may use a questionnaire to measure changes in the subjective states of his experimental subjects. He needs to observe the experiment in order to analyze the process that goes on and to account for the changes observed in his before-and-after measurements. He may need to interview the experimental subjects after the experiment in order to throw further light upon the process and to probe for personality influences in differential responses to the process. In fact, some well-known social psychological experiments can be criticized for their failure to provide observations of process and interview data on the reactions of the experimental subjects.

If these methods are indeed complementary rather than competitive, it follows that a student of social anthropology, social organization, and social psychology should develop some competence in each of them. In fact, this rarely happens in the United States.

The graduate student in anthropology must not only master social anthropology; he must also develop some competence in one or more of the fields of archaeology, physical anthropology, and linguistics. Since these fields do not use the same theories and research methods as social anthropology, what he learns in one field does not contribute to his learning in another. Therefore, the requirement of mastery of these really separate and distinct fields simply takes away time from that available to concentrate on social anthropology.

A generation or more ago, it was assumed that the well-trained social anthropologist should have a mastery of the literature regarding every culture in every part of the world, for which there was some literature. The proliferation of research reports has made this manifestly impossible. Today, the social anthropologist is expected to have a comprehensive knowledge of one area of the world and some comparative background in other areas. But even for one area of the world, such as Latin America, Africa, or Southeast Asia, the literature grows so rapidly that the area specialist is hard pressed to keep up with it. It thus becomes very difficult for the student of social anthropology to find the time to take even a single course in questionnaire survey methods, let along the courses in statistics that would be necessary to enable him to analyze the data he can gather with surveys.

In sociology, recent years have seen an extraordinary development of questionnaire survey methods, along with progress in machine data-processing and computers. The well-trained sociologist today is expected to have a solid command of statistics, plus some grounding in mathematics; and he must learn to move from simple correlation coefficients and tests of significance to scaling, factor analysis, and other more elaborate statistical or mathematical schemes.

The young student of sociology who wants to gain the required mastery of statistics, mathematics, and systems of data-processing, must spend a considerable part of his time on this subject through his period of study. The effort required to master this one methodology is thus likely to crowd out any other methodologies. This specialization tends to be further emphasized by the strong belief on the part of many sociologists that questionnaire surveys represent the really only thoroughly scientific method. They see anthropological methods of interviewing and observation as being simply impressionistic and of no scientific value, except insofar as they might give the sociologist ideas as to how to improve his scientific measurements with a survey.

We thus see within sociology an extraordinary specialization upon questionnaire surveys, with ever-increasing refinements in the methods of analyzing survey data, so that sociologists tend to forget the narrow range of phenomena that can be measured by the questionnaire.

Social psychologists tend to have more methodological breadth in their training, learning to experiment as well as to do surveys. But they too tend to share the sociologist's distrust of anthropological field methods.

While all social scientists will give lip service to the maxim that the nature of the problem should determine the research method or methods used, actually we find in the behavioral sciences today that each specialist tends to have his favorite method and tends to use it on every problem that interests him.

This discussion leads us to two main points:

1. The present boundaries and definitions of disciplines among the fields of anthropology, sociology, and psychology are simply a product of history. They have no justification in any logic of theory or research methods. If he had a chance to start over with a clean slate, no man in his right mind would draw the disciplinary boundaries as they stand today.

2. Within each discipline, the trend in growth has been toward increasing specialization, so that the specialist tends to develop ever more refined methods for analyzing his very partial view of human society.

HOW TO PICK A RESEARCH MAN

These conclusions have at least two important implications for action:

1. It is misleading and unprofitable to think of research problems in terms of disciplinary lines. If we think that the problem is economic, sociological, psychological, or anthro-

pological, then we are naturally inclined to think that we should find a good economist, sociologist, psychologist, or anthropologist to tackle it. This sort of approach may lead us to a man who has a good professional reputation but who is unqualified by experience, research methods at his command, or intellectual interest in the problem.

We need rather to ask questions such as these: Should the problem be defined as one of individual motivation? Of the relation of the individual to his peer group? Of intergroup relations? Of leadership? Would the researcher be studying small groups? An organization? A set of interorganizational relations? A community? What research instruments should be used: Psychological tests? Questionnaire surveys? Laboratory experiments? Field experiments? Interviewing and observation?

As we find our answers to these questions, we will find them leading us to the man or men who are qualified by experience, knowledge, skill, and interest to tackle the research problems we have in mind. Of course, I do not mean to imply that it is easy to find answers to such questions or to find the men to fit the answers. I am simply suggesting that if we define problems in terms of what individuals will probably have to do in order to solve them and then look about us for people who have shown some skill at doing these things, we are much more likely to make sound decisions than we are if we are swayed by the mystique of one or another discipline.

2. Knowledge is not advanced through specialization alone. If indeed we are suffering in the social sciences from excessive specialization, we may find the next breakthroughs through pursuing the integration of knowledge across fields rather than through pushing specialization farther.

CASE EXAMPLES

Let us bring these ideas to bear on some hypothetical examples.

We might begin with a questionnaire survey study of a training program, for the questionnaire is the most popular instrument in the behavioral sciences today; and it is the one most likely to be picked up by the economist who ventures across disciplinary boundary lines. Let us say that the questionnaire has demonstrated that the trainees who show the pattern of attitudes *XYZ* are (a) more likely to complete the training program, and (b) more likely get jobs within two months of completing the program than other fellow trainees who do not show pattern *XYZ*. The man of action —and also the theorist—should greet this finding by saying, "That is interesting, but so what?"

The finding obviously points to the next question: how is pattern of attitudes *XYZ* produced? To the extent that these attitudes are a product of experience before entering the training program, the questionnaire can provide us only with limited and partial answers. The questionnaire may provide demographic data upon the trainees: information regarding age, education, composition of the family, father's occupation, father's employment record, and so on. It may also provide some information about the respondent's *perception* of his relations with his father, his mother, and perhaps others. The questionnaire does not provide data on *process*—on the flow of experience and interpersonal relations that has formed the attitudes not being measured. If we wish to get at the process, we have to go beyond the questionnaire and use methods such as intensive interviewing of our subjects and observation of them in various social situations.

Such studies of child development may be of great

importance in the long run, but they do not, of course, tell us much about what may be done with this particular group of trainees at this particular time—and others like them. If we want to face up to that question (and still remain with the pattern *XYZ* attitude finding), we might ask whether the training program itself has any effect in building pattern *XYZ*. For this purpose, we could apply a questionnaire at the beginning of the program and the same questionnaire at a later period. If we found a change in the direction of pattern *XYZ*, we might plausibly attribute it to the training program —providing we could rule out the possibility that the trainees had simply learned to verbalize what the trainers considered to be appropriate attitudes.

But note that even if we are able to establish a link between a change toward pattern *XYZ* and the training program, we have not resolved the underlying scientific question. We may have proven that the change has been caused by the training program, but then we have to ask: what is that training program? It is just at this point that we find many research projects deficient. The investigator tends to assume that the formal description of the training program tells him all he needs to know about the nature of the program and concentrates simply upon his before-and-after attitude measures. Training programs tend to be described in the language of educational administration. There may be very little similarity between what the trainer or the administrator of the training program reports is going on or what has gone on and what a trained research man would find if he observed the training sessions and then followed up with interviews with trainer, trainees, and others associated with them.

In other words, it does us no practical good to know that a given training program reached a certain objective unless we can also discover what features of that program contributed toward that objective. Only as we make these systematic observational studies, can we have some confidence in being able to reproduce a program that has proven effective.

It is not my purpose with this case to cast aspersions upon the value of questionnaires. I am simply seeking to point out that, for many research projects, the questionnaire by itself will tell only part of the story. Indeed, the questionnaire findings will take on greatly enhanced value, insofar as they are integrated with the findings of other methods.

I would also like to point to one important area of investigation which is not readily accessible to a questionnaire and where questionnaires may prove to be of little value. I refer to the study of interorganizational relations.

In making comparative evaluations of the poverty program in a number of cities, Mitchell Svirdoff[3] focused attention upon this area of investigation. He said that the comparative effectiveness of these programs depended in large measure upon the degree of interorganizational integration that was achieved within each city. I suspect that those who have studied social agencies would be inclined to agree with this judgement. In any large metropolitan area, a large number of agencies can now claim rights to a slice of the poor people. Do these agencies simply compete with each other? Or has it been possible to achieve some integration in their activities?

Up to this point, research has focused largely upon the poor people themselves. I suggest that any number of studies at this level, no matter how good they are, will not lead us very far toward the solution of the complex institutional and interinstitutional problems of this field. Now and then we might lay off the poor people for a while and examine the behavior of individuals and organizations that are trying to help them—or to push them around.

Who can do this sort of study? Again, I suggest the type of answer I have given earlier. It could be a political scientist, a sociologist, a social psychologist, an anthropologist, or an economist—but it must be one who has some competence in the study of organizations and interorganizational relations. While no well-developed theoretical framework is yet available for the study of interorganizational relations, a combination of concepts and ideas from social organization and collective bargaining research may prove useful to us.

Where no organization has control of other organizations, their relations cannot be understood in terms of a system of authority. Following the lead of George Homans [4] and Peter Blau, [5] we may look at interorganizational relations as being based upon *exchanges,* and then examine the nature of the exchanges which take place. Richard Walton and Robert McKersie [6] have provided a framework focusing on distributive versus integrative issues, as a means of explaining conflict or cooperation between organizations.

BASIC VERSUS APPLIED RESEARCH?

When we begin talking about applied research, we run up against a well-established prejudice that applied research is, from a scientific standpoint, an inferior type of activity. On this point, let me quote the late Chester I. Barnard, when he took the National Science Foundation to task for its effort to distinguish between basic research and applied research:

> As one example, we have Karl Jansky's discovery of radio signals from outer space. Jansky, according to the report, was not engaged in basic research; he merely made a basic discovery. Here the confusion arises from labeling research according to the motives for which it is carried on; there is an element of snobbery involved which ought not to be encouraged. After all, Louis Pasteur made his great contributions to the foundations of bacteriology in trying to find solutions to the practical problems of the French silk and wine industries. The whole discussion demonstrates that the dichotomy between basic and applied research can be overemphasized.[7]

I find it more useful to distinguish between service research (or information gathering) and basic research. A service research project is one in which the investigator simply seeks information of use to a particular organization, without any regard to the general applicability of his findings, beyond that organization. Whenever the investigator seeks to gain knowledge that may help to establish certain uniformities of human behavior, he is engaged in basic research. His project may be good research or bad research, but that is a different issue.

In other words, basic research may be of two types: applied and nonapplied. By nonapplied, I mean simply that there is no provision for the application of knowledge within the research design. This does not mean, of course, that only applied research is useful in the solution of practical problems. Depending upon the state of knowledge regarding the problem under investigation, it may be the most useful thing an investigator can do to carry out a research project designed to make an advance in theory and/or research methods, without any plan for the immediate application of the knowledge gained. It is always a legitimate question whether a given area of knowledge has reached a point where it is useful to plan an applied research project or whether further nonapplied studies are necessary before the applied project will pay off.

PROBLEMS OF APPLYING RESEARCH KNOWLEDGE

Within this general context, let us face another problem. Anyone with experience in this field knows that there is a great deal more behavioral science knowledge available than is being currently applied in industry or government. Why?

We all know of research reports that have simply found

their way into filing cabinets without having any impact upon behavior. Nor is this simply because the written word does not communicate as effectively as face-to-face conversation, though this is a part of the problem.

Suppose, at the conclusion of the research project, the research man delivers an oral report to a group of administrators in the organization that sponsored the study. As Everett C. Hughes[8] has commented, the administrators tend to respond almost simultaneously with two characteristic comments: (1) "It isn't true; and (2) "You haven't told me anything I didn't already know."

These two statements are often uttered in practically the same mouthful by a single individual. Is this illogical? Of course it is, but such illogicality should alert us to an underlying problem between the research men and the key people in the organization under study. The administrators have been hit suddenly by what appears to be criticism of their own behavior, and they naturally react defensively.

We will not solve this probelm through any effort to be tactful and diplomatic in a single situation. We will only solve the problem as we conceive of the application of research findings as a social process—the research application process. Ideas do not automatically jump off the pages of the research report and put themselves into practice, nor can the same jump be achieved simply through one good group discussion.

Industry has departments of research *and* development. In the field of agriculture, a long history points in the same direction. The research findings arrived at in laboratories and experiment stations are channeled into the extension organization, whose members carry them to the farmers and their organizations. We have to think in terms of a process that flows from research to extension to application and back to research again.

How NOT to Do It. To show what process means, let us get down to cases. I shall focus on a training program, first illustrating how not to do it and then trying to sketch out an approach based on what we so far have learned about the research application process.

Some years ago, a colleague told me that a large company had decided to set up a training program for its 140 foremen. Would I like to join him in conducting the training program and also perhaps in developing some research connected with it?

Managing to contain my enthusiasm, I pointed out that the research so far done on human relations training programs for supervisors had failed to find that they did any good. Therefore, if we were going to throw ourselves into such an enterprise, we ought to try out some new approach.

I further argued that before we could provide very useful training for these foremen, we ought to know a good deal more than we did about the nature of their jobs and of their relations with workers, their superiors, industrial engineers, personnel men, and so on. I suggested that we do this research first, then design our training program on the basis of what we found, and at the same time design the research that we would do around the training program.

I also advised against training 140 foreman all at once. If we put the first step on a pilot basis, with one or two small groups of foremen, we could try out our new methods of training, and we could also try out our research ideas and instruments. According to the results of the pilot effort, we could then proceed to a larger-scale training and research operation.

My colleague put my proposals to the training director of the company and a few days later, told me his response. The training director said that he had been trying for three years to persuade top management to support a training program for the foremen. When he finally received their endorsement, he was determined to go ahead, with *all* the foremen, just as fast as possible, before top management changed its mind. He was very much in favor of research, he said, so much so that he had arranged to give us three weeks before the kick-off sessions with the foremen to do research, to plan the training program, and to organize the study of the training program. At the risk of being considered a poor team player, I opted out of the program.

I should emphasize that these events took place some years ago. If a similar proposal came to us today, I believe we would tell the training director politely, but firmly, to go somewhere else to get his training services.

I am not arguing that no training should be done unless the program is integrated with an adequately planned and executed research project. This would be highly unrealistic. A federal or state agency that has a mandate to provide training programs cannot realistically refuse to provide these services. To the extent that the demand exceeds the supply of talent and money available, the agency can pick and choose among requests. Even so, the administrators of the agency will have to recognize that for most of the programs, they will just have to do the best they can without any research. Certainly this is a better policy than to try to tack on a little research, which will be largely window dressing, with every program. It seems to me much more important, now and then, when the conditions are right and the talent is available, to try to do a research-training job as it really should be done.

Integrating Research and Action. In the first place, the research men and those designing and carrying out the training should plan jointly. It is a waste of time and effort simply to tack on research activities after the training has been planned. If the research is to evaluate the effectiveness of the training program, that evaluation must be carried out in terms of progress toward certain objectives. It is important to agree on objectives that the trainers want to aim for and that the research men consider feasible from the standpoint of their ability to measure progress toward these objectives.

Furthermore, the research men should have an opportunity to make suggestions regarding training plans and training methods. These are ordinarily thought to be the sole responsibility of the teacher, but I would argue that the improvement of training programs must depend in large measure upon their being better grounded in behavioral science knowledge. For example, Lawrence Williams [9] has reported a case where behavioral science findings have been used with apparent success in reorganizing the sequence of assignments in a craft training program for pupils in a depressed area. The principles involved here have to do with the relationship between delayed gratification and social class. It has now been well established in psychological and sociological research that middle-class individuals accept much more readily than do lower-class individuals assignments which involve a long-range goal, with little or no immediate payoffs.

Thus, if we are dealing with lower-class individuals, it is a mistake to start them on exercises that have no immediate payoff or on a long-term project which will be rewarding to them only upon completion. In the training program in question, the pupils had an opportunity to show off at home something that they had made in the very first session of the class. As the training program preceeded, the assignments involved steadily increasing time periods for completion. This approach appeared to be much more successful with this group of students than can be expected when the principles of delayed gratification and social class are not taken into account.

Especially when large-scale enterprises are under consideration, it is important to plan first a pilot operation, so that both trainers and research men have an opportunity to try out their methods. This should also give the administrators a much more realistic view of what they might expect from a large-scale research and training program, than if they undertook it without some pilot testing.

For example, a colleague has told me about a study contracted by the health department of a large city to a research organization. The research was tied in with a campaign to get the citizens to go to clinics to get certain kinds of health check-ups. The aim was to find out what variables were associated with going or not going to these clinics. The researchers put a large number of variables into their questionnaire and carried out a $100,000 study. After all the data had been put on punch cards and ground through innumerable computer runs, there was just one finding that emerged at an appropriate level of statistical significance. It was this: the closer a man lived to the clinic, the more he tended to go to that clinic.

The head of the Health Department did not regard this finding as being worth $100,000. Such an experience no doubt discouraged the administrator from pushing farther with social research. Perhaps this unfortunate outcome might have been avoided if the research problem had been tackled on a pilot basis first, enabling the administrators and the research men to get a more realistic idea of what they were likely to conclude and of the relationship of costs to values of research findings.

Planning for research should include more than simply the development of the formal research instruments. If we are to learn what went on in the training program that might have led to the changes we hope to measure, we need to observe the sessions themselves and also interview the trainees and the trainer from time to time, in order to get a systematic record of the process.

Before a final written report is submitted, the researchers should organize feedback sessions in which they give preliminary reports on their findings and their interpretations of the data. Since feedback comes relatively late in the research process, investigators tend to give little thought to this step until they are about to reach it. I feel strongly that the researchers and the trainers and administrators should reach an understanding before the beginning of the program regarding feedback sessions, at least in general terms. It is important at the outset to have an understanding of what research data can be communicated and what may not be communicable. If this is not done, the researchers and the administrators and trainers may have quite different expectations as to what should be reported in the feedback sessions.

Feedback sessions are sometimes looked upon strictly as efforts in diplomacy on the part of the researchers. It is well recognized that a written report will get a better reception if there has been some prior discussion of its contents with those most concerned. At the very least, this kind of experience enables the researcher to get a better feel for emotionally sensitive areas so that he does not inadvertently use emotionally loaded words in the written statement.

It is a mistake to look upon feedback simply as a means of "softening up" the agency for the written report. In my own experience, I have found such feedback sessions exceedingly valuable to the researcher, quite beyond the functions of diplomacy. Sometimes genuine errors have been pointed out to me, which of course would be much more awkward to cope with after a written report has been submitted. More frequently, I am told that my information is correct on a certain point, but that I only have part of the story. My informant then tells me the other part, which can sometimes turn out to be a very valuable contribution indeed. Finally, there are questions of the interpretation of data. I have often received alternative interpretations of a given finding, which had not occurred to me before. In some cases, I have had to take these interpretations into account in the final report.

If he treats the members of the organization simply as subjects to be studied, the researcher is bound to run into resistance, particularly when he presents his findings. The research man who can treat members of the organization as participants in the study, including the feedback process, will find that he not only gets better acceptance of his research, but also learns much more from the members of the organization.

In an evaluation study, a final step should involve the evaluation of the research itself, and this too can be carried on jointly by the researchers and the officers of the organization under study. The administrators need not be asked to tear the research apart, but they might at least be asked how the research might be directed so as to be more helpful in the future.

The assumption involved in this final step is that research and development should be a continuous process. For administrators and research men to get the most out of working together, they should not think of a given research project as a one-time experience. The people involved on both sides need to learn a new set of roles. They also need to recognize that the payoff to the organization is not simply in the final product of the research. I have often heard administrators in organizations comment that they have learned a good deal from the research process itself. At the very least, the questions asked by the investigator may lead them to reflect about things they have taken for granted; and, as they seek to explain what is going on to the investigator, they learn to understand their own organization better. By the same token, as the investigator becomes more familiar with the people and the problems of the organization, he improves his own ability to formulate meaningful and researchable questions and also in his ability to fit the research into the organization with a minimum of disturbance.

In building a research program that will lead to practical

payoffs, we need to think in terms of continuities and avoid a scattering of one-shot operations.

FUTURE PROSPECTS

I have presented a rather dismal picture of the state of the behavioral sciences, particularly on the following points:

1. Overspecialization, which prevents us from dealing effectively with interrelated aspects of the same problem.
2. The prevalence of the one-method man, who applies his favorite method to any problem that interests him.
3. Snobbishness, which divides the world of research into basic and applied, thus luring the intellectual elite toward the problems that are most remote from practical application.
4. The consequent failure to design, develop, evaluate, and redesign application processes that increase our abilities to transform theoretical knowledge into socially useful outcomes.

Perhaps there were signs of healthy changes developing even in 1966, when the first draft of this paper was written. Those trends are clearer now.

The one-method man is no longer king. I no longer startle people when I tell them that the questionnaire is *not* really the only scientific method for sociologists—or for anybody else. In fact, there is growing recognition of the sterility of many studies based solely on the questionnaire. While this swing in professional opinion is unlikely to throw the questionnaire completely into the discard, there is now a real danger of underestimating the potential of that method, especially when it is used in combination with other methods.

Reaction against the questionnaire has led to the popularity of something called "ethnomethodology." I recently discovered that this was what I was doing when I started hanging around on Boston street corners in 1936—but we called it participant observation, then. Whatever we call the method, we seem to be enjoying a resurgence of interest in studies based on field observation.

This emphasis on observation is not likely to be a short-lived fad. It meets real needs felt both by students of the behavioral sciences and by practitioners who seek to use behavioral science findings. Students feel the need to do research that is "relevant" as they find themselves examining real live social processes. Men concerned with deriving action and policy recommendations from research are also recognizing the practical merits of observational field studies. Speaking about some of the research on poverty programs the Office of Manpower Policy, Evaluation and Research (Dept. of Labor) was then supporting, Curtis Aller commented:

> When the research men do a questionnaire study, we have to wait six months to a year after the data are all in before they can carry out their analysis and tell us what they have found out. With the participant observer, it is quite different. By the time he comes out of the field—if not before—he can tell us a great deal about the nature of the program he is studying. He can point out to us problems of policies or procedures that we can do something about and that we never would have discovered through a questionnaire survey.[10]

The academic ivory tower is now under fire as never before. No longer does the man who is studying practical problems have to defend his problem choice to his academic colleagues. To be sure, he may have to defend himself from his students if he appears to be studying only those research problems that "the establishment" will finance, but at least the legitimacy of practical concerns is no longer at issue.

The fall of the ivory tower is not without its perils. The "radical sociology" many enthusiasts are now trying to build may not turn out to be any more scientifically productive than the old model. My quarrel with sociology's most eminent theorist, Talcott Parsons, is not over the alleged conservative bias of his framework. I have simply found Parsonian theory of very little practical use in predicting or controlling human behavior. I hope that any new emerging "radical" social theory will be subjected to the same practical tests that Parsonianism has failed.

Finally, there is a growing recognition of the need to focus systematic attention on the process of research utilization. In fact, institutions are even being created to give emphasis to research on the utilization of scientific knowledge.[11]

While we cannot yet boast over the contributions of the behavioral sciences to manpower research, with such trends now under way, there are grounds for at least the diplomatic expression of "cautious optimism."

NOTES

1. J. K. Galbraith, "The Language of Economics," *Fortune* (December 1962) pp. 128–30, 169–71.

2. Everett C. Hagen, *On the Theory of Social Change* (Homewood, Ill.: Richard C. Irwin and Co., 1963).

3. Mitchell Svirdoff, Comment made in Sub-Committee on Research, National Manpower Advisory Committee.

4. George Homans, *Social Behavior: Its Elementary Forms* (New York: Harcourt, Brace & World, 1961).

5. Peter Blau, *Exchange and Power in Social Life* (New York: Wiley, 1964).

6. Richard Walton and Robert McKensie, *A Behavioral Theory of Labor Negotiations* (New York: McGraw-Hill, 1965). See also Richard Walton, J. M. Dutton, and H. G. Fitch, "A Study of Conflict in the Process, Structure and Attitudes of Lateral Relationships," in A. H. Rubenstein and C. J. Haberstroh, eds., *Some Theories of Organization*, rev. ed. (Homewood, Ill.: Irwin Dorsey, 1966), pp. 444–65.

7. Chester I. Barnard "A National Science Policy," *Scientific American*, 197 (November 1957), 45–49.

8. Personal conversation.

9. Personal conversation.

10. Curtis Aller, Comment made at meeting of Sub-Committee on Research, National Manpower Advisory Committee.

11. For example, the Center for Research on the Utilization of Scientific Knowledge (CRUSK), in the Institute for Social Research at the University of Michigan.

DANIEL BELL

THE CORPORATION AND SOCIETY IN THE 1970s

OVER the last few years, there has been a notable change in public attitudes toward the corporation. Only twelve years ago, writing in Edward S. Mason's magisterial compendium on *The Corporation in Modern Society*, Eugene V. Rostow could comment:

> In reviewing the literature about the current development of [the large, publicly-held] corporations, and about possible programs for their reform, one is struck by the atmosphere of relative peace. There seems to be no general conviction abroad that reform is needed. The vehement feelings of the early thirties, expressing a sense of betrayal and frustration at a depression blamed on twelve years of business leadership, are almost entirely absent.

The reason for that tolerant and even benign attitude towards the corporation in the 1950s is not hard to find. Apart from the general sense of social peace induced by the Eisenhower administration (a peace maintained, in part, by the mobilization of the sentiments of society against an external enemy), a new and seemingly satisfactory conception of the role of the corporation in the society had arisen.

For 75 years, going back to 1890 when Congress passed the Sherman Antitrust Act, the corporation had been viewed with populist suspicion because of its size. Size, in the American lexicon, means power, and the bigness of business was perceived as both an economic and political threat to democracy. Economic size was equated with market power, or the ability to control (within limits) the price of products offered for sale. Large scale assets were equated with undue influence, either in a local community or state, or in the nation itself.

But in the more than half century's experience with antitrust, a new economic sophistication had been developed. One was the important distinction between size and market control, and the realiziation that the two are not completely related. The two biggest manufacturing companies today are Standard Oil of New Jersey and General Motors, with $19.2 billion and $14.1 billion respectively in assets. GM has about 55 percent of United States' automotive production; but Standard Oil, though larger than GM, has only about 9 percent of domestic oil refining and an even small percentage of production.

Size clearly, is not a good predictor of market control. Market control is measured by "concentration ratios," i.e., the sales of the largest four companies, in a product line, as a percentage of total product sales. But it seems reasonably clear that, since the turn of the century, the concentration ratios have gone down considerably and that, in most industries, there is not increasing concentration but rather a ceaseless flux.[1]

But the more important shift was a change in ideology. The idea took hold that "size" was less relevant than "performance." Performance itself is an elusive criteria. It embraces the idea of receptivity to innovation; willingness to expand capacity (one of the chief charges by liberal economists in the 1940s against such "monopolistic" industries as aluminum and steel was that they were unwilling to expand capacity); the reflection of increased productivity in better quality, higher wages, and steady, if not lower, prices; and similar indices of responsiveness to the needs of the society.

The clearest mark of performance was growth. The fear of the 1930s, after all, was stagnation. Liberal economists such as Alvin Hansen had predicted, in fact, that the economy had achieved such a state of "maturity" that there was no longer the possibility of expansion. The facts belied these fears. New technological frontiers opened up after the war; and the large corporations took the initiative.

A vigorous, large company could present its case to the public that size was immaterial, so long as the corporation displayed those hallmarks of dynamism that added up to "performance." In fact, as J. K. Galbraith argued in his book, *American Capitalism*, size was an asset because it enabled the large corporation to underwrite technological progress.

> It is admirably equipped for financing technical development. Its organization provides strong incentives for undertaking development and for putting it into use . . . The power that enables the firm to have some influence on price insures that the resulting gains will not be passed onto the public by imitators (who have stood none of the costs of development) before the outlay for development can be recouped. *In this way market power protects the incentive to technical development.* (Italics in the original.)

Here was a strong and sophisticated defense of bigness by the criteria of performance. And, to a considerable extent, the ideology of American business in the postwar years became its ability to perform. The justification of the corporation no longer lay, primarily in the natural right of private property, but in its role as an instrument for providing more and more goods to the people. Because the corporation seemed to be performing this role adequately, criticism of it did, indeed, become muted, so that by the end of the 1950s the corporation had established a new legitimacy in American life.

THE NEW CRITICISM

Today that legitimacy is being challenged, or at least the tolerant and benign attitude toward the corporation has receded. The paradox is that the ground of the new criticism is no longer size or bigness (though some old populist echoes persist), but performance itself. A feeling has begun to spread in the country that corporate performance has made the society uglier, dirtier, trashier, more polluted, and noxious. The sense of identity between the self-interest of the corporation and the public interest has been replaced by a sense of incongruence.

Any issue that becomes ideological becomes distorted. The facts of spoliation of countryside and the reduction of various amenities are obvious; the reasons less so. One evident cause is the sheer increase of numbers of persons in the society and a change in social habits. Take, for example, the national parks: in 1930, the number of visitor-days (one person staying twelve hours) was 3 million in a population of 122 million, by 1960, it was 79 million, in a population of 179 million; and in 1968, there were 157 million visitor-days in a population of 200 million. The results are described vividly in an account in *The New York Times:*

Yosemite, only a day's drive from San Francisco and Los Angeles, is generally considered the most overcrowded park. Congestion reaches its peak on major holidays and this Labor Day weekend was no exception.

The constant roar in the background was not a waterfall but traffic. Transistor radios blared forth the latest rock tunes. Parking was at a premium. Dozens of children clambered over the rocks at the base of Yosemite Falls. Campsites, pounded into dust by incessant use, were more crowded than a ghetto. Even in remote areas, campers were seldom out of sight of each other. The whole experience was something like visiting Disneyland on a Sunday.

Moreover, if we take pollution of the air and water as the criterion of social ill, then clearly all sections of the society are at fault: The farmer who, by seeking to increase food production, uses more nitrate fertilizer and thus pollutes the rivers of the country; the individual automobile owner who, seeking greater mobility, spews noxious gas into the atmosphere; the Atomic Energy Commission which, in seeking to expand nuclear power, may be responsible for thermal pollution of the waters; and the corporation whose smokestacks emit smog-creating gases in the air, or whose waste products pollute the lakes.

But if one takes the attitude that everyone is to blame—and simply ends with the moral exhortation for each person to restrain his behavior—then one misses the important point. Such a situation itself points to the fact that the allocative mechanism of society, the proper distribution of costs and resources, is not working. In a free society, the socially optimal distribution of resources and goods exists where the market reflects the true economic cost of an item. But where private costs and social costs diverge, as A.C. Pigou pointed out fifty years ago, then the allocation of goods becomes skewed. When the owner of a factory has no incentive to take account of costs to others of the pollution he generates because these costs are not charged to him, factory output (or automobile mileage in the case of a car owner) will be at a higher level than is socially optimal.

The growing problem for modern society is this increasing divergence of private costs and social costs (what economists call technically an "externality," because such costs are not "internalized" by a firm in its own cost accounting). But along with this awareness there arises, too, the question whether the strict conception of costs—and return on investment—that is the rationale of the accounting procedures of the firm are at all adequate today. In other words, perhaps the older definition of "performance" is too narrow. The question that then arises involves, not just the "social responsibility" of any particular corporation, but the "rightness" of the broader pattern of social organization and of the social goals of the society. And, to the extent that the corporation has been the institution integral to the existing pattern, it becomes the starting point of a new inquiry.

Perhaps we can see the quite radical difference between these two perspectives by setting up two models, which I shall call the *economizing* mode and the *sociologizing* mode, as polar extremes within which the actions of the corporation can be estimated and judged.

THE ECONOMIZING MODE

Beginning little more than 150 years ago, modern Western society was able to master a secret denied to all previous societies—a steady increase of wealth and a rising standard of living by peaceful means. Almost all previous societies had sought wealth by war, plunder, expropriation, tax-farming, or other means of extortion. Economic life, in the shorthand of game theory, was a zero-sum game; one group of winners could benefit only at the expense of another group of losers. The secret mastered by modern Western society was *productivity,* the ability to gain a more than proportional output from a given expenditure of capital, or a given exertion of labor; or, more simply, society could now get "more with less effort or less cost." Economic life could be a non zero-sum game; everyone could end up a winner, though with differential gains.

In the popular view, productivity was made possible by the introduction of machinery or, more specifically, the discovery of new forms of power, mechanical or electrical, hitched to an engine. Clearly much of this view is true. But productivity, as a concept, became possible only through a new "supporting system" which dictated the placement of machines in a new way. To put the matter less abstractly, modern industrial society is a product of two "new men," the engineer and the economist, and of the concept which unites the two—the concept of efficiency. For the engineer, the design of a machine and its placement vis-à-vis other machines is a problem of finding the "one best way" to extract maximum output within a given physical layout. The economist introduces a calculus of monetary costs, within the framework of relative prices, as a means of finding the most appropriate mix of men and machines in the organization of production.

Modern industrial life, in contrast with traditional society, has been revolutionized by these innovations. The new sciences have introduced a distinctive mode of life. We can call it *economizing*. Economizing is the science of the best allocation of scarce resources among competing ends; it is the essential technique for the reduction of "waste"—as this is measured by the calculus stipulated by the regnant accounting technique. The conditions of economizing are a market mechanism as the arbiter of allocation, and a fluid price system which is responsive to the shifting patterns of supply and demand.

Economics itself, over the past hundred years, has developed a rigorous and elegant general system of theory to explain the relative prices of goods and services and of the factors in production, the allocation of those factors to various uses, the level of employment, and the level of prices. With economics, comes a rational division of labor, specialization of function, complementarity of relations, the use of production functions (the best mix of capital and labor at relative prices), programming (the best ordering of scheduling of mixed batches in production or in transportation), etc. The words we associate with economizing are "maximization," "optimization," "least cost"—in short, the components of a conception of rationality. But this conception of rationality it should be pointed out, was intended by its utilitarian founders as a rationality of *means*, a way of best satisfying a given *end*. The ends of life themselves were never given; they were seen as multiple or varied, to be chosen freely by the members of society. Economics would seek to satisfy these choices in the "best way," i.e., the most efficient means possible in order to "maximize" satisfaction.

For an understanding of the economizing mode, this distinction between rational means and a plurality of ends must be emphasized. Modern industrial society, being a liberal society, has never felt the need to define its ends or to establish such collective decision-making. No conscious social decision was made to "transform" society 200 years ago. No conclave met, as in a French constituent assembly or an American constitutional convention, to declare a new social order. Yet it is quite clear what the new goals of the new industrial society were to be—the ends that became "given" all involved the rising material output of goods. And other, traditional modes of life (the existence of artisan skills and crafts, the family hearth as a site of work) were sacrificed to the new system for the attainment of these economic ends.

Commonplace as this history may be, the singular fact needs to be emphasized. Unlike political change, no one "voted" for these dicisions in some collective fashion, no one assessed (or could assess) the consequences of these changes. Yet a whole new way of life, based on the utilitarian calculus or the economizing mode, gradually began to transform the whole of society.

THE CORPORATION: A NEW SOCIAL INVENTION

Productivity is a technique, steadily rising output of goods is an end; for the two to be realized they have to be institutionalized in some renewable system of organization. That institution was the corporation.

Much of economic history and some of economic theory has focused on the entrepreneur as the singularly important person who, sensing new opportunities, breaks the cake of custom and innovates new areas of economic life. Much of contemporary sociological theory has dealt with the manager as the faceless technocrat who runs a routinized operation. But to understand the corporation, one has to turn not to the entrepreneur (and the myths about him) or the manager (and the caricatures that are drawn of him), but to a figure historically and sociologically intermediate between the two—the organizer.

The church and the army have been the historic models or organizational life. The business corporation, which took its present shape in the first decades of the twentieth century, was the one new social invention to be added to these historic forms. The men who created that form—Theodore N. Vail who put together AT&T, Walter Teagle of Standard Oil of New Jersey, Alfred P. Sloan of GM—designed an instrument which coordinates men, materials, and markets for the production of goods and services at least cost with the best possible return on capital investment. They did so by introducing the idea of functional rationality, of *economizing*, as a new mode of ordering social relations.

Of the three, only Alfred P. Sloan has put down directly the principles he employed. His account, *My Years With*

General Motors, is fascinating, and one can take his sketch as prototypical of the corporate mode of mid-century America. The most striking aspect of Mr. Sloan's book is its language. Sloan's key terms are *concept, methodology,* and *rationality.* Throughout the book, Sloan uses these terms to explain the innovations he made in General Motors: "Durant had no systematic financial methodology. It was not his way of doing business." "The spacing of our product line of ten cars in seven lines in early 1921 reveals its irrationality." "In product variety only Buick and Cadillac had clear divisional concepts of their place in the market."

The language is not an accident or an affectation. It is surprising only to those who associate such language with the academy and not with the analytical necessities of organization. The language derives in part from Sloan's training as an engineer (he took a degree at MIT in 1895); but more, it derives directly from the revolution in organization that Sloan introduced: the initiation of detailed planning, of statistical methods and of financial controls. In explaining why he relied on market research and forecasting rather than salesmen's intuition, he remarked: ". . . In the automobile industry you cannot operate without programming and planning. It is a matter of respecting figures on the future as a guide."

The reasons for the success of General Motors can be attributed, in simplified fashion, to two elements: A market strategy based on a "clear concept" of product lines and an organizational form which combined decentralization of operations with coordination of policy.[2] The organizational structure of General Motors is commonplace now, and has been widely copied by most large corporations. At the time of its innovation, it was a novelty. Stated most simply the principle of organization is to have a complete breakdown of the costs of each unit, and to exercise control of operating divisions through stringent budgets. Before the system was instituted, division in GM sold their parts to other divisions (e.g., a battery division to a car division) on the basis of cost plus a predetermined percentage. But the corporation at the top did not know which units were profitable and which not. "It was natural for the divisions to compete for investment funds," Sloan wrote, "but it was irrational for the general officers of the company not to know where to place the money to best advantage."

What Sloan did was to treat each division as a separate company, with the corporate group at the top acting as a "holding company," and to measure the performance of each division by the rate of return on investment consistent with attainable volume. The rate of return is thus a measure of performance and a means of ranking each division, not on the basis of its absolute profit alone, but on the rate of return on capital invested. The measure, in short, is the margin of profit multiplied by the rate of turnover of invested capital. Through these measures, the corporate group at the top could determine how to allocate the corporation's money in order to achieve a maximum return for the whole.

All aspects of corporate policy became subordinated to that end. In specifying the corporation's philosophy, Sloan was explicit:

> To this end [he writes] we made the assumptions of the business process explicit. We presumed that the first purpose in making a capital investment is the establishment of a business that will pay satisfactory dividends and preserve and increase its capital value. The primary object of the corporation, therefore, we declared, was to make money not just motor cars. Positive statements like this have a flavor that has gone out of fashion; but I still think that the ABC's of business have merit for reaching policy conclusions.

The economizing system of each corporation locks with each other to create a social system. Earnings per share of common stock becomes the balance wheel around which the system turns. If the earnings of a firm drop, it may find it difficult to attract capital, or may have to pay more for capital vis-à-vis other firms. Thus, the allocation of capital in the economy follows the same principle as it does within the corporation. Locked thus into competition, the degree of freedom of any single corporation to break away from this measuring rod—the rate of return on investment—is limited. Any change in the system has to be a change in the entire system.

Profitability and productivity, thus, are the indices of corporate success. They are the tests of meeting the demands of the marketplace and the demand for the efficient distribution of resources within the firm and between members of the society. This is the rationale for the *economizing* mode for the corporation, as for the economy.

LIMITS OF THE ECONOMIZING MODE

The theoretical virtue of the market is that it coordinates human interdependence in some optimal fashion, in accordance with the expressed preferences of buyers and sellers (within any given distribution of income). But what ultimately provides direction for the economy, as Veblen pointed out long ago, is not the price system but *the value system of the culture* in which the economy is embedded. The price system is only a mechanism for the relative allocation of goods and services within the framework of the *kinds of demand* generated. Accordingly, economic guidance can only be as efficacious as the cultural system which shapes it.

The value system of industrial society (communist as well as capitalist) has been centered around the desirability of economic growth; and the cultural value of Western society, particularly American society, has been the increase of private-consumption economic goods. There are, however, three drawbacks (at least) to this system.

The most important consideration is that it measures only economic goods. But as E. J. Mishan has pointed out, and as a once popular refrain once had it, "the best things in life are free." Clean air, beautiful scenery, pure water, sunshine, to say nothing of the imponderables such as ease of meeting friends, satisfaction in work, etc.—they are "free goods" either because they are so abundant that there is little or no cost, or because they are not appropriable and saleable. Such free goods contribute greatly to our total welfare. But in our present accounting schemes, priced at zero, they add nothing to the economist's measure of wealth. Nor, when they disappear, do they show up as subtractions from wealth.

The second consideration is that growth, as measured by our present economic accounting, tends to generate more and more "spillovers" which become costs borne directly by other private parties or distributed among the society as a whole. These are what economists call "externalities." Externalities (or "external costs"), as economists define the term, is the unintended or unplanned impact, the "fallout" on Third Party C (and often D,E, and F, as well), of a private transaction between parties A and B. The result is a social cost (though frequently a social benefit, too). The most obvious example of a social cost is air pollution—the result, in part, of the increasing number of private cars in the society. In every elementary economics textbook, air was once the classic illustration of the "free good." Yet the irony is that in the next thirty years one of the most scarce resources we may have, (in the sense of proportionately sharply rising costs) will be clean air. The costs of automobile disposal are not charged to the automobile owner; similarly, the costs of salvaging a depressed coal mining community are not charged to the companies selling the competing fuels which may have driven coal off the market.

The third problem with the economizing mode is that the value system of American society emphasizes, as the primary consideration, the satisfaction of individual private consumption; the result is an imbalance between public goods and private goods. In the popular psychology, taxes are not considered as the necessary purchase of public services that an individual cannot purchase for himself, but as money "taken away from *me* by *them*." Taxes, thus, are not considered as an addition to welfare, but as subtractions from it. This is reinforced by politicians who claim that taxes are too "high" (but by what standard?) rather than asking: Are there needs which can be met only by public goods, and what are the taxes buying?

Thus, if one is trying to assess welfare (or the quality of life) in some optimal fashion, the problem is not only the simple commitment to economic growth, but the nature of the accounting and costing system of the economizing mode which has served to mask many of its deficiencies. Our fascination with Gross National Product is a good illustration.

GNP PRIVATE COSTS AND SOCIAL COSTS

Conventionally we measure economic welfare primarily through the figures of Gross National Product. GNP was a marvelous economic concept. Developed largely by Simon Kuznets and his colleagues at the National Bureau of Economic Research in the late 1930s, it first came into government use in 1945 and is the basis of the framework of the United States National Economic Accounts. These accounts allow us to sketch the macroeconomic levels of activity in the society, and through them to measure economic shortfalls the potentials of full employment revenues and the like, as a means of deciding on economic policy. But there are several drawbacks as well, particularly if we are concerned not only with wealth but the welfare of the society.

GNP measures the value of goods and services bought and sold in the market. But the measure itself is only "additive." It does not discriminate between a genuine addition to welfare and what, in effect, may be a subtraction but is counted as an economic plus. Thus, in the conventional example, the output of a steel mill is a value added to GNP. But if the steel mill pollutes a lake, and then uses additional resources to clean up the lake, that new expenditure is also added to GNP. Similarly an increase in environmental deterioration over time would not show up as a decline in real output because the flow of benefits from the environment is not counted as an output to begin with (e.g., the usability of a lake or river for swimming). But expenditures designed to reduce environmental deterioration would show up as increased real output.

More important, however, is the fact that in assessing *public* services we do not have a means of estimating actual benefits or values. In items that are sold in the market, such as automobiles or clothing, we have market prices as the value individuals place on the products. But how do we value publicly provided services such as health, or education, or protection? Our accounting system does so only by the "input" costs, not by the output values. Thus the "output" of police services is measured by salaries paid to members of the Police Department, the costs of police cars, etc., not by the social and economic value of crimes prevented or violators apprehended; the value of health services is measured by the costs of doctor's fees and drugs, not by the reduction of time lost on account of illness; the value of education is measured by the cost of teachers' salaries, equipment, etc., not by the value imputable to the gain in pupil knowledge.

This is a central problem in the question of how much money should be spent on "public goods." People grumble over taxes, but there is no way, at present, of showing that the benefits received for these services may be far greater than the costs. And while there is no way of knowing, it is likely that public services of this kind are "undervalued," and therefore less appreciated.

The second limitation of the accounting system, which derives from the growing existence of externalities is the divergence between private and social costs. The idea of social costs is an old one, going back 150 years to the socialist economist Sismondi. But it was not until about fifty years ago, when A.C. Pigou wrote his *Economics of Welfare*, that the phenomenon of social costs was integrated into the conceptual system of neoclassical equilibrium economics. Pigou pointed out that the investment of additional resources may throw costs "upon people not directly concerned" such as the "uncompensated damage done to surrounding woods from railway engines." [3]

But for almost half a century, this idea of divergence between private cost and social cost was almost completely neglected. Now with the rising concern with environmental spoliation, the second-order consequences of technological change and the increase in "externalities," the problem has moved into the center of social policy. In the next decade one of the major social questions will be the determination of who is to pay the costs of such externalities, and how the amounts will be assessed. Which costs ought to be borne by the parties that generate the costs, and which, legitimately, should be borne by the society as a whole, will be one of the most difficult questions in the political economy of the future. What we have now is only the beginning awareness of the problem. What we lack is a genuine total cost matrix which, for particular instances, would be able to assess the costs and benefits of particular actions and policies.[4]

THE SOCIOLOGIZING MODE

Important as all these issues are, they do not go to the heart of the matter, which is that the economizing mode is based on the proposition that *individual* satisfaction is the unit is which costs and benefits are to be reckoned. This is an atomistic view of society and reflects the utilitarian fallacy that the sum total of individual decisions is equivalent to a social decision. Yet the aggregate of individual decisions has collective effects far beyond the power of any individual to manage, and which often vitiate the individual's desires. Thus, every individual may value the freedom and mobility which a personal automobile provides, yet the aggregate effect of so many autos on the roads at once can lead to clogged transportation. We might all accept, in the abstract, the principle that the automobile has become a vehicle of uglification; yet lacking a social decision about which alternative modes of transportation might best serve an area, I might have, willy-nilly, to go out and buy a car. Each of us, individually, may see the consequences of an individual action, but lacking a social mechanism to assess it, we become helpless, drift, and thereby accelerate it.

In effect, in contrast to the economizing mode of thought, one can specify—I apologize for the heavy-handed clumsiness—a sociologizing mode, or the effort to judge a society's needs in more conscious fashion,[5] and (to use an old-fashioned terminology) to do so on the basis of some explicit conception of the "public interest."

Two fundamental questions are involved.

First, the conscious establishment of social justice by the inclusion of all persons *into* the society. If the value system of a society is made more explicit as a means of guiding the allocative system (pricing) of a society, this value system must also establish, however roughly, the "right" distribution of income in the society, the minimum income available to all citizens, etc.

The second is the relative size of the public and the private sector. Economic goods, to put it in textbook fashion, are of two types, individual and social. Individual goods are "divisible;" each person buys the goods or services he wants—clothes, appliances, automobiles—on the basis of free consumer choice. Social goods are not "divisible" into individual items of possession, but are a communal service—national defense, police and fire protection, public parks, water resources, highways, and the like. These goods and services are not sold to individual consumers and are not adjusted to individual tastes. The nature and amounts of these goods must be set by a single decision, applicable jointly to all persons. Social goods are subject, therefore, to communal or political, rather than individual demand.

A man cannot ask for and individually buy in the market place his share of unpolluted air, even if he were willing to pay extra for it. These are actions that have to be taken in coordinated fashion through public channels. We can assign the costs of air pollution to its source, whether industrial, municipal, or individual, in order to force culprits to reduce the pollution, or we can use the money for remedial measures. In the same way, the laying out of roads, the planning of cities, the control of congestion, the organization of health care, the cleaning up of environmental pollution, the support of education—all these, necessarily, become matters of public policy, of public concern and often (though not necessarily) of public funding.

To say, in effect, that the public sector of the society has to be expanded, is not to assume, naively, that the failures of the market will now be remedied. Each arena has its own problems, and the beginning of political wisdom is to recognize the ineluctable difficulties in each. Public decision-making can easily be as irrational and counter-productive as private decision-making. The major sociological problem ahead will be the test of our ability to *foresee* the effects of social and technological change and to *construct alternative courses* in accordance with different valuations of ends, at different costs.

VARIETIES OF PLANNING

A considerable amount of planning goes on already. Every major corporation today necessarily operates in accordance with a one-year fiscal plan and a five-year market strategy in order to meet competition or to expand its size. Each company plans singly and each introduces its own new technologies—yet no one monitors the collective effects. The same is true of the planning of various government agencies. In considering social effects, one finds this kind of planning unsatisfactory.

The first flaw is the fallacy inherent in single-purpose planning itself.[6] Most engineers, developers, industrialists, and government officials are single-purpose planners. The objective they have in mind is related almost solely to the immediate problem at hand—whether it be a power site, a highway, a canal, a river development–and even when cost-benefit analysis is used (as in the case of the Army Corps of Engineers) there is little awareness of, and almost no attempt to measure, the multiple consequences (i.e., the second-order and third-order effects) of the new system.

The second is the failure to make the necessary distinction between, as Veblen put it, the technological and institutional processes, or, in the terminology used by a panel of the National Academy of Sciences, between the "technologies" and "the supporting system." The automobile, the SST, pesticides, drugs—all these are technologies in the physical engineering sense of the term. The support system is the organization of production and distribution, or more generally the economic and legal matrix in which the technology is embedded. The simple point is that there is no "technological imperative." no exact one-to-one correspondence between a particular technology and a specific supporting system. As Jack Burnham pointed out in a pungent way: "When we buy an automobile we no longer buy an object in the old sense of the word, but instead we purchase a three-to-five-year lease for participation in the state-recognized private transportation system, a highway system, a traffic safety system, an industrial parts-replacement system, a costly insurance system . . ." [7]

One may, therefore, depending on the problem, seek to change either the technology (the gasoline engine) or the support system (unrestricted private use of the roads). But what this allows us to do is to compare alternative modes, at alternative costs, and to design national "technology assessment." [8] With few exceptions, the decision about the future use of a technology today is made by the economic or institutional interests who will primarily benefit from it. But as the panel of the National Academy of Sciences argues: "Decisions concerning the development and application of new technologies must not be allowed to rest solely on their immediate utility to their sponsors and users. Timely consideration must be given to their long-term sacrifices entailed by their use and proliferation, and to potentially injurious effects upon sectors of society and the environment often quite remote from the places of production and application."

In rather inchoate fashion, assessment and decisional systems already exist in the federal government. The Federal Water Pollution Control Administration, the National Air Pollution Control Administration, and the Environmental Control Administration, all are empowered to make studies of consequences; but they have less power to establish controls. Some agencies, such as the Atomic Energy Commission both promote new technology (e.g., nuclear power) and assess the consequences. But what may be needed are *independent* boards to make assessment and propose remedial actions to the executive or to Congress. Whatever the final structures may be, it is clear that some social decision mechanisms will have to emerge in the next few years to make such assessments of second-order effects of technological and social change. New and large powers will be vested in administrative boards. New and complex tasks will confront the Congress.

And for the private corporation, a new principle in the relations of corporations to public policy will soon be emerging. Just as it has been public policy to provide tax inducements to help corporations expand plant capacity (by investment credits, or more rapid depreciation allowances), so it will be public policy to provide tax penalties either to force corporations to bear the burdens of social costs generated by the firm, or to favor an alternative technology or supporting system if the social costs can be minimized by the alternative system or the social benefits enhanced. Given the collective effects of private decisions, this involvement of public policy in corporate policy is inescapable.

Just as we may be moving into technology assessment, so we shall have to cope with social assessments as well. For example, the social map of the United States was redrawn after World War II by the rapid expansion of the suburbs and the extraordinary rise in suburban home ownership. But all this was made possible only as a matter of public policy: by federal guarantee of mortgages; by low down payments by veterans (often as little as 10 percent down on a purchase price) so that "owning" became cheaper than renting; and by the policy of permitting the deduction of interest payments on mortgages from income taxes. But no one questioned the existing "support system" of large numbers of small developers creating tracts of unattached houses in mechanical grids.

There can be, let us say, three alternative models of suburban development: one, a pattern of detached homes with private walkways and separate garages; the second, a set of "cluster houses" with the sharing of common auxiliary facilities (e.g., garaging); and third, high-rise apartment houses with large green spaces. Each of these developments has vastly different "social costs" which are borne by the community, not by the developer (the pattern of roads, auxiliary land use, the location of schools, etc.). Yet these social costs are rarely, if ever, taken into consideration. There is no "total cost matrix" to make a buyer aware of what the alternative styles could cost him in terms of the secondary costs he and the community would have to pay as a result of his choice. Nor has public policy ever sought to make such a determination.

Now, I am not arguing that consumers should be required to take one or another of the patterns. But intelligent public policy—because it is public monies that are facilitating this social change—should inquire into the alternative total cost matrices of the different patterns, and of the consequences of maintaining or changing existing institutional patterns of home building and development. It is not a matter of "interference" or "non-interference" in the society; *any* action (including non-action) is bound to strengthen or weaken one or another vested interest. It is a matter of making the choices and consequences explicit.

THE CORPORATION AS A SOCIOLOGICAL INSTITUTION

In traditional corporate law, property is defined as things (res), but the major lesson which corporations have learned in the last thirty years is that a corporation, while producing things, is made up of people, and that one cannot treat people—at least managerial and white collar personnel—as things.

Corporations are institutions for economizing; but they are also ways of life for their members. Until the early years of the twentieth century, the life of most Americans was bounded by the isolated small town, the church, and the family. The small town has virtually disappeared; the church has lost much of its emotional hold on people; and the tight bond between family and occupation, which gave a unity to life—the family farm, the family business, or the family occupation which the son inherited—has been sundered. The breakup of that traditional way of life, and the consequent sense of uprootedness and disorientation, is the source of what sociologists call *anomie*.

Emile Durkheim, the French sociologist who coined that term, thought that for *anomie* to be resolved there must be a group which could provide a sense of kindredness and common purpose for its members. Political society, he thought, was too amorphous and too distant. The answer, he said, lay in the occupational group, the profession, which could provide a new ethic for society. One of Durkheim's chief expositors, Elton Mayo of the Harvard Business School, thought that this purpose could be most effectively realized in the business corporation.

For a significant number of persons, this has necessarily become the case. The "four wishes" which the late sociologist W.I. Thomas thought were basic to human experience—the wish for security, for new experience, for response, and for recognition—can for these men only be obtained within the corporate milieu. Much of this led, twenty years ago, to the creation of the derogatory expression, "the organization man," as signifying a new kind of conformity. If the image were meant to suggest that previously men had been free and individualist and now were uniform and identical, the history was mythical and the irony was simply a new ideology. For life in the small town had been largely narrow and bigoted—one has only to recall Sinclair Lewis' *Main Street*—and the world of organizations offered an authentic, fresh challenge and opportunity. Corporations can be forces for conformity; and they can equally be arenas for personal initiative.

A business corporation, like a university, or a government agency, or a large hospital—each with its hierarchy and status system—is now a lifetime experience for many of its members. Necessarily, therefore, it can no longer be an instrument satisfying a single end—in the case of the business corporation, only turning out its goods and services—but it has to be a satisfactory way of life for its members. It not only has to satisfy its customers; it has to be agreeable to its "self."

A business corporation, however, is subject to different constraints, and has a somewhat different ethos, from a university or a government agency or a hospital. Corporations, unlike the other three, are competitive and have to be profitable. (And the profits, moreover, are often a major support—through taxes—of the other three.) Even so, if we set up a continuum, with *economizing* at one end of the scale (in which all aspects of organization are single-mindedly reduced to becoming means to the goals of production and profit) and *sociologizing* at the other (in which all workers are guaranteed lifetime jobs, and the satisfaction of the work force becomes the primary levy on resources), then in the last thirty years the corporation has been moving steadily, for almost all its employees, towards the sociologizing end of the scale. One has only to note, in the rising percentage of "fringe benefit costs"—the index of that shift—vacations, disability pay, health insurance, supplementary unemployment benefits, pensions, and the like.

All of this, historically, was inescapable. To the extent that the traditional sources of social support (the small town, church and family), have crumbled in society, new kinds of organizations, particularly the corporation, have taken their place; and these inevitably become the arenas in which the demands for security, justice, and esteem are made. To think of the business corporation, then, simply as an economic instrument is to fail totally to understand the meaning of the social changes of the last half century.

THE BALANCE OF OBLIGATION

When one uses the phrase the "social responsibility" of the corporation, one is not indulging in rhetoric (though many corporate officials are), or thinking of *noblesse oblige* (which fewer corporate officials do), or assuming that some subversive doctrine is being smuggled into society (as some laissez-faire economists suggest), but simply accepting a cardinal socio-psychological fact about human attachments. Unless one assumes that loyalty and identification are simply monetary transactions, or that employment is simply a limited relation of service-for-payment, then the corporation is a social world, with social obligations to its members, as well as an economizing instrument competitively providing goods at least cost to an economic world of consumers.

But what is the balance of obligation, and how far can one go in either direction? Perhaps the best way of trying to deal with this question is to confront some questions which have already emerged or which may be emerging in the next decade.

Satisfaction on the Job. The trite observation from the "human relations" literature of twenty years ago was that a man more satisfied with his job was likely to have higher morale and be more productive. Thus, the mechanical layout of work, set down by the engineer, was modified to take into account the findings of industrial psychologists and sociologists. The increase in costs could be justified by the more than proportional increase in productivity.

But what if a change in job patterns increases satisfaction but does *not* increase productivity? What is the corporation to do? The conventional answer is that the primary obligation of the corporation is to profits and that marginal increases in costs can only be justified by marginal increases in productivity. But let us take a variant of this problem. When a corporation hires more women, and these women ask for child-care centers to be paid for and maintained by the company, is it obligated to do so? The question is not just of treating such centers as a necessary cost to attract female labor when one has a tight labor market, but of a change in social values which would permit women who want to work to go back to work during the years when their children are young. A child-care center is a necessary component of job satisfaction for young women, even though it may add costs to a company far beyond the "gains" in productivity from such women. Does the conventional principle still hold?

Minority Employment. Does a corporation have a special obligation to take on a larger proportion of persons from minority groups which have suffered historical disadvantage—even if such persons are less able than a competitor for the job? And if the employment of such a person increases training costs and may lead to lower productivity? The problem, in principle is no different from that of a university which may have to set aside a special quota and, sometimes, given the limited number of places, exclude "majority" group persons who on the formal criteria of merit (e.g., test scores, grades) may be more qualified. The question of merit versus social justice is, as most complex moral problems, a question of "right" versus "right," rather than right versus wrong. Where there is such a conflict of right, how does one balance one's obligations?

Relative Pay. How does one decide what a man is worth? A pure market principle, of competing supply and demand, only reflects relative scarcities, but relative scarcity is not identical with social justice. In most American industry, a distinction is still maintained between blue-collar work, wherein a man is paid by the piece or the hour, and white-collar work wherein a man is paid by the week or month. A few corporations—IBM, Texas Instruments—have abolished the distinction, but not many have followed that lead. What is the rationale for this invidious status distinction?

Within the corporation itself, the differential between the lowest paid (often the common labor rate) and the average of the top executive group may be about 25:1 or higher. On what basis is this spread justified? The original rationale was the market. But increasingly the market becomes less relevant for the determination of the relative differences between "grades" of labor and persons. Elliot Jaques, the English industrial psychologist, has sought to work out a principle of "equitable" pay on the basis of differential responsibility between jobs—as measured, for example, by the amount of independent time a man has to do a job and the degree of supervision. There may be other such "formal" systems. But because human beings want and need a clear rationale for the differences in reward among them, some principle of social justice for social distinctions will have to be articulated.

Responsibility to a Community. An old problem, but one which recurs as increasingly the corporation becomes the way of life for its members. Beyond the payment of taxes, what obligations does a corporation have to the local community where it locates its plants and headquarters? What are its responsibilities in creating amenities and a more satisfactory social and cultural environment?

Responsibility for the Environment. In the last few years, the corporation, along with the rest of the society, has learned that the environment cannot be treated as a "free good." How the costs are to be divided will be, as I have already indicated, one of the most difficult technical-political issues of the decade.

The Confrontation with Moral Issues. The corporation, like the university, has always pleaded that on moral questions it is "value-neutral." As a corporation, its obligation is to seek the best return on investment. But value neutrality is no longer so easily possible. The difficulty arising from American private investment in South Africa illustrates the problem. In the classic morality tale of fifty years ago, the example was one of the local church which gained an income from properties on which brothels were located. The church could always claim a trade-off by arguing that it saved as many souls as it lost bodies. Such a calculus was never entirely convincing. A corporation's claim that it saves as many bodies as it loses souls is not likely to be more so.

What all this adds up to is that, on the continuum I have drawn of the *economizing* and *sociologizing* modes, the balance of attention shifts more and more to the latter. And, while on the particular questions I have cited which the corporation will face in the next decade, there are no exact answers or ready-made formulae, the standpoint from which the decisions will be considered will, more and more, be made from the sociological viewpoint.

THE TURNING POINT FOR THE CORPORATION

The question of "social responsibility" is, I believe, the crux of a debate that will become crucial in the next few years. One position has been put forth by Milton Friedman:

> what does it mean to say that the corporate executive has a 'social responsibility' in his capacity as businessman? If this statement is not pure rhetoric, it must mean that he is to act in some way that is not in the interest of his employers. For example, that he is to refrain from increasing the price of the product in order to contribute to the social objective of preventing inflation, even though a

> price increase would be in the best interests of his corporation. Or that he is to make expenditures on reducing pollution beyond the amount that is in the best interests of the corporation or that is reguired by law in order to contribute to the social objective of improving the environment. Or that, at the expense of corporate profits, he is to hire 'hard-core' unemployed instead of better qualified available workmen to contribute to the social objective of reducing poverty . . .
>
> In a free-enterprise, private property system, a corporate executive is an employee of the owners of the business. He has direct responsibility to his employers. That responsibility is to conduct the business in accordance with their desires, which generally will be to make as much money as possible while conforming to the basic rules of the society, both those embodied in law and those embodied in ethical custom.[9]

There are two different kinds of answers to Friedman. Both were given recently by Alden Clausen, the new president and chief executive officer of the Bank of America, the biggest bank in the world.

For Clausen, one crucial question is: in what social context does the corporation operate today? As a recent article in *Fortune*, by John Davenport, reported: "To keep this giant money machine profitably growing is the first business of Alden Winship (Tom) Clausen . . . It is of some significance that . . . his thoughts turn often to: how to alleviate if not cure the blight now spreading at Hunter's Point and south of Market Street (in San Francisco); how to crack the city's hard-core unemployment; how to cope with student unrest at Berkeley or down the peninsula at Stanford."

In defending these objectives, Clausen confronted directly the views of Friedman. As the article in *Fortune* reported:

> At the moment Clausen and his associates are less interested in modifying their bank's capital structure than in charting a course through a period when capitalism itself is under intense attack . . .
>
> . . . Business, he argued, has to concern itself with nonbusiness problems today if it wants to be around tomorrow. The Friedman view is okay in the short pull. 'But in the long pull, nobody can

expect to make profits—or have any meaningful use for profits—if the whole fabric of society is being ripped to shreds.'

There is, equally, a different question, apart from social expediency: Below the surface of this clash of views, there lies an important but seldomly explicated confronted question about the nature of the corporation. Friedman sees the corporation as fundamentally an 'artificial person' and the corporate manager as simply an agent of individual shareholders. Clausen sees the corporation as having a kind of life of its own, and hence having a certain freedom of choice in balancing its contribution to the long-range needs of the community against the immediate demands of owners.

And, as the writer John Davenport, himself a distinguished conservative, comments: There may be dangers lurking in Clausen's view of corporate autonomy, but there is surely something unrealistic in the view that society is just an atomized collection of individuals.[10]

The heart of the matter is the question of the nature of the corporation. Is the corporation primarily an instrument of "owners"—legally the stockholders—or is it an autonomous enterprise which, despite its particular history, has become—or should become—an instrument for service to society in a system of pluralist powers?

A classic debate on that question was initiated 40 years ago in the pages of the *Harvard Law Review* by A. A. Berle and Merrick Dodd. Berle held to the view, at the time (he later revised his views) that all corporate powers are powers in trust for the benefit of the stockholders. Dodd argued that legally such was the case, but the use of private property was deeply affected with a public interest and that the directors should be viewed as trustees for the enterprise as a whole—for the corporation viewed as an institution—and not merely as "attorneys for the stockholders." Berle responded that, since one could not offer "a clear and reasonably enforceable scheme of responsibilities to someone else," Dodd's proposal would place the control of the organization entirely in the hands of management. The problem, as he saw it, was: If there is not a prior legal statement of responsibility to stockholders, how does one prevent management from exercising arbitrary social and political power, or from becoming overreaching and self-seeking?

This legal—and sociological—issue remains. Is the manager primarily a trustee for absentee investors? Or is the role of the manager, as Frank Abrams, when he was chairman of the board of Standard Oil of New Jersey, put it, to conduct his affairs "in such a way as to maintain an equitable and working balance among the claims of the various directly interested groups—stockholders, employees, customers and the public at large."

PRIVATE PROPERTY OR PRIVATE ENTERPRISE?

The modern business corporation has lost many of the historic features of traditional capitalism, yet it has, for lack of a new rationale, retained the old ideology—and finds itself trapped by it.

Unhappy is a society that has run out of words to describe what is going on. So Thurman Arnold observed in connection with the language of private property—the myths and folklore of capitalism—which even thirty years ago was hopelessly out of date. *The point is that today ownership is simply a legal fiction.*

A stockholder is an owner because, in theory, he has put up equity capital and taken a risk. But only a minor proportion of corporate capital today is raised through the sale of equity capital. A more significant portion of capital comes through self-financing, by the success of the enterprise itself. In the last decade, more than 60 percent of the capital investment of the nation's 1,000 largest manufacturing firms was financed internally. Retained capital is the basis of the rise in net assets of large corporations. And the growth of retained capital is the product of managerial skill. (Equally, a large portion of new capital is raised by debentures, which become a fixed charge against earnings, rather than through floating equity or risk stock. Debentures hinge on the stability of the company and the prospect of repayment—again a managerial problem.)

If one were to follow the logic of Friedman's argument, as he does—it is his strength and weakness that he always follows the logic of his argument, to the very end—one would have to outlaw or at least discourage self-financing. Under the "pure" theory of market capitalism, a firm risks a stockholder's capital and then pays back any profits in the form of dividends—to its legal owners, the stockholders. If it seeks to risk that money again, it should ask those stockholders to reinvest that money, rather than withhold it from them and reinvest it by managerial decision. Friedman argues that it is only the "double taxation" (through corporate and personal income tax) of dividends that prevents such a desirable state of affairs from emerging. But I should say that such a state of affairs is neither desirable nor possible. Given the pattern of stock ownership today—particularly with the growth of mutual funds, pension funds and trust funds—the stockholder is often an "in-and-out" person with little continuing interest in the enterprise. Such an in-and-out procedure may be a useful discipline for management and a measure of economic performance—but then it becomes a form of countervailing power, not ownership. True owners are involved directly and psychologically in the fate of an enterprise; and this description better fits the employees of the corporation, not its stockholders. For these employees, the corporation is a social institution which they inhabit. It is politically and morally unthinkable that their lives should be at the mercy of a financial speculator.

In other words, the corporation may be a *private enterprise* institution, but it is not really a *private property* institution. (If the assets of the enterprise are primarily the skill of its managerial employees, not machinery or things—and this is preeminently true in the science-based industries, in communications, and in the so-called "knowledge industries"—then property is anyway of lesser importance.) And if ownership is largely a legal fiction, then one ought to adopt a more realistic attitude to it. One can treat stockholders not as "owners" but as legitimate claimants to some fixed share of the profits of a corporation—and to nothing more.

THE MEANING OF "A CORPORATION"

What then is a corporation? If one goes back to the original meaning of the term, as a social invention of the late Middle Ages to meet some novel problems, a corporation was an instrument for self-governance for groups carrying on a common activity (artisan guilds, local boroughs, ecclesiastical bodies); it often had common economic assets, and its existence would persist beyond the lives of its individual members. Those who were "members" of the corporation were those directly responsible for its activities, those who were the legatees of the past members, and those chosen to carry on the work.

A business corporation today—like a university today—can be viewed in this original sociological conception of the term. Indeed, if one begins to look on the business corporation more and more on the model of the university, then the fallacy of ownership becomes more apparent. Who "owns" Harvard or the University of Chicago? Legally the "corporation," as composed by the overseers or the trustees. But in any sociological sense this is meaningless. The university is a self-selective ongoing enterprise of its members (administration, faculty, students, and alumni, with differential responsibilities and obligations) who seek to carry out its purposes with due regard to the interests of the particular community which constitutes the university—and also to the larger community that makes the university possible.

As a business institution, the "corporation" is the management and the board of directors, operating as trustees for members of the enterprise as a whole—not just stockholders, but workers and consumers too—and with due regard to the interests of society as a whole. But if this view is accepted, there is a significant logical corollary—that the constituencies which make up the corporation themselves have to be represented within the board of corporate power. Without that, there is no effective countervailing power to that of executive management. More important, without such representation, there would be a serious question about the "legitimacy" of managerial power.

How such constituencies might be represented is a question to be explored. A dozen years ago, Bayless Manning, Jr., until recently the Dean of the Stanford Law School, sought to picture the corporation as if it were in law what it often is in fact, as a kind of "voting trust" wherein the stockholder delegates all his rights, except that of collecting dividends, to the directors. In order to establish some check on the board of directors, he proposed a "second chamber" an "extrinsic body," which would review decisions of the board where conflicts of interest arose—such as compensation of officers, contributions to other enterprises (universities, community efforts, etc.) not directly related to a company's business, clashes with a public interest, etc.

It is beyond the scope of this essay, and the competence of the author, to estimate the viability of these—or other—specific proposals. The problem is there; it is not going to go away; and discussion of possible resolutions is anything but premature.

FROM BITTERNESS TO BANALITY

As a debate on these issues continues, one important consideration should be kept in mind—the bitterness of one generation is often the banality of another. Who, today, gives a second thought to Savings Bank Life Insurance? Yet this idea, authored by Louis D. Brandeis in Massachusetts, was fought for five months in passage through the legislature and was marked by one of the bitterest fights ever witnessed on Beacon Hill. (One line of attack was that people would not voluntarily seek insurance, and that they would not take it out at all if the expensive system of soliciting by agents were done away with.) The issue gave Brandeis a national reputation, and eventually brought Brandeis to the Supreme Court. The reputation remained, but the issue itself soon faded.

The lesson, however, was not, and is still not wholly learned—reforms will never be as sweeping in their effects as their proponents hope, and the results will rarely be as damaging and apocalyptic as the opponents fear. Workmen's compensation was an issue that inflamed a generation of radicals and was fought by industry on the ground that it would relieve the workman of "individual responsibility" for his actions; yet who today would deny that industrial safety is a legitimate cost of factory operations?

Such reforms are always an expression of a revision—implicit or explicit—in the American "public philosophy." This kind of "revisionism" is inevitable as men and societies change, and as the dominant values assume a new shape. The private enterprise system has been the primary institution of Western society not because of its coercive power but because its values—economizing and increasing output of material goods—were congruent with the major consumer values of the society. With all its obvious imperfections the system "worked." Today, however, those values are themselves being questioned, not in the way socialists and radicals questioned them a generation ago—that they were achieved at the cost of exploiting the worker—but at the very core, the creation of more private goods at the expense of other social values. I return to a point made earlier that unlike the polity, no one, meeting collectively "voted in" our market economy. But now votes are being taken.

It seems clear to me that, today, we in America are moving away from a society based on a private-enterprise market system toward one in which the most important economic decisions will be made at the political level, in terms of consciously-defined "goals" and "priorities." The dangers inherent in such a shift are familiar enough to anyone acquainted with the liberal tradition. In the past, there was an "unspoken consensus," and the public philosophy did not need to be articulated. And this was a strength, for articulation often invites trials by force when implicit differences are made manifest. Today, however, there is a visible change from market to non-market political decision-making. The market disperses responsibility: the political center is visible, the question of who gains and who loses is clear, and government becomes a cockpit.

But to be hypnotized by such dangers is little less than frivolous. No social or economic order has a writ of immortality, and the consumer-oriented free-enterprise society no longer satisfies the citizenry, as once it did. So it will have to change, in order that something we still recognize as a liberal society might survive.

Whether such a change will represent "progress" is a nice metaphysical question that I, for one, do not know how to answer. This was a society "designed" by Locke and Smith and it rested on the premises of individualism and market rationality in which the varied ends desired by individuals would be maximized by free exchange. We now move to a communal ethic, without that community being, as yet, wholly defined. In a sense, the movement away from governance by political economy to governance by political philosophy—for that is the meaning of the shift—is a return to pre-capitalist modes of social thought. But whether this be progress or regress, it clearly makes it incumbent upon us to think more candidly and rigorously about our values, and about the kind of world we wish to live in.

NOTES

1. The stereotype that the big company has a big market share is obviously supported by many examples. Only it is refuted by even more. If one looks at the "symbolic" examples of concentration, it is quite clear that in no industry today is concentration at a comparable level with the period after the great wave of consolidations, from 1898 to 1902. As pointed out by Professor Segall of the University of Chicago: In 1900, International Harvester produced 85 percent of the nation's harvesting machines. In 1902, National Biscuit controlled 70 percent of the biscuit output. In 1901, American Can turned out 90 percent of its industry's output. In 1902, Corn Products had 80 percent of its industry's capacity. In 1902, U. S. Leather accounted for more than 60 percent of leather output; Distillers Securities provided more than 60 percent of whiskey output; International Paper produced 60 percent of all newsprint. In 1900, American Sugar Refining refined virtually all the sugar in the country. For a comprehensive discussion of the contemporary degree of concentration see M. A. Adelman, "The Two Faces of Economic Concentration," *The Public Interest*, 21 (Fall 1970).

2. This market strategy and organizational form allowed GM to come from behind to oust Ford, a genius at production techniques, from the leading position in the market. In 1921, Ford had 60 percent of the car and truck market and almost complete control of the low-price field. Chevrolet, GM's entry in the low-price field, had only 4 percent of the market. To meet Ford head-on in price competition would have been suicidal. Sloan's strategy was not to undercut the Ford price but to top it somewhat, seeking to skim off that layer of buyers who would be willing to go to a higher

price on the assumption they were getting a better car. By successive "upgrading" of items, largely through annual model changes, GM won the larger share. In effect, GM countered "style" to "utility" and won.

3. In his book, Pigou gave dozens of examples of similar "disservices": the destruction of neighborhoods by the construction of factories in residential districts; the costs to the consumers of competitive advertising; the increase in expenditures for police and prisons because of the rising sale of liquor; the overrunning of a neighbor's land by rabbits originating from game preserves; the costs of diplomacy and armies because of the rise of foreign investments, etc.

In this country the theme was elaborated by John Maurice Clark of Columbia, who, in his studies in the Economics of Overhead Costs (Chicago: University of Chicago Press, 1923), drew a distinction between social and market values and between social and market costs. For Clark, as Allan Gruchy points out, the business concept of cost excluded many important social costs such as communal health hazards, unemployment, and other costs associated with business fluctuations. Clark's concern was to bring commercial efficiency closer to social efficiency, and with making the economic system account for social values, clean air, scenic beauty, etc., as well as market values.

4. I do not minimize the technical and political difficulties of establishing such a matrix. Let me provide a "homely" example of a problem which, many years ago, first brought the social cost problem to my personal attention.

In New York City when I was a boy, snow was removed from the streets by the hiring of extra trucks which would cart mounds of it away and dump it in the river. Many years later, Paul Screvane, who was the Commissioner of Sanitation, ordered his men to push the snow into the middle of the streets, where it was churned into slush by passing cars. Perhaps he did it because the costs of hiring trucks had gone up exorbitantly, or because he wanted to demonstrate an outstanding record in office so that he could run for mayor. The sanitation department showed a commendable record of economy. But (as I figured out from the records of the Industry and Commerce Association), after each snowfall the cleaning and dyeing bills in the city went up substantially, because the passing cars would splatter the clothes of the innocent bystander.

Now, which was the "rational" solution? One could say that

Screvane's method was highly irrational, because it passed the costs of snow removal onto the backs of the unfortunate pedestrians, and if the cleaning and dyeing bills were higher than the cost of hiring additional trucks, it was truly a misallocation of resources. Yet one could also say that if the trucks had been hired, direct city expenses would have been increased and taxes would have to go up, increasing the resentments of the taxpayers in the city, so that the system of "Russian roulette" whereby a random group of bystanders bore the costs might have a greater "political" rationality than economic cost benefit analysis.

5. One can say, theoretically, that the price system could manage the problem, e.g., when the costs of individual congestion became high it would then become profitable for alternative modes of transportation to compete with the private car. But the price system, in this instance, relies on *trial and error* to assess the result. The difficulty is that such assessments, *after the fact*, are likely to be futile—an enormous amount of resources would have been misallocated, and a preemptive "system" of transportation will have been established. Under such a system, clogged highways will eventually result in the building of more highways.

6. For an elaboration of this point, see Harold Gilliam, "The Fallacy of Single-Purpose Planning," *Daedalus*, 96 (Fall 1967), 1142, on America's changing environment.

7. Jack Burnham, *Beyond Modern Sculpture* (New York: G. Braziller, 1968) If one asks what a sculptor is doing in discussing the automobile system, his argument is cast in the context of the disappearance of "objects" in contemporary society and its replacement of "systems."

8. The idea of "technology assessment" grew largely out of the studies of the House of Science and Astronautics Committee under the leadership of Congressman Daddario. Two panels, one in the National Academy of Sciences and one in the National Academy of Engineering were set up to test the feasibility of the idea. The National Academy of Sciences Panel, under the direction of Harvey Brooks, agreed that assessment was possible and proposed a number of ways in which the process could be implemented in government. The Engineering panel undertook three studies—of subsonic aircraft noise, of computer-assisted instruction, and of multiphasic health screening—to further this idea. Both reports on Technology Assessment were published by the Morse Committee in July 1969.

9. From "The Social Responsibility of Business Is to Increase Its

Profits," in *The Sunday Times Magazine*, September 13, 1970, p. 32. The argument is elaborated in Milton Friedman, *Capitalism and Freedom* (Chicago: University of Chicago Press, 1962).

10. John Davenport, "Bank of America Is Not for Burning," *Fortune*, LXXXIII (January 1971), 91.

PART FIVE

THE REV. THEODORE M. HESBURGH, C.S.C.

TRIBUTE TO ELI GINZBERG

IN 1968 the United States Commission on Civil Rights issued a publication, *Mobility in the Negro Community: Guidelines for Research on Social and Economic Progress*, prepared by Eli Ginzberg and an associate. Its theme, the full utilization of all human resources, conditions of race, creed, or color notwithstanding, is symbolic of Dr. Ginzberg's career —a career that has continuously stressed the grave wrong imbedded in society's failure to utilize men's skills properly and the still graver wrong in not providing opportunity for all men to develop and use their skills.

I see a parallel between his career and the lifespan of the Commission on Civil Rights: Both have sought to enrich the human experience. Someone has to do the long, hard work and study and factually analyze the elements upon which change can be based. Someone has to do the prodding of the conscience of men with the right kind of ammunition that cannot be waved aside because the prodding is based on the facts. There are moments of action in this process, but they are fairly few and far between and are interlocked with long periods of tough, grinding work. But this makes action both possible and effective. The work of Eli Ginzberg and that of the Commission has been of this nature and both have had profound effect on the process of change.

For Eli Ginzberg the involvement in change began almost thirty years ago, in 1942, with his book, *Grass on the Slag Heaps: The Story of the Welsh Miners*. Only a rare eye and sensitive soul would have been cognizant of the plight of Welsh miners caught in a morass of poverty between the two wars since it, seemingly, had no effect on his own life. Ah, but it did as, in actuality, it affected all men, just as the plight of America's deprived today has its impact on our total society. In that book and in all that he has done since to point the way toward the conservation and utilization of human resources, Eli Ginzberg has given us blueprints by which we can bring about those changes in our social and economic structures that will end those inequities in our society that are contrary to everything we profess.

Ours is an age which can be described in many shattering terms. War, fear, deprivation engulf us; we are confronted by indifference where there should be commitment; the values that history has proved to be enduringly affirmative are being questioned; above all, we are dismayed by the wanton waste of human resources at every turn of the road. Paradoxically, these miseries flourish in an epoch of glorious creativity, magnificent human ingenuity, and incomparable skill which has reached its climax in man's most brilliant scientific triumph. Riches abound, but we are surrounded by a poverty of the spirit.

Being fully aware of the disasters of the achievements of this moment of history, I look with hope at this time in the story of mankind and call it an Age of Awakening. For, with all its drawbacks, it is an age in which man's social conscience has become more sensitive than ever before, a living part of his being. The Commission's studies have shown that not yet all, but many, have begun to see the worthlessness of old mores. They are recognizing that life must be reconstituted in terms of man's relationships to his fellow men; they see with clear vision that the best of our traditions must be cherished but those which serve an evil purpose must be discarded from out lives. This is what the generation gap is all about.

The Commission and Eli Ginzberg share the same goals and walk common paths. How appropriate it is then that he has been an active member of the Commission's New York State Advisory Committee since 1962. Within this span of time, Dr. Ginzberg has provided wise and dedicated counsel as the Commission has fulfilled its role in the process of social change.

The Commission, established by Congress in 1957, has its roots in several historic moments in American history. The first, undoubtedly, was the Supreme Court decision of 1954 that segregation of schools by race was unconstitutional. The second, perhaps, was that memorable move by the Negro community to shed its centuries-old fetters by instigating the Montgomery, Alabama, bus boycott in 1955. For this was no single gesture of defying the tradition of moving to the back of the bus. This was a people's rebellion against white America's imposed penalty for having a dark skin.

In the decade and a half that have passed since then, many gains have been made, many insights developed. Tragedies have occurred, devastating hostilities have been revealed, and immense heroism has been displayed. The flame has dimmed from time to time, but it has never been extinguished. We have not yet reached our goals but—we have begun!

I repeat what I have said often before: the first phase of the civil rights movement accomplished and wrote into federal law what I would call a national conscience of civil rights. The Commission has cultivated this.

It is a fact-finding agency with no enforcement powers of its own but its assiduous work in exploring inequities in all spheres of man's life has led to corrective actions by those who possess the power to take such actions. Surely the passage of the Civil Rights Act of 1964 and the Voting Rights Act of 1965 can be numbered among the foremost of these. But I venture to say that the Commission's most lasting and meaningful service will be found to have been in its contribution to the entire concept of the Age of Awakening. It has helped make society aware that families of minority groups are living in subhuman circumstances and literally starving because decent employment and decent housing are denied them; aware that the children of such families are being deprived of an adequate education making it a certainty they will grow into illiterate, psychologically stunted adults trapped in a cycle to nowhere; aware that minority group members are often forbidden due process of law under unspeakable circumstances; aware that this is taking place mainly because of the color of their skin.

The arithmetical process is as simple as adding two and two to make four. No people can reach its potential in any area of its life unless its members have adequate jobs that bring in adequate earnings. With financial security, many other problems that beset minority groups will be lightened. I do not say *all* because the problem is not one of money alone. Unfortunately, it is more intricate than that. The utilization of manpower wisely and imaginatively goes beyond finding jobs for people. Its philosophy encompasses all of man's social and psychological needs. Its full relization will come when, in the immortal words of Martin Luther King, Jr., spoken on that unforgettable August 28, 1963, when the

March on Washington took place " . . . the bright day of justice emerges."

But time is running out. Our whole social structure, our very civilization is in peril. Just as three decades ago when Professor Ginzberg said of the Welsh situation: "Years passed before the English populace became aware of the depressed areas and more passed while the problems were being analyzed. Action was long delayed. No reason . . . was more potent than the belief that the problems . . . affected only a relatively few people. . . ." or when André Gide, writing in his diary during the German occupation of France, [*Pages de Journal*] 1944, deplored the lack of sympathetic imagination which caused people to accept coolly the sufferings of others which they were not forced to undergo, so today, too much time has been lost in ignorance, indifference, meaningless verbiage, and the theory that the only people involved were those who count least.

What tragic folly! Some of it has been intentional and some, perhaps more pathetic, has been due to imperviousness. Whatever the reason, in this Age of Awakening, no one can now claim to be unaware nor offer a justifiable excuse to stand aside in the overwhelming effort to find an affirmative solution to America's problem of race relations. No man is an island.

The Commission on Civil Rights has been a strong source for good in helping awaken the Nation to the racial dilemma of this country. Its investigations, public hearings, State Advisory Committee meetings, and publications have opened the way for all men to see the attritions taking place in our land.

It has revealed the inequities that exist to an almost unbelievable degree in American life. The Commission has helped make man's sense of moral responsibility begin to come into full being.

A very basic conviction since the Commission began is that

our main job is education. We are educating Secretaries in their Departments about what should be done to remove inequities from their programs, we are educating Congress about what should be done in the field of legislation and the sometimes hidden implications of certain measures; we are, hopefully, assisting the Executive Branch in the role it should play; and we are indirectly educating our 51 State Advisory Committees by giving its members information which they can use locally. I have a feeling deep inside that if the American people really knew the dimension of the problem and its human aspects we would be able to step up the tempo of change.

The importance of this type of activity is often only dimly perceived against the panoply of more glamorous actions, but if there is to be progress, there has first to be the gathering of facts and the effective dissemination of those facts, and this is the role of the Commission as an institutional entity in social change.

In 1957, when the Commission came into being, three years after the Supreme Court decision on school desegregation, the home of Martin Luther King, Jr. was bombed in Montgomery, a riot occurred when Autherine J. Lucy was admitted to the University of Alabama, and Tennessee National Guardsmen had to be called out to disperse mobs demonstrating against school desegregation in Clinton, Tennessee. These were difficult days, but the time was right for arousing consciences and initiating change.

From its very first report, issued in 1959, education of the young has been a primary focus of the Commission. Two basic premises were stated in the first report that remain valid today: "(1) that the American system of public education should be preserved without impairment, and (2) that the recently recognized constitutional right to be free of racial discrimination in public education is to be realized."

In its first report, the Commission made a number of recommendations on education, many of which were subsequently written into law. The Commission recommended that it be authorized to serve as a clearinghouse for information in the desegregation of school districts, and it was given this function under Title V of the Civil Rights Act of 1964.

It is recommended that it be authorized to establish advisory, mediation, and conciliation services with respect to desegregation of schools, and Title X of the Civil Rights Act of 1964 established the Community Relations Service to perform these functions.

Three Commissioners recommended that Federal agencies withhold funds from any institution of higher learning which refused to admit, on racial grounds, students otherwise qualified for admission, and this recommendation was enacted by Title VI of the Civil Rights Act of 1964.

As the years passed, other recommendations made by the Commission were subsequently embodied into law. These recommendations included federal sponsorship of educational programs designed to assist public school students handicapped scholastically as a result of inferior educational opportunity and training; authorization for the Attorney-General to intervene or to initiate suits in certain cases involving the enforcement of the constitutional rights of individual persons denied equal protection of the laws with respect to public higher education; authorization for the Attorney-General to initiate suits to desegregate public schools; and the implementation of Title VI of the Civil Rights Act of 1964 requiring all school districts receiving federal funds to submit assurance of compliance with the act.

The Commission has never viewed educational segregation as simply a violation of the law. In 1967, it issued a report, *Racial Isolation in the Public Schools,* which concluded that racial isolation, whether caused by *de jure* segregation, discriminatory housing patterns, or other factors, results in serious educational harm to the children of minority groups.

Conversely, integration significantly boosted the educational achievement of these children.

I have seen nothing during the succeeding years that has caused any change of heart. Education is the capstone of the trilogy of problems that must be solved if racial justice is to become real. The other two parts—employment and housing—are certainly of major importance, but quality education offers the best long-range solution.

As I have noted before, Professor Ginzberg was among the first to recognize that injustices done to minority groups per se had a deleterious effect on the entire society. In *The Negro Potential,* written in collaboration with three other scholars in 1956, he found that the Negro in the United States is the nation's single most underdeveloped human resource and urged that more opportunities be opened to make better and wiser use of that strength. In the years that have passed, he and his colleagues would, I am certain, enlarge this finding and plea and would agree with the Commission that Mexican-Americans, Puerto Ricans, Oriental Americans, Indians, and such poverty-stricken groups as the Appalachian whites be given the same opportunities as members of the majority group and, thus, be enabled to enrich this nation by the distinctive cultural contributions they can bring to its life force.

Sayings become trite because they are true. I find truth in reflecting that man has learned to live the powerful life; now he must learn to live the good life.

No thinking person today is unaffected by the problems which beset our youth nor can he be left unshaken by its tragic despair. For that, as I see it, is what the current "rebellion" represents—unresolved problems and tragic despair. I know from close personal experience that there is real cause for anxiety. Yet I have seen at close range and have worked with several generations of young people and I can say this as a fact: this young generation is probably the most idealistic and the most committed to social justice and the preservation of human rights of any generation in America's history. Because this generation is young, because it still lacks true sophistication and maturity, its members often express themselves and their ideals badly. But the *desire* is there! They are trying, however fumblingly, to build a better world in which each human being shall have an equitable share. This young generation is our potential reservoir of manpower resources. It must have direction, yes. But it must be the right direction—toward seeking to help these young people as they work for a unified country in which, as the distinguished social psychologist Kenneth B. Clark has said: "We shall have achieved racial maturity."

No man or woman can do a job until he is prepared for it psychologically and professionally. The nation's strength will be depleted until its manpower resources are replenished by concrete programs to restore them.

The Commission knows this and through its investigations and publications stresses the need for nationwide provision of sound, broad, creative education. This means education that will be integrated, democratic, unbiased and, thus, meaningful for all children. Such education will obviously have to be furnished in good buildings, whether in individual schools or educational complexes, provided with the most modern and all-inclusive teaching equipment, including textbooks which cover the full complement of cultural contributions of all ethnic groups. Such education will be provided by competent, integrated, understanding administrators and faculty who have respect for cultural pluralism, that quality which has made America varied and admirable.

Because we must face the hard reality that many minority group children are suffering the effects of a deprived infancy and early childhood, we must put our best heads together to devise the most efficacious methods that exist to help them overcome these handicaps. All children, unless they are sick and need special education, should be regarded from the start as potential college material. I would like to expunge the words "vocational education" from the vocabularies of schools minority group children attend. Since this is impossible, and probably impractical, let us put it last on the list of suggestions when it is automatically prompted by the color of a child's skin or his ancestry. Counselors often remind me of Pavlov's dog! A minority group child does *not* necessarily need to evoke the image of the vocational school! Which leads me to point out that the counseling system, even at highly regarded schools, is often horrifying. Usually deficient in number of counselors, the work is often sandwiched in as an unpleasant chore between harried teaching schedules. Trained counselors, and enough of them, should be part of the permanent staff who bring empathy to the atmosphere and, where appropriate, are able to function in more than one language. A child's first language, if it is not English, should become a source of pride, not of shame, to him. Need we really be so provincial? Counselors, incidentally, should be hired as counselors and not as teachers. Each is a full-time job!

All this takes money and I would hope that federal and state and local administrators would recognize the imperative need for spending it on adequate education for the youth of our nation. Quality desegregated education is not a miracle to be achieved overnight. Too much must first be undone. But yesterday is gone, today is here, and tomorrow is coming. Some progress has been noted by the Commission and others who are particularly aware, but some is not enough. Only all is enough! I have no illusions about the ease with which this can be accomplished. It is already proving to be about as hard a problem to solve as any that has ever faced this nation. The Commission has studied the matter thoroughly; it has held public hearings on it in all parts of the country; its members know the extent of the resistance. But that resistance need not have a stranglehold on us. The good of our children, which means the good of our country, must prevail and our own efforts must be to rally to our country's aid in this time of moral crisis.

Crisis is a strong word and I use it advisedly. But I see education as the foundation on which all our other efforts to attain racial equality and a unified nation must rest. When every educable child has been educated under optimum circumstances, we will be a nation of enlightened men in every sense. Superstitions will have been exploded; schools will be filled with able teachers of diversified backgrounds who are qualified to teach children of diversified backgrounds; universities will increase the number of their graduates who are competent to function in expanding fields of interest; husbands will be able to provide for their families and stable homes will result; children will be born healthier and they will not die before their time.

As Hosea Williams, one of the lieutenants of the late Dr. Martin Luther King, Jr., said at the Commission's Alabama hearing in Montgomery in 1968: " . . . We are not saying in our Poor People's Campaign that the Rockefellers and the Kennedys and the Fords should not be millionaires. But we are certainly saying that while there are millionaires, we must not have the Buttermilk Bottoms in Atlanta, Georgia; we must not have the Watts in Los Angeles; we must not have the West Sides of Chicago or the Harlems of New York. . . . Now all our program is designed to do is that every man in this country can get a job, one that he finds fulfillment and creativity in. . . ."

I, too, rejoice that many Americans are affluent and I have no wish to see them stripped of their wealth. But I have every wish to see all Americans given equality of opportunity and, above all, not be denied it for reasons that have no place in the American democratic tradition.

Perhaps I speak of the millennium. I trust the solution is nearer than that. But when that day comes, even when that day is on the decisive way to becoming, we shall, indeed, be fulfilled in our manpower resources—a nation materially rich, morally hardy. The work of men like Eli Ginzberg has already shown signs of budding. In that day it will burst into bloom. What is mainly needed today is the vision and the leadership, from top to bottom, to make the promises of our Constitution come true.

The age which I prefer to regard as the Age of Awakening, represents a striving for human equality, for human development, for an end to the poverty, the hunger, the illness, the ignorance, the homelessness that beset and cloud the lives of so many of our fellow Americans today. In the efforts of men like Eli Ginzberg lie the means of achieving those goals and bringing America a unification of spirit that it has not enjoyed before.

Noteworthy as are the achievements of such men toward this end, it cannot be accomplished without the cooperation of our total society. It will not happen if the most knowledgeable, the most intelligent, the most powerful people in our midst do not join those who are already devoting themselves to solving this problem. The job must be done at all levels. The sooner it is done on the local level, the sooner it will be completed.

If ideas are needed, where are the knowledgeable? If more intelligent administration is needed, where are the intelligent? If power and affluence are needed, are they being put into the service of those whose survival depends on them or are they being kept by their owners for their own selfish purposes?

What I am calling for, I suppose, is for more Eli Ginzbergs in the world, for a greater understanding of the deep human problems, for a more meaningful involvement in the current revolution of human development and human opportunity that will bring us all to a better day. What I am calling for is an ever-widening and deepening concern with what the Commission on Civil Rights and the Conservation of Human Resources Project labor for: a conscious effort to uncover the ills of a society weakened by deprivation on the basis of race and a continuous charting of a course for their cure. In the academic sense, of course, the professionals do the research. But in the most cogent sense, each human being who helps in the effort to wipe out injustice is doing research. No positive effort can fail to leave its mark and that mark will be for good.

Unfortunately, I must utter a word of caution. Too many people *mean* to do good. That is, they mean to do no harm. But many "good citizens" would be horrified to know that their unthinking acts of omission serve the same dreadful ends as do the conscious acts of commission. Guard against lip service only. When men *really* hold jobs commensurate with their ability; when their promotions on a fair basis are *really* assured so they have a goal to aspire to ; when any family can *really* live alongside any other family in amity; when children are *really* given equal, understanding, and ungrudging opportunity to receive a sound education and prepare themselves for a fruitful life, then we shall see the fulfillment of Martin Luther King, Jr.'s dream.

The federal government, that institution which is the prototype and must be the backbone for all efforts to conserve our human resources, has not been exempt from the formidable obstacles which beset all who would make the dream a reality. The old adage: "Where there are human beings, there is human frailty" holds true here as elsewhere. But the record of the federal government is not negligible.

It was the federal government which established the Commission on Civil Rights and other federal agencies whose programs are concerned with civil rights. It was the federal government which placed an equal opportunity officer on the staff of each of its agencies to ensure that no one is deprived of his rights because of his race, color, or country of origin. It was the federal government which has enacted legislation and signed into law the various civil rights acts which mark the last decade and a half as fifteen years of civil rights progress. It is the federal government which is expending its resources so that minority group members may direct their own businesses and thus be independent of others.

But it would be both banal and misleading to assume that the goal has been reached. Although less and less the dominant society is yielding to the evils of the age and, instead, is rising to resist them, we have far, far to go. At the Commission we learned early that political and civil rights under the general heading of equal protection of the laws must mean more than nondiscriminatory laws and machinery; they must include the greater social and economic rights—the human rights—to the individual and pour his abilities into the mainstream of American life. Only so can it be enriched, unified, and become a source of new outer and inner strength to all.

I repeat, we must, above all, safeguard the future of our youth. We are three decades away from the end of the twentieth century. Children born in 1970 will be just 30 years old when the year 2000 is reached.

What heritage will we have left them? Their future is in our hands and will be determined by what we do now. Of all our human resources, that future is our most precious and highest trust. In the last analysis, it is the future of those children and theirs which bind us together to work for a unified nation.

Eli Ginzberg has been in the vanguard of those who have recognized this and have offered tangible ways to achieve it. According to Jewish folklore no greater blessing can be bestowed upon a man than to wish him a lifespan of one hundred and twenty years. In this spirit, I salute Professor Ginzberg at the half-way mark. He is already a landmark in the effort to make America "one nation, indivisible, with liberty and justice for all."

ROBERT M. MAC IVER

PERSONAL POSTSCRIPT

I AM delighted to have the opportunity to contribute to this Festschrift in honor of my good friend and colleague Eli Ginzberg. I know no one more deserving of this honor.

I have been acquainted with Eli since I was a professor of political theory at Columbia University. He attended my courses in this subject and proved himself to be a distinguished student, an avid learner, and a thinker in his own right who was both ingenious and inventive. I admired his independence, his initiative, his aptitudes, and his courtesy. He learned as he questioned, and he questioned as he learned. I recall that some of the older and more staid professors at the adult School of Business at Columbia considered him "brash," but they soon concluded that it was simply because he did not accept as gospel the words of wisdom delivered by his seniors.

I kept in touch with him when he became a lecturer and in

due course a professor. There was something very disarming and likeable about him. He was admirable on the rostrum, a spontaneous and effective speaker, never at a loss for the apt formulation. His research interests were not restricted to recent works of learning and to cold facts but extended to the more humane problems of the oppressed and the downtrodden.

He devoted himself to the plight of the inhabitants of our inner cities, the blacks and to a degree the Puerto Ricans. With the influx to the cities of the North of segregated blacks from the Southern states and Italians from the miserable poverty of life in Sicily and the south of Italy, and of Eastern Europeans seeking more freedom and better employment, the ghettos of New York City and other large cities throughout the country were ever more congested. Eli Ginzberg drafted, edited, and wrote an amazing number of volumes, often aided by able assistants. Several of his writings were on topics that probably were nearest to his heart: the plight of the poor migrant or immigrant subject of discrimination and prejudice by the white majority.

His research output has been amazing and extraordinarily comprehensive. It may truly be said of Eli Ginzberg that "Nothing human is alien to him." While the problems of youth, especially of the youth of our slums who have been neglected, denied opportunity and subjected to prejudice and discrimination, have been of major concern to him, he ranged far and wide in his effort to awaken the white majority to make the "land of opportunity" live up to its promises.

He began, however, with more distant topics. The plight of the Welsh miners, the economics of the Bible, the laissez-faire doctrine of Adam Smith, the problems of the unemployed, of the uneducated, the management of health services and of Army recruiting. He has been in the forefront of research on manpower problems, both military and civilian, strategies for developing human resources, manpower strategies for developing nations, as well as for our own human resources, the problems of being Jewish in the United States, certain problems of business management, the life styles of educated women, progress in East Asia, and more besides.

Only a valorous, indefatigable spirit could carry anyone through all that labor—but he revelled in work. Only a most unusual intellectual could explore and report on such a range of topics. He went on mission after mission to the countries he wrote about, sometimes under White House auspices, sometimes on his own initiative. And he did it all with a happy tranquillity and a sense of dedication.

He could never have accomplished so amazing and totally efficient an output had he not known how to choose thoroughly qualified assistants, how to instruct them and how to test their reports, but the finished work was always his own. He knew how and what to delegate his well-trained assistants to do, and made the most effective use of their reports. Eli himself has all the expertise he needs for the various areas of research and reconnaissance his many-sided work demands. He has the sympathetic approach that enables him to get to first base with his respondents.

I was a trustee of the National Manpower Council of which he was then director. It was planned and directed by Eli, who obtained the funds requested for its maintenance over a period of several years and who selected a board of highly distinguished men, heads of foundations, eminent leaders in science, journalism, trade union officials, government leaders as well as leaders in religion and law.

The Council explored every area of public service, governmental and civilian. It met rather frequently, was financed by the Ford Foundation, and possessed the official backing of President Eisenhower, who himself had an affection for Eli. Its executive director under Eli was Henry David, who took every care to consult all the trustees on all the many issues under study, the conclusions of which engaged their respective interests. The President had expressed concern over the large number of draftees who had been rejected by the draft board as unfit for service. The Board was invited to propose remedial measures, industrial and educational training systems, and medical services for the removal of the disabilities of so many young people across the nation. It was a call for improvement and redirection of our welfare services.

As a member of the board of trustees of the National Manpower Council, therefore, I had an excellent opportunity to see Eli in action. Very unobtrusively he listened and observed, noting not only the proposals of the Board, but also the warmth, indifference, or degree of enthusiasm of the responses of the various members. Occasionally, they might go off into somewhat irrelevant discussion, and he would quietly recall them to the queston at issue. He never forced his own opinions, meantime, on the group he led.

Every year, often in early spring, he would visit some countries far afield and when he returned with a store of information, he would report on it to our government and he would visit us and tell us the story. His observations were always keen and Eli never lacked the capacity to tell the tale with sprightly conviction and zest.

Eli and Ruth Ginzberg are a well matched pair, which in this case does not mean they are alike but that they are complementary, which is far more interesting. "Ruthie" has a caustic wit, and when she thinks Eli is getting on his high horse, talking too freely about his travels and what he has observed or done, she calls him to order. He retorts quietly, and the sparring goes on. Ruth is a lady of high ability. She acts as his top secretary and first critic. She writes well on her own account.

The Ginzbergs have a cozy summer home on Martha's Vineyard, an island that attracts remarkable numbers of distinguished people, educators, artists, authors, performing artists, journalists, and important political figures. It has also been our own summer home for a great many years. We see much more of the Ginzbergs when we are both at our summer homes on the island. The evening usually begins with a discussion of the international scene, and of national political problems, and in fact, in the old Latin phrase, *de omnibus et quibusd am diis,* about anything or everything.

Eli is a most unusual person, unlike anyone else I have ever known with his combination of keen intelligence, comprehensive range of interests, empathy in his approach to all kinds of people, both "underdogs" and the highly priviliged, ability both to write and to speak clearly, fluently, and effectively, a fine raconteur, and an incisive critic of sham, slovenly scholarship, and badly reasoned conclusions. He stands foursquare to all the winds that blow.

GEORGE P. SHULTZ

A PERSONAL TRIBUTE TO ELI GINZBERG

FOR the past thirty years, Eli Ginzberg has been uniquely associated with the origin of many of the most important developments in the manpower field—both in the government and in the academic world. His role has been that of an innovator and stimulator of ideas.

This penchant for initiation has been a key element in his career. The list of original ideas which came from his thinking is long and important. But let me turn to another side of the man—to Eli the Counselor.

From 1964 to 1968 I served with Eli on the National Manpower Policy Task Force, a group of academics set up to advise the Secretary of Labor on manpower research and policy priorities. In 1967 we served together on a White House Task Force to study urban employment problems. Eli's sparkle, dynamism, and depth of knowledge was a major factor in the success of both these efforts.

I appreciated his important role as Counselor even more fully when I became Secretary of Labor. In that office I spent many an hour listening to and participating in the discussions of the National Manpower Advisory Committee chaired by Professor Ginzberg. My most vivid memories of this Committee's work are not the long discussions but rather the remarkable letters which he would send to me and the Secretary of Health, Education, and Welfare summarizing the Committee's recommendations and observations.

These letters should be studied as models of precision, tact, and wisdom. His unusual ability to synthesize and summarize the deliberations of committees made up of people of quite different backgrounds was constantly demonstrated through the NMAC letters. He was able to "feel" a consensus without soliciting votes and bring forth agreement of Committee members on some of the more difficult problems of our society.

As a cabinet official, I studied these letters with care, knowing full well that I was reading more than the deliberations of a committee, that I was in the fortunate position of hearing from a wise counselor who has read extensively, studied long, observed carefully and could deal with practical issues.[1]

Eli Ginzberg's father, Louis Ginzberg, was a famous teacher, scholar, and humanitarian. He once wrote to a friend, "As a proud father, I was particularly pleased to find in your poem a reference to Eli. On reaching old age, one lives his life in the lives of his children, and any praise bestowed upon them is taken by the fond parent to be paid to him, though in truth he could claim, at most, fifty percent for himself."

These reminiscences are dedicated to Eli Ginzberg—respected teacher, scholar, and humanitarian. Although his father is not here to read these learned essays and these reminiscences in this Festschrift in "praise bestowed upon . . ."

his son—I wish to conclude by offering a salutation that Louis Ginzberg would appreciate: To Eli—*L'chayim!*

NOTES

1. These letters have recently been published in *Manpower Advice for Government: Letters of the National Manpower Advisory Committee* (Eli Ginzberg, Chairman) *to Secretaries of Labor and HEW, 1962–1971* (Washington, D.C.: U.S. Department of Labor).—Ed.

ELI GINZBERG
A SELECTIVE BIBLIOGRAPHY
1932 - 1972

Studies in the Economics of the Bible. Philadelphia: Jewish Publication Society, 1932.

The House of Adam Smith. New York: Columbia University Press, 1934.

The Illusion of Economic Stability. New York: Harper & Row, 1939.

Report to American Jews: On Overseas Relief, Palestine, and Refugees in the U.S. New York: Harper & Row, 1942.

Grass on the Slag Heaps: The Story of the Welsh Miners. New York: Harper & Row, 1942.

The Unemployed: I. Interpretation; II. Case Studies. Eli Ginzberg, Ethel L. Ginsburg, Dorothy L. Lynn, L. Mildred Vickers, and Sol W. Ginsburg, M.D. New York: Harper & Row, 1943.

The Labor Leader: An Exploratory Study. Eli Ginzberg, assisted by Joseph Carwell. New York: Macmillan, 1948.

A Program for the Nursing Profession. The Committee on the Function of Nursing, Eli Ginzberg, chairman. New York: Macmillan, 1948.

A Pattern for Hospital Care. New York: King's Crown Press, 1949.

Agenda for American Jews. New York: King's Crown Press, 1950.

Occupational Choice: An Approach to a General Theory. Eli Ginzberg, Sol W. Ginsburg, M.D., Sidney Axelrad, and John L. Herma. New York: Columbia University Press, 1951.

The Uneducated. Eli Ginzberg and Douglas W. Bray. New York: Columbia University Press, 1933.

Psychiatry and Military Manpower Policy: A Reappraisal of the Experience of World War II. Eli Ginzberg, Sol W. Ginsburg, M.D., and John L. Herma. New York: Columbia University Press, 1953.

What Makes an Executive? Report of a Round Table on Executive Potential and Performance. Eli Ginzberg, chairman, New York: Columbia University Press, 1955.

The Negro Potential. Eli Ginzberg, with the assistance of James K. Anderson, Douglas W. Bray, and Robert W. Smuts. New York: Columbia University Press, 1955.

Effecting Change in Large Organizations. Eli Ginzberg and Ewing W. Reilley assisted by Douglas W. Bray and John L. Herma. New York: Columbia University Press, 1956.

Human Resources: The Wealth of a Nation. New York: Simon & Schuster, 1958.

The Ineffective Soldier: Lessons for Management and the Nation. 3 vols. New York: Columbia University Press, 1959.

I. *The Lost Divisions*. Eli Ginzberg, James K. Anderson, Sol W. Ginsburg, M.D., and John L. Herma.

II. *Breakdown and Recovery*. Eli Ginzberg, John B. Miner, James K. Anderson, Sol W. Ginsburg, M.D., and John L. Herma.

III. *Patterns of Performance*. Eli Ginzberg, James K. Anderson, Sol W. Ginsburg, M.D., John L. Herma, Douglas W. Bray, William Jordan, and Major Francis J. Ryan.

The Nation's Children. 3 vols. Edited by Eli Ginzberg. New York, Columbia University Press, 1960.

I. *The Family and Social Change*.

II. *Development and Education*.

III. *Problems and Prospects*.

Values and Ideals of American Youth. Edited by Eli Ginzberg, with a Foreword by John W. Gardner. New York: Columbia University Press, 1961.

Planning for Better Hospital Care. Eli Ginzberg and Peter Rogatz, M.D. New York: King's Crown Press, 1961.

The Optimistic Tradition and American Youth. Eli Ginzberg, James K. Anderson, and John L. Herma. New York: Columbia University Press, 1962.

The American Worker in the Twentieth Century: A History through Autobiographies. Eli Ginzberg and Hyman Berman. New York: Free Press, 1963.

Democratic Values and the Rights of Management. Eli Ginzberg and Ivar Berg, with John L. Herma and James K. Anderson. New York: Columbia University Press, 1963.

Technology and Social Change. Edited by Eli Ginzberg. New York: Columbia University Press, 1964.

The Troublesome Presence: American Democracy and the Negro. Eli Ginzberg and Alfred S. Eichner. New York: Free Press, 1964.

Talent and Performance. Eli Ginzberg and John L. Herma, with Ivar Berg, Carol A. Brown, Alice M. Yohalem, James K. Anderson, and Lois Lipper. New York: Columbia University Press, 1964.

The Negro Challenge to the Business Community. Edited by Eli Ginzberg. New York: McGraw-Hill, 1964.

The Pluralistic Economy. Eli Ginzberg, Dale L. Hiestand, and Beatrice G. Reubens. New York: McGraw-Hill, 1965.

Life Styles of Educated Women. Eli Ginzberg, Ivar Berg, Carol A. Brown, John L. Herma, Alice M. Yohalem, and Sherry Gorelick. New York: Columbia University Press, 1966.

Educated American Women: Self-Portraits. Eli Ginzberg and Alice M. Yohalem. New York: Columbia University Press, 1966.

The Development of Human Resources. New York: McGraw-Hill, 1966.

Keeper of the Law: Louis Ginzberg. Philadelphia: Jewish Publication Society, 1966.

Manpower Strategy for Developing Countries. Eli Ginzberg and Herbert A. Smith, New York: Columbia University Press, 1967.

The Middle-Class Negro in the White Man's World. Eli Ginzberg, with Vincent Bryan, Grace T. Hamilton, John L. Herma, and Alice Yohalem. New York: Columbia University Press, 1967.

Manpower strategy for the Metropolis. Eli Ginzberg and the Conservation of Human Resources Staff. New York: Columbia University Press, 1968.

Manpower Agenda for America. New York: McGraw-Hill, 1968

Business Leadership and the Negro Crisis. Edited by Eli Ginzberg. New York: McGraw-Hill, 1968.

Men, Money, and Medicine. Eli Ginzberg with Miriam Ostow. New York: Columbia University Press, 1969.

Urban Health Services: The Case of New York. Eli Ginzberg and the Conservation of Human Resources Staff. New York: Columbia University Press, 1971.

Career Guidance: Who Needs It, Who Provides It, Who Can Improve It. New York: McGraw-Hill, 1971.

Manpower for Development: Perspectives on Five Continents. New York: Praeger, 1971.

Manpower Advice for Government: Letters of the National Manpower Advisory Committee (Eli Ginzberg, Chairman) *to Secretaries of Labor and HEW,* 1962–1971. Washington D.C.: U.S. Department of Labor.

Corporate Lib: Women's Challenge to Management. Edited by Eli Ginzberg and Alice M. Yohalem. New York: Praeger, in press.

New York Is Very Much Alive. Eli Ginzberg and the Conservation of Human Resources Staff. New York: McGraw-Hill, in press.